Adobe® Acrobat® 6.0
Professional

Classroom in a Book®

Adobe

Adobe Press books are published by Peachpit Press, Berkeley, CA. To report errors, please send a note to errata@peachpit.com.

Printed in the U. S. A.

ISBN# 0-321-24743-4

9 8 7 6 5 4 3 2 1

Contents

Creating Adobe PDF from Web Pages

Modifying PDF Files

Using Acrobat Professional in a Document Review Cycle

Using Acrobat's Engineering and Technical Features

Creating PDF Forms

Using Adobe Acrobat for Professional Publishing

Index

Getting Started

Adobe® Acrobat® 6.0 Professional is the essential tool for universal document exchange. You can use Acrobat Professional to publish virtually any document in Portable Document Format (PDF), preserving the exact look and content of the original, complete with fonts and graphics.

Distribute your PDF documents by e-mail or store them on the World Wide Web, an intranet, a file system, or a CD. Other users can view your work on the Microsoft® Windows®, Mac® OS, and UNIX® platforms. Add interactive elements such as custom hyperlinks and sound clips. Streamline your document review process with Acrobat comments and digital signatures, and use Acrobat to place security locks on sensitive files.

About Classroom in a Book

Adobe Acrobat 6.0 Professional Classroom in a Book® is part of the official training series for Adobe graphics and publishing software. The lessons are designed to let you learn at your own pace. If you're new to Adobe Acrobat Professional, you'll learn the fundamental concepts and features you'll need to master the program. If you've been using Acrobat Professional for a while, you'll find Classroom in a Book teaches many advanced features, including tips and techniques for using this latest version.

The lessons in this edition include information on the new Adobe Acrobat Professional user interface, new ways of creating Adobe PDF files, more powerful methods of repurposing the content of Adobe PDF files for use in other applications, and new tools for reviewing and commenting on Adobe PDF documents, as well as information on making your documents more accessible, reading and organizing eBooks, and creating photo albums to share with friends and family.

Although each lesson provides step-by-step instructions for specific projects, there's room for exploration and experimentation. You can follow the book from start to finish or do only the lessons that match your interests and needs.

Prerequisites

Before beginning to use *Adobe Acrobat 6.0 Professional Classroom in a Book*, you should have a working knowledge of your computer and its operating system. Make sure you know how to use the mouse, standard menus and commands, and how to open, save, and close files. If you need to review these techniques, see the printed or online documentation included with your system.

Installing Adobe Acrobat Professional

Before you begin using *Adobe Acrobat 6.0 Professional Classroom in a Book*, make sure that your system is set up correctly and that you've installed the required software and hardware. You must purchase Adobe Acrobat 6.0 Professional software separately. For system requirements and complete instructions on installing the software, see the *HowTo-Install.rtf* file on the application CD.

You must install the application from the Adobe Acrobat 6.0 Professional CD onto your hard drive; you cannot run the program from the CD. Follow the on-screen installation instructions.

Make sure your serial number is accessible before installing the application. You can find the serial number on the registration card or CD sleeve.

Starting Adobe Acrobat Professional

You start Acrobat Professional just as you would any other software application.

• On Windows, choose Start > Programs > Adobe Acrobat 6.0 Professional.

• On Mac OS, open the Adobe Acrobat 6.0 Professional folder, and double-click the Acrobat 6.0 Professional program icon.

Note: To run Acrobat 6.0 Professional on Mac OS, you must have Mac OS X, version 10.2.2 or later.

The Adobe Acrobat Professional application window appears. You can now open a PDF document or create a new one and start working.

Copying the Classroom in a Book files

The *Adobe Acrobat 6.0 Professional Classroom in a Book* CD includes folders containing all the electronic files for the lessons. Each lesson has its own folder, and you must copy the folders to your hard drive to do the lessons. To save room on your drive, you can install only the necessary folder for each lesson as you need it, and remove it when you're done.

To install the Classroom in a Book files:

1 Insert the *Adobe Acrobat 6.0 Professional Classroom in a Book* CD into your CD-ROM drive.

2 Create a folder named AA6_CIB on your hard drive.

3 Copy the lessons you want to the hard drive:

• To copy all of the lessons, drag the Lessons Art folder from the CD into the AA6_CIB folder.

• To copy a single lesson, drag the individual lesson folder from the CD into the AA6_CIB folder.

If you are installing the files on Windows, you may need to unlock them before using them. You don't need to unlock the files if you are installing them on Mac OS or later versions of Windows.

4 On earlier versions of Windows, such as Windows 98, unlock the files you copied as necessary:

• If you copied all of the lessons, double click the unlock.bat file in the AA6_CIB/Lessons Art folder.

• If you copied a single lesson, drag the unlock.bat file from the Lessons folder on the CD into the AA6_CIB folder. Then double-click the unlock.bat file in the AA6_CIB folder.

Note: If as you work through the lessons, you overwrite the lesson files, you can restore the original files by recopying the corresponding lesson folder from the Classroom in a Book CD to the AA6_CIB folder on your hard drive.

Additional resources

Adobe Acrobat 6.0 Professional Classroom in a Book is not meant to replace documentation provided with the Adobe Acrobat 6.0 Professional program. Only the commands and options used in the lessons are explained in this book. For comprehensive information about program features, refer to these resources:

• The How To pane, which gives concise steps for completing common tasks. If this pane doesn't open automatically, choose Help > How To > How To Window, or click the How To button on the Acrobat toolbar.

• The Complete Acrobat 6.0 online Help included with the Adobe Acrobat 6.0 Professional software, which you can view by choosing Help > Complete Acrobat 6.0 Help. This guide contains a complete description of all features.

• The Adobe Web site (www.adobe.com/products/acrobat/), which you can view by choosing Help > Acrobat Online if you have a connection to the World Wide Web.

Adobe certification

The Adobe Training and Certification Programs are designed to help Adobe customers improve and promote their product proficiency skills. The Adobe Certified Expert (ACE) program is designed to recognize the high-level skills of expert users. Adobe Certified Training Providers (ACTP) use only Adobe Certified Experts to teach Adobe software classes. Available in either ACTP classrooms or on-site, the ACE program is the best way to master Adobe products. For Adobe Certified Training Programs information, visit the Partnering with Adobe Web site at http://partners.adobe.com/.

Lesson 1

1 Introducing Acrobat Professional

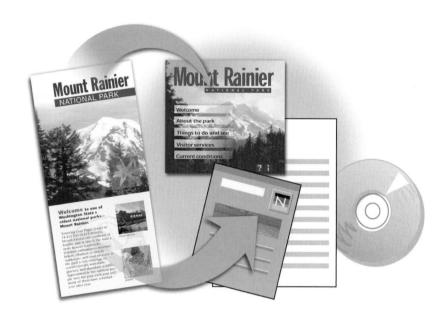

Quality publishing tools are within reach of more people than ever before, and easy access to the Internet and to CD recorders enables wider distribution of electronic publications. Acrobat Professional helps you create electronic documents quickly and easily—and Adobe® Reader® can provide your audience free access to them.

In this lesson, you'll do the following:

• Review the main features of Acrobat Professional.

• Look at the differences between electronic documents designed for printing and viewing online.

• Identify the types of formatting and design decisions you need to make when creating an electronic publication.

This lesson will take about 30 minutes to complete.

If needed, copy the Lesson01 folder onto your hard drive.

Note: Windows users may need to unlock the lesson files before using them. For information, see "Copying the Classroom in a Book files" on page 3.

Getting started

Adobe Portable Document Format (PDF) is a universal file format that preserves all of the fonts, formatting, colors, and graphics of any source document, regardless of the application and platform used to create it. Adobe PDF files are compact and can be shared, viewed, navigated, and printed exactly as intended by anyone with the free Adobe Reader. You can convert any document to Adobe PDF using Acrobat Professional software.

• Adobe PDF preserves the exact layout, fonts, and text formatting of electronic documents, regardless of the computer system or platform used to view these documents.

• PDF documents can contain multiple languages, such as Japanese and English, on the same page.

• PDF documents print predictably with proper margins and page breaks.

• PDF files can be secured with passwords to lock against undesired changes or printing, or to limit access to confidential documents.

• The view magnification of a PDF page can be changed using controls in Acrobat Professional or Adobe Reader. This feature can be especially useful for zooming in on graphics or diagrams containing intricate details.

About Acrobat

Acrobat Professional lets you create, work with, read, and print Portable Document Format (PDF) documents.

Creating Adobe PDF

Your workflow and the types of documents you use determine how you create an Adobe PDF file.

• Use Distiller® to convert almost any file to Adobe PDF, including those created with drawing, page-layout, or image-editing programs.

• Use Acrobat PDFMaker to create Adobe PDF files from within Microsoft Office for Windows applications. Simply click the Convert to Adobe PDF button (🗎) on the Microsoft Office toolbar.

• Use the Create PDF commands to quickly convert a variety of file formats to Adobe PDF and open them in Acrobat.

• Use an application's Print command to create Adobe PDF directly from within common authoring applications.

• Scan paper documents and convert them to Adobe PDF.

• Use the Create PDF from Web Page command to download Web pages and convert them to Adobe PDF.

Lesson 3, "Converting Microsoft Office Files;" Lesson 4, "Converting Files to Adobe PDF;" and Lesson 6, "Creating Adobe PDF from Web Pages" give step-by-step instructions for creating Adobe PDF using several of these methods.

Working with PDF files

Working with PDF files has never been easier.

• Add hyperlinks, electronic bookmarks, and page actions to create a rich online experience. (Lesson 7, "Modifying PDF Files;" Lesson 9, "Putting Documents Online;" and Lesson 10, "Optimizing Online Document Design.")

• Use the powerful new content repurposing tools to re-use content in other applications by saving text in other file formats, extracting images in image formats, and converting PDF pages to image formats. (Lesson 7, "Modifying PDF Files.")

• Use built-in or third-party security handlers to add sophisticated protection to your confidential PDF documents, preventing users from copying text and graphics, printing a document, or even opening a file. Add digital signatures to approve the content and format of a document. (Lesson 11, "Adding Signatures and Security.")

• Add comments and files, and markup text in a totally electronic document review cycle. (Lesson 8, "Using Acrobat Professional in a Document Review Cycle.")

• Fill in electronic forms and add signature fields to documents. (Lesson 12, "Filling Out Forms.")

• Convert your pictures to Adobe PDF and create "slideshows" to share with friends and family. (Lesson 14, "Working with Pictures and Images.")

Reading PDF files

You can read PDF documents using Acrobat Professional, Acrobat Professional, or Adobe Reader. You can publish your PDF documents on network and Web servers, CDs, and disks.

Adobe Reader can be downloaded free of charge for all platforms from the Adobe Web site at www.adobe.com. If you need to read a PDF document and have not purchased Acrobat Professional or Acrobat Professional, you would use Adobe Reader to do so.

Adobe PDF on the World Wide Web

The World Wide Web has greatly expanded the possibilities of delivering electronic documents to a wide and varied audience. Because Web browsers can be configured to run other applications inside the browser window, you can post PDF files as part of a Web site. Your users can then download or view these files inside the browser window using Adobe Reader.

When including a PDF file as part of your Web page, you should direct your users to the Adobe Web site so that the first time they look at a PDF document, they can download Reader free of charge.

PDF documents can be viewed one page at a time and printed from the Web. With page-at-a-time downloading, the Web server sends only the requested page to the user, decreasing downloading time. In addition, the user can easily print selected pages or all pages from the document. PDF is a suitable format for publishing long electronic documents on the Web. PDF documents print predictably, with proper margins and page breaks.

You can download and convert Web pages to Adobe PDF, making it easy to save, distribute, and print Web pages.

Looking at some examples

Publishing your document electronically is a flexible way to distribute information. Using Adobe PDF, you can create documents for printing, for multimedia presentations, or for distribution on a CD or over a network. In this lesson, you'll take a look at some electronic documents designed for printing on paper and at some designed for online reading.

1 Start Acrobat Professional.

2 Choose File > Open. Select Introduc.pdf in the Lesson01 folder, and click Open. If necessary, use the scroll bars to bring the bottom part of the page into view.

The previews in this document are links to the corresponding electronic documents. The top three previews link to documents designed to be both distributed and viewed electronically; the bottom three previews link to documents intended to be distributed online, but also printed out for reading.

3 Click the Schedule preview in the bottom row to open the corresponding PDF file.

This document is a work schedule that has been converted to Adobe PDF for easy electronic distribution.

4 Look at the status bar at the bottom of the document window. Notice that the page size (lower left) is a standard 8.5-by-11 inches, a suitable size for printing on a desktop printer.

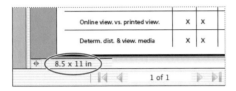

You might glance at the schedule online, but you'd also want to print out a hard-copy version for handy reference.

5 Click the Previous View button (⬤) in the status bar to return to the previews in the Introduc.pdf document.

Another example of a publication designed for printing is the Documentation file. This text-intensive document is much easier to read in printed format than online.

6 Click the Documentation preview in the bottom row to look at the file, and then click the Previous View button to return to the previews.

7 Click the Slide Show preview in the top row to open that document.

This document is a marketing presentation designed to be shown and viewed exclusively on-screen. Notice that the presentation opens in Full Screen mode to occupy all available space on the monitor.

8 Press Enter or Return several times to page through the presentation. The colorful graphics, large type size, and horizontal page layout have been designed for optimal display on a monitor.

The Full Screen preference settings in Acrobat Professional let you control how pages display in this mode. For example, you can have a full-screen document with each page displayed automatically for a certain number of seconds.

9 Press the Escape key to exit Full Screen mode.

10 Click the Previous View button until you return to the previews in the Introduc.pdf document.

An online help publication and an electronic catalog are further examples of documents for which on-screen viewing is suitable and even preferred. Electronic publishing offers intuitive navigational features, such as hypertext links, which are well-suited for publications meant to be browsed or used as quick reference guides.

Designing documents for online viewing

Once you have identified the final format for your publication, you can begin to make the design and production decisions that will help make the publication attractive and easy to use. If you're simply converting an existing paper document to electronic format, you'll inevitably weigh the benefits of reworking the design against the time and cost required to do so. If your publication will be viewed on-screen and on paper, you'll need to make the design accommodate the different requirements of both.

First you'll take a look at a document designed to be browsed online but printed out for closer viewing.

1 In the Introduc.pdf file, click the Brochure preview at the bottom of the page to open the corresponding document.

This document is a printed brochure that was converted unchanged to electronic format. Converting a document to Adobe PDF is a good way to distribute it cheaply and easily. It also enables you to use features such as hypertext links to make navigation of the online brochure both easy and intuitive.

2 If necessary, click the Fit Page button (🗋) to view the entire page. Click the Next Page button (▶) in the toolbar a few times to page through the brochure.

Notice that while the online brochure is useful for quick browsing and printing of selected pages, it is not designed to be read on-screen. The long and narrow pages are inconveniently shaped for the screen, and the small image and type sizes make reading a strain for the user.

Now you'll look at the same brochure redesigned and optimized for online reading. The topics in the brochure have been reorganized as a series of nested and linked topic screens that lead the reader through the document.

3 Click the Previous View button (⊙) until you return to the Introduc.pdf file, and click the Park Kiosk preview at the top of the page to open that document.

4 If necessary, click the Fit Page button to view the entire page.

Notice that the horizontal page orientation is well-suited for display on a monitor.

5 Click About the Park to activate that link.

The About the Park topic screen appears, with its own list of subtopics. Notice how the larger image and type sizes make this document easier to view than the online brochure.

Notice also the use of sans serif fonts in the publication. Sans serif fonts have simpler and cleaner shapes than serif fonts, making them easier to read on-screen.

6 Click Flora & Fauna to jump to that topic screen. Then click Lowland Forest to view a specific information screen about the Olympic Elk in this region.

Notice that the pages of the original brochure have been redesigned to accommodate a navigational structure based on self-contained, screen-sized units.

The formatting considerations of on-screen publications—fonts, page size, layout, color, and resolution—are the same as those of other kinds of publications; however, each element must be reevaluated in the context of on-screen viewing. Decisions about issues such as color and resolution, which in traditional publishing may require a trade-off between quality and cost, may require a parallel trade-off between quality and file size in electronic publishing. Once you have determined the page elements that are important to you, you need to choose the publishing tools and format that will best maintain the desired elements.

7 Click the Previous View button until you return to the Introduc.pdf file.

8 Click the Online Booklet preview to see another example of a PDF document designed for online viewing.

9 Choose Window > Close All to close any open PDF files.

In this lesson, you have examined a variety of electronic documents designed in different file formats for different purposes. Later on in this book, you'll get some hands-on practice in creating and tailoring your own electronic documents.

Review questions

1 Describe some of the features of Acrobat 6.0 Professional.

2 How do electronic documents designed for printing differ from documents optimized for online use?

3 What hardware and software do you need to view PDF documents?

4 What kinds of media can you use to distribute PDF documents?

5 What kinds of fonts or typefaces and type sizes are best suited for on-screen display?

Review answers

1 Acrobat 6.0 Professional is used for creating, modifying, printing, and viewing PDF documents. Among the things you can do with Acrobat are add hyperlinks, electronic bookmarks, and page actions to PDF documents; add password protection to prevent users from copying text and graphics, printing a document, or even opening a file; digitally sign documents; add comments and files, and markup text; and add signature fields to existing documents.

2 Electronic documents designed for paper output tend to be longer, text-intensive documents. Optimized online documents have been redesigned for optimal display on a monitor and may contain more graphics and screen-based navigational features.

3 You can view PDF documents on Windows, Mac OS, or UNIX computer systems. In addition to a computer, you need Adobe Reader, Acrobat Professional, or Acrobat Professional to view PDF documents.

4 You can distribute PDF documents via floppy disk, CD, electronic mail, corporate intranet, or the World Wide Web. You can also print PDF documents and distribute them as printed documents.

5 Large fonts or typefaces with simple, clean shapes display most clearly on the screen. Sans serif fonts are more suitable than serif fonts, which contain embellishments more suitable for the printed page.

Lesson 2

2 Getting to Know the Work Area

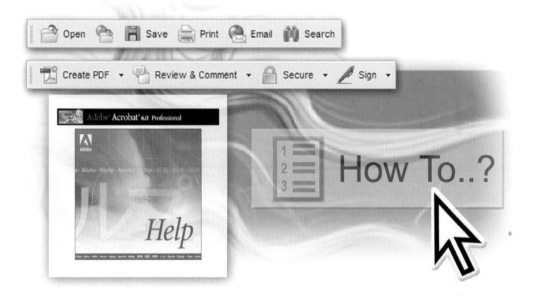

In this lesson, you'll familiarize yourself with the Complete Acrobat 6.0 Help, the Acrobat toolbars, and the Acrobat work area. You'll learn how to navigate through an Adobe PDF document, paging through an online document using controls built into Adobe Acrobat 6.0 Professional. You'll also get some tips on printing help topics.

In this lesson, you'll learn how to do the following:

- Use the Complete Acrobat 6.0 Help and the How To window.

- Work with Acrobat tools and navigation pane.

- Page through an Adobe PDF document using Acrobat's built-in navigational controls.

- Change how an Adobe PDF document scrolls and displays in the document window.

- Change the magnification of a view.

- Retrace your viewing path through a document.

This lesson will take about 60 minutes to complete.

If needed, remove the previous lesson folder from your hard drive and copy the Lesson02 folder onto it.

Note: Windows users may need to unlock the lesson files before using them. For information, see "Copying the Classroom in a Book files" on page 3.

Getting started

You'll practice navigating through a PDF version of a document. This document was created using Adobe FrameMaker® and then converted to Adobe PDF.

1 Start Acrobat Professional.

2 Choose File > Open. Select Illus_Excerpt.pdf in the Lesson02 folder, and click Open. Then choose File > Save As, rename the file **Illus_Excerpt1.pdf**, and save it in the Lesson02 folder.

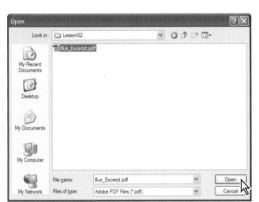 

On Windows

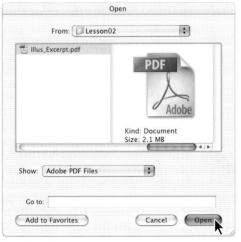 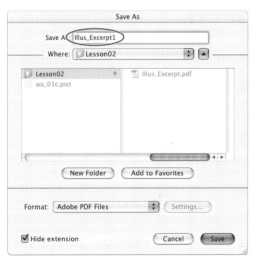

On Mac OS

Using the How To window

The How To window opens automatically on the right side of your Document window when you first open Acrobat Professional. This How To window lists several topic areas. Each of these topic areas links to a page that lists some of the more common tasks that you're likely to perform. The How To page also has a convenient link to the Complete Acrobat 6.0 Help. (For information on using the complete help system, see "Using the Complete Acrobat 6.0 Help" on page 50.)

In this section of the lesson, you'll learn how to hide the How To window when you don't need it and how to show it and use it to get information quickly.

The How To window offers links to step-by-step instructions for completing common tasks.

1 Click the Hide button at the top of the window to close the How To window.

2 Click the How To button (▤) on the Acrobat toolbar to reopen the How To window.

Click the Hide button to close the window.   *Click the How To button to open the window.*

If you want the How To window to open each time you launch Acrobat, make sure the Show How To Window at Startup option is checked. The option is checked when the box contains a check mark.

On Mac OS, when you hide the How To window, you can maximize the document window by clicking the Mac OS Zoom button. Subsequently, when you open and close the How To window, the document window remains maximized. On Windows, the document window is maximized automatically whenever the How To window is closed.

3 Click the Hide button at the top of the How To window.

You can also open the How To window by choosing a How To topic from the How To menu on the toolbar.

4 Click the arrow next to the How To button on the toolbar, and choose Review & Comment.

You can open the How To window by choosing a topic from the How To menu.

The How To window opens and displays a list of tasks related to reviewing and commenting. Use the scroll bar on the right of the How To window to scroll down the list if necessary.

5 Under the Create Comments heading in the How To window, click the Add a Note link.

Before you follow the steps for adding a note, take a look at how easy it is to navigate through the How To window.

6 Click the Back button (◀) at the top of the How To window once to return to the complete list of review and commenting topics. Click the Forward button (▶) to return to the steps explaining how to add a note.

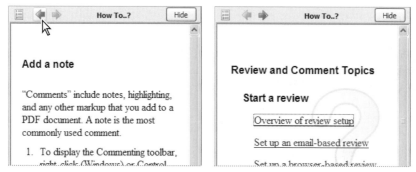

Use the Back and Forward buttons to navigate through the How To windows.

7 Click the Home Page button (▦) to return to the home page.

8 Click the Review & Comment link to return to the Review and Comment Topics window.

💡 *Always use the Back and Forward buttons to navigate through the How To windows. Clicking the Home Page button returns you to the list of How To topics but erases the navigation path associated with the Back and Forward buttons.*

Now you'll use the step-by-step instructions in the How To window to learn how to add a note to your PDF document.

9 Click the Add a Note link under Create Comments.

10 Follow the step-by-step instructions in the How To window to add a note. You can leave the note empty if you like.

Now you'll look at the additional links at the bottom of the Add a Note window. At the bottom of each set of step-by-step procedures, you'll find a link back to the complete list of tasks for this group of help topics. (In this case, "Review and Comment Topics.") In some cases, you'll also have a link to the topic in the complete online help system. (In this case, "Adding note comments.")

You also have links to related procedures. For example, you might decide that you need to delete the note that you've just added.

11 To find out how to delete a note, click the Select, Move, and Delete Comments link in the How To window. Clicking this link displays a new How To window that explains how to delete a note. Go ahead and follow the direction to delete the note you just added.

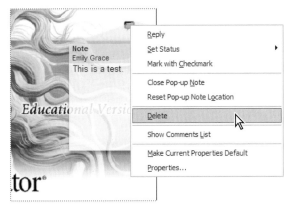

Right-click (Windows) or Control-click (Mac OS) the note,
and choose Delete or Delete Comment to remove the comment.

12 When you've finished, click the Home Page button ( ) at the top of the How To window.

Clicking the Home Page button always returns you to the list of topic areas, which also contains the link to the complete help system.

13 Click the Hide button to close the How To window.

14 Click the Close button on the Commenting toolbar to close the toolbar.

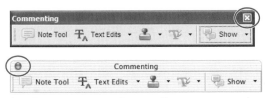

Click the Close button to close a toolbar.

 The step-by-step procedures presented in the How To window provide limited background information on procedures. For more in-depth information, you should always use the Complete Acrobat 6.0 Help.

Using the Acrobat tools, toolbars, and task buttons

When you first launch Acrobat Professional, a default set of toolbars and task buttons are displayed. The toolbars contain commonly used tools and commands for managing your Adobe PDF files, scrolling, zooming, selecting text and images, and rotating pages.

Task buttons on the toolbar give you access to additional commands and toolbars.

This section introduces the default toolbars and task buttons and shows you how to select tools, including hidden tools, how to open additional toolbars, and how to arrange the toolbars. As you work through the lessons in this book, you'll learn more about each tool's specific function.

To see the name of a toolbar, position the pointer over the toolbar's separator bar. A separator bar is located at the beginning of each toolbar.

Separator bar.

The File toolbar contains the Open, Create PDF from Web Page, Save, Print, Email, and Search buttons.

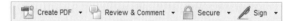

The Tasks toolbar contains the Create PDF, Review & Comment, Secure, Sign, Picture Tasks task, and eBooks buttons. (The eBooks button is hidden by default. The Picture Tasks button is not available unless you have an appropriate file open. See Lesson 14.)

Click the arrow next to any task button to show a menu of commands and associated tool and toolbars, as well as a link to the How To window for that task.

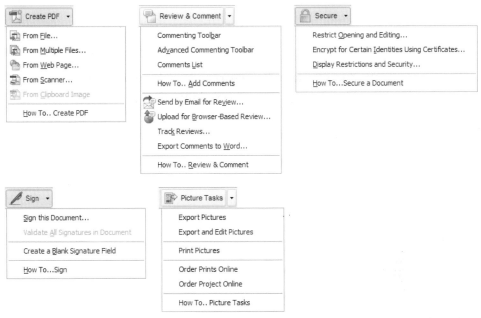

Note: *The commands available vary by platform. Also, the Picture Tasks button is not present on the Tasks toolbar unless you open a document that contains pictures created with the Adobe Photoshop® family of products, or unless you open a PDF file created by Acrobat from a JPEG source file.*

The Basic toolbar contains the Hand, Select Text, and Snapshot tools and related hidden tools.

The Zoom toolbar contains the Zoom In, Actual Size, Fit Page, Fit Width, Zoom Out, and Magnification tools and related hidden tools.

The Rotate View toolbar contains the Rotate Clockwise, Rotate Counterclockwise tools.

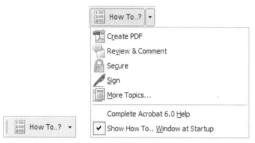

The How To task button.

Selecting tools

The default tool in Acrobat is the Hand tool (🖐).

1 To select a different tool, you click the tool icon in the toolbar. A selected tool usually remains active until you select a different tool.

2 Click the Actual Size button (⬜) to display the page at 100%.

3 Click the Zoom In tool (🔍). Notice that when you move the pointer into the document pane, the pointer changes to a magnifying glass (🔍).

4 Click in the document pane. The view of the document is magnified.

5 Click the arrow next to the Zoom In tool, and select the Zoom Out tool (🔍).

6 Click in the document pane again. The view of the document returns to 100%.

7 Select the Hand tool.

The presence of an arrow or small triangle to the right of a tool icon indicates the presence of additional hidden tools.

💡 *You can temporarily revert to the Hand tool while you have another tool selected by pressing the space bar. When you release the space bar, your other tool is the selected tool again.*

Using the Tools menu

You can also access hidden tools using the Tools menu. In the prior section, you used the arrow next to the Zoom In tool ( ) to reveal the Zoom Out tool ( ). Now you'll use the Tools menu to access the same tool.

1 Choose Tools > Zoom > Zoom Out. The hand changes to the magnifying glass containing a minus sign.

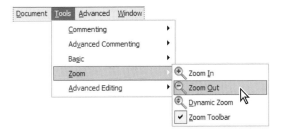

2 Select the Hand tool ( ).

Take a few minutes to explore some of the tools you can access from this menu. The Tools menu offers a convenient way to access many of the hidden tools without crowding the toolbar area with unnecessary toolbars. When you are finished, be sure to select the Hand tool.

Docking toolbars

You can often display hidden tools in a separate toolbar and dock the toolbar in the main toolbar area.

1 Click on the arrow next to the Select Text tool ( ). When the list of additional tools appears, click Show Selection Toolbar.

The selection tools are displayed on a floating toolbar. You can leave the floating toolbar as is, or dock it with the other toolbars.

2 To dock a floating toolbar, drag it by its separator bar or title bar and drop it in the toolbar area.

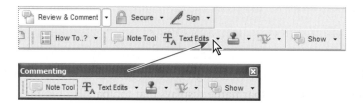

You can drag toolbars to a new location in the toolbar area. You can also drag toolbars from the toolbar area into the document pane or navigation pane. The toolbar area holds up to three rows of toolbars.

Practice moving toolbars in and out of the toolbar area.

If your toolbar area becomes cluttered as you expand some of the hidden toolbars, you can create more space by hiding the tool button labels. Choose View > Toolbars > Tool Button Labels to hide or show all the labels. Acrobat also automatically hides labels selectively as the toolbar area becomes full.

Using keyboard shortcuts to select tools

You can set your Acrobat Professional preferences so that you can use a keyboard shortcut to select tools.

1. *Choose Edit > Preferences (Windows) or Acrobat > Preferences (Mac OS), and select General in the left pane.*

2. *Click the check box next to the Use Single-Key Accelerators to Access Tools option. A checkmark appears in the box when this option is selected.*

3. *Click OK to apply the change.*

Now when you position the cursor over a tool, you'll see a letter in parentheses following the tool name. This is the keyboard shortcut for that tool.

4. *Move the cursor over the Select Text tool and notice that the tooltip now contains the letter "V." This is the keyboard shortcut.*

5. *Move the cursor into the document pane, and press "V" on the keyboard. The cursor changes from a hand to a selection cursor.*

6. *Click the Hand tool.*

Customizing toolbars

You can customize your toolbars, putting the ones you use most frequently together in the most convenient location.

1 To hide a toolbar, select the Hand tool ( ), choose View > Toolbars, and choose a name of a toolbar (such as Basic) from the menu. A checkmark appears next to the name of any toolbar that is currently visible. Selecting a checked toolbar name hides that toolbar. Selecting an unchecked toolbar name displays that toolbar. Try hiding and showing different toolbar combinations.

You can also show or hide a toolbar by right-clicking (Windows) or Control-clicking (Mac OS) in the toolbar area, and then selecting the toolbar name from the context menu.

2 To show the Basic toolbar again, right-click (Windows) or Control-click (Mac OS) in the toolbar area and choose Basic from the menu.

3 To move a toolbar, drag it by the separator bar. Release the mouse button when the toolbar is located in its new position. Try dragging a toolbar to another location in the toolbar area or into the document pane. For example, drag a toolbar from the upper row to the lower row. Then drag the bar back to its original location and reattach it.

Locking toolbars

If you customize the arrangement of toolbars in the toolbar area, you can save your arrangement by locking the toolbars. Locking the toolbars preserves your arrangement, even after you close and restart Acrobat Professional. (You cannot lock the position of a floating toolbar.)

1 To preserve the arrangement of toolbars in the toolbar area, choose View > Toolbars > Lock Toolbars.

When toolbars are locked, the separator bars are hidden. We recommend that you don't lock toolbar configurations until you're confident of the toolbars that you'll use most often.

2 To unlock toolbars, choose View > Toolbars > Lock Toolbars again.

Resetting toolbars

After you have rearranged the toolbars, you can revert to the Acrobat default toolbar arrangement by choosing View > Toolbars > Reset Toolbars. The Reset Toolbars command can be used to reset locked toolbars but you need to unlock the toolbars before you can rearrange them again.

Experiment with expanding and collapsing toolbars, and repositioning them.

When you're finished, we recommend that you reset the toolbars before continuing with the lessons in this book.

Using Acrobat panels

Acrobat provides panels to help you organize and keep track of a document's bookmarks, page thumbnails, comments, signatures, articles, and destinations. Panels can be docked inside the navigation pane or floated over the work area. They can also be grouped with other panels. This section introduces the navigation pane and shows you how to display panels. As you work through later lessons in this book, you'll learn more about each panel's specific function.

Displaying panels

You can display panels in a variety of ways. Experiment with several techniques:

• To show the navigation pane as you work, click the tab of the panel that you want to open, or click the Navigation Pane button ( ) in the status bar at the bottom of the Acrobat window. To close the navigation pane, click the tab of the active panel (the panel that you are currently viewing), or click the Navigation Pane button.

• To show or hide a panel, choose the panel's name from the View > Navigation Tabs menu. If the navigation pane is closed, no names are checked. The name of the panel that is currently active is checked.

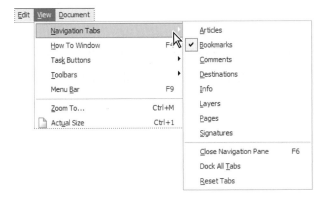

Changing the panel display

You can change the panel display in a variety of ways.

If necessary, click the Navigation Pane button in the status bar to open the navigation pane, and then experiment with several techniques for changing the panel display:

• To change the width of the navigation pane while it's visible, drag the pane's right border.

• To bring a panel to the front of a group of panels, click the panel's tab.

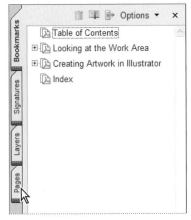 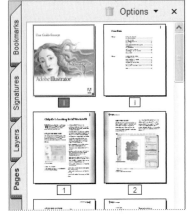

Click a panel's tab to bring it to the front.

- To move a panel to its own floating window, drag the panel's tab to the document pane. To return the panel to the navigation pane, drag the panel's tab back into the navigation pane.

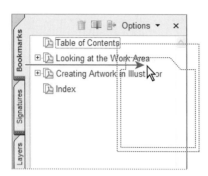

- To display the Options menu for a panel, click the Options button at the top of the panel. Drag to select a command. To hide a panel menu without making a selection, click in the blank space in the navigation pane.

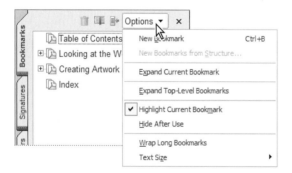

The Comments window, which appears across the bottom of the document pane, has a unique set of buttons and commands that help you manage comments in a PDF document. For information on using this panel, see Lesson 8, "Using Acrobat Professional in a Document Review Cycle."

Using context menus

In addition to menus at the top of your screen, context menus display commands relevant to the active tool, selection, or panel.

1 If necessary, click the Navigation Pane button (◀▶) in the status bar to open the navigation pane, and click the Bookmarks tab.

2 Position the pointer over the Table of Contents bookmark in the Bookmarks panel and right-click (Windows) or Control-click (Mac OS). After you have looked at the commands available in the context menu, click in a blank area anywhere outside the context menu to close it without choosing a command. You'll learn more about these commands in later lessons.

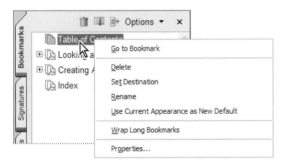

About the on-screen display

Take a look at the status bar located at the bottom of the document window and the Zoom toolbar located at the top of the document window. Notice that the document size is given in inches (7.5 x 8.4).

The magnification shown in the status bar does not refer to the printed size of the page, but rather to how the page is displayed on-screen. Acrobat determines the on-screen display of a page by treating the page as a 72 ppi (pixels-per-inch) image. For example, if your page has a print size of 2-by-2 inches, Acrobat treats the page as if it were 144 pixels wide and 144 pixels high (72 x 2 = 144). At 100% view, each pixel in the page is represented by 1 screen pixel on your monitor.

How large the page actually appears on-screen depends on your monitor size and your monitor resolution setting. For example, when you increase the resolution of your monitor, you increase the number of screen pixels within the same monitor area. This results in smaller screen pixels and a smaller displayed page, since the number of pixels in the page itself stays constant. The following illustration shows the variation among 100% displays of the same page on different monitors.

Pixel dimensions and monitor resolution

Regardless of the print size specified for an image, the size of an image on-screen is determined by the pixel dimensions of the image and the monitor size and setting. A large monitor set to 640-by-480 pixels uses larger pixels than a small monitor with the same setting. In most cases, default PC monitor settings display 96 pixels per inch, and default Macintosh monitor settings display approximately 72 pixels per inch.

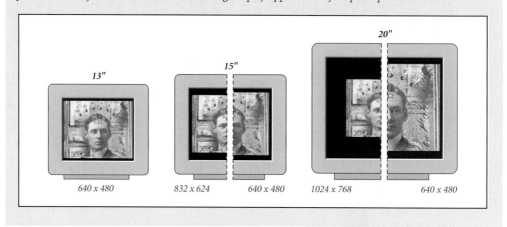

Setting up a work area

As you become more familiar with Acrobat Professional, you'll want to rearrange your toolbars so that the tools you use most often are always close at hand and the navigation panels are arranged for easy access. While you're working with the lessons in this book, however, we suggest that you set up your work area as described in this section.

Closing the How To window

Because the How To window takes up quite a lot of space, we'll close it. You learned earlier in the lesson how to open the window when you need it or how to access the How To topics from the Task button.

1 Click the How To button (▤) on the toolbar to open the How To window.

2 In the How To window, verify that the check box next to the option Show How To Window at Startup is empty. If it isn't empty, click the check box to remove the check mark. This action stops the How To window opening automatically whenever you start Acrobat. Then click the Hide button at the top of the window.

When you're finished with these lessons, you can reset the How To window to open automatically each time you start Acrobat by choosing Show How To .. Window at Startup from the How To task button menu.

Organizing the toolbars

You'll start work with the default toolbar arrangement. As you progress through the lessons, you'll open and close additional toolbars as needed.

1 Choose View > Toolbars > Reset Toolbars to return to the default toolbar configuration.

2 Choose View > Toolbars, and verify that there is no check mark next to the Lock Toolbars command. The toolbars should *not* be locked.

3 Choose View > Toolbars, and verify that there is a check mark next to the Tool Button Labels command. The tool button labels should be on.

Navigating the document

Acrobat provides a variety of ways for you to move through and adjust the magnification of a PDF document. For example, you can scroll through the document using the scroll bar at the right side of the window, or you can turn pages as in a traditional book using the browse buttons in the Navigation toolbar (which is closed by default) or the status bar at the bottom of the document pane. You can also jump to a specific page using the status bar at the bottom of the window or the page thumbnails in the Pages panel.

Browsing the document

1 If needed, click the Navigation Pane button (◀▶) in the status bar or click the current tab to hide the navigation pane, and if you're not on the first page of the document, click the First Page button (▐◀) in the status bar.

2 Click the Fit Width button (▢).

3 Make sure that the Single Page button (▢) on the status bar is selected.

4 Select the Hand tool (🖐) in the toolbar, position your pointer over the document. Hold down the mouse button. Notice that the hand pointer changes to a closed hand when you hold down the mouse button.

5 Drag the closed hand up and down in the window to move the page around on the screen. This is similar to moving a piece of paper around on a desktop.

Drag with Hand tool to move page.   *Result.*

6 Press Enter or Return to display the next part of the page. You can press Enter or Return repeatedly to view the document from start to finish in screen-sized sections.

7 Click the Fit Page button (▢) to display the entire page in the window. If needed, click the First Page button to go back to page 1.

8 Position the pointer over the down arrow in the scroll bar, and click once.

The document scrolls automatically to display all of page 2. In the next step, you'll control how PDF pages scroll and display.

9 Click the Continuous button (⊟) in the status bar, and then use the scroll bar to scroll to page 3.

The Continuous option displays pages end to end like frames in a filmstrip.

10 Now click the Continuous - Facing button () in the status bar to display page spreads, with left- and right-hand pages facing each other, as on a layout board.

Continuous option.   *Continuous - Facing option.*

11 Click the First Page button to go back to page 1.

In keeping with the conventions of printed books, a PDF document always begins with a right-hand page.

12 Click the Single Page button (☐) to return to the original page layout.

You can use the page box in the status bar to switch directly to a specific page.

13 Move the pointer over the page box until it changes to an I-beam, and click to highlight the current page number.

14 Type 4 to replace the current page number, and press Enter or Return.

You should now be viewing page 4.

The scroll bar also lets you navigate to a specific page.

15 Begin dragging the scroll box upward in the scroll bar. As you drag, a page status box appears. When page 1 appears in the status box, release the mouse.

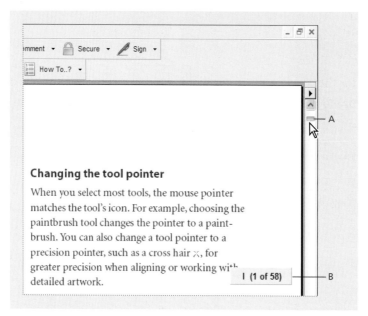

Changing the tool pointer

When you select most tools, the mouse pointer matches the tool's icon. For example, choosing the paintbrush tool changes the pointer to a paintbrush. You can also change a tool pointer to a precision pointer, such as a cross hair ⨯, for greater precision when aligning or working with detailed artwork.

A. Scroll box B. Page status box

You should now be back at the beginning of the document.

Browsing with page thumbnails

Page thumbnails are miniature previews of your document pages that are displayed in the Pages panel, which is docked in the navigation pane to the left of the document pane.

In this part of the lesson, you'll use page thumbnails to navigate and change the view of pages. In Lesson 7, "Modifying PDF Files," you'll learn how to use page thumbnails to reorder pages in a document.

1 Click the Fit Width button (▱) to view the full width of the page. You should be looking at page 1 (3 of 58).

2 Click the Pages tab in the navigation pane to open and bring the Pages panel to the front.

Page thumbnails for every page in the document are displayed automatically in the navigation pane. The page thumbnails represent both the content and page orientation of the pages in the document. Page-number boxes appear beneath each page thumbnail.

You may need to use the scroll bar to view all the page thumbnails.

3 Click the page 3 thumbnail to go to page 3.

The page number for the page thumbnail is highlighted, and a full-width view of page 3 appears in the document window, centered on the point that you clicked.

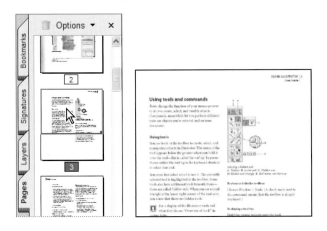

Take a look at the page 3 thumbnail. The rectangle inside the page thumbnail, called the page-view box, represents the area displayed in the current page view. You can use the page-view box to adjust the area and magnification being viewed.

4 Position the pointer over the lower right corner of the page-view box. Notice that the pointer turns into a double-headed arrow.

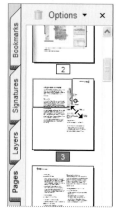

Drag lower right corner   *Result.*
of page-view box upward.

5 Drag to shrink the page-view box, and release the mouse button. Take a look at the Zoom toolbar and notice that the magnification level has increased to accommodate the smaller area being viewed.

6 Now position the pointer over the bottom border of the page-view box. Notice that the pointer changes to a hand.

7 Drag the page-view box within the page thumbnail, and watch the view change in the document window.

8 Drag the page-view box down to focus your view on the image at the bottom of the page.

Page thumbnails provide a convenient way to monitor and adjust your page view in a document.

9 Click the Pages tab to hide the navigation pane.

Changing the page view magnification

You can change the magnification of the page view using controls in the toolbar, or by clicking or dragging in the page with the Zoom In ( ) or Zoom Out tool ( ).

1 Click the Fit Width button ( ). This control adjusts the magnification to spread the page across the whole width of your screen. A new magnification appears in the Zoom toolbar.

2 Click the Previous Page button ( ) to move to page 2. Notice that the magnification remains the same.

3 Click the Actual Size button ( ) to return the page to a 100% view.

4 Click the arrow to the right of the magnification pop-up menu in the Zoom toolbar to display the preset magnification options. Drag to choose 200% for the magnification.

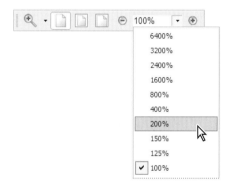

You can also enter a specific value for the magnification.

5 Move the pointer over the magnification box in the Zoom toolbar, and click to highlight the current magnification.

6 Type 75 to replace the current magnification, and press Enter or Return.

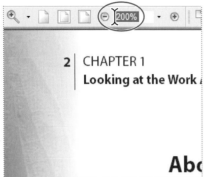

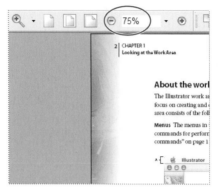

Click to highlight magnification.

Type in new magnification, and press Enter or Return.

7 Now click the Actual Size button ( ) to display the page at 100% in the window.

Next you'll use the Zoom In tool to magnify a specific portion of a page.

8 Type 3 in the page box, and press Enter or Return to go to page 3. Then select the Zoom In tool ( ) in the toolbar.

9 Click in the top right section of the page to increase the magnification. Notice that the view centers around the point you clicked. Click in the top right section of the page once more to increase the magnification again.

10 Hold down Ctrl (Windows) or Option (Mac OS). Notice that the zoom pointer now appears with a minus sign, indicating that the Zoom Out tool ( ) is active.

11 With Ctrl or Option held down, click in the document to decrease the magnification. Ctrl-click or Option-click once more to decrease the magnification again, and then release Ctrl or Option.

The page should be displayed at 100% again.

Now you'll drag the Zoom In tool to magnify the image.

12 Click the Next Page button to go to page 3, and position the pointer near the top left of the image, and drag over the text as shown in the following illustration.

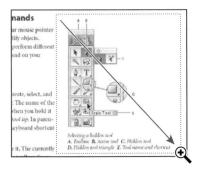

Marquee-zooming.

The view zooms in on the area you enclosed. This is called *marquee-zooming.*

Using the Dynamic Zoom tool

The Dynamic Zoom tool lets you zoom in or out by dragging the mouse up or down.

1. *Click the arrow next to the Zoom In tool, and choose Dynamic Zoom.*

2. *Click in the document pane, and drag upward to magnify the view, and drag down to reduce the view. You can switch from the Zoom In or Zoom Out tool to the Dynamic Zoom tool, by pressing the Shift key. When you release the Shift key, you switch back to the Zoom In or Zoom Out tool.*

Following links

In a PDF document, you don't always have to view pages in sequence. You can jump immediately from one section of a document to another using custom navigational aids such as links.

One benefit of placing a document online is that you can convert traditional cross-references into links, which users can use to jump directly to the referenced section or file. For example, you can make each item under the contents list into a link that jumps to its corresponding section. You can also use links to add interactivity to traditional book elements such as glossaries and indexes. In this lesson you'll follow links; in later lessons, you'll create links.

Now you'll try out an existing link.

1 Click the Previous Page button (◀) in the status bar several times to return to the Contents page, and click the Fit Page button (▢) so that you can view the entire page.

2 Select the Hand tool (✋). Move the pointer over the Creating Artwork in Illustrator heading in the Contents. The Hand tool changes to a pointing finger, indicating the presence of a link. Click to follow the link.

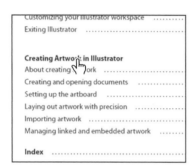

This item links to the chapter on Creating Artwork in Illustrator.

3 Click the Previous View button (◉) to return to your previous view of the Contents.

You can click the Previous View button at any time to retrace your viewing path through a document. The Next View button (◉) lets you reverse the action of your last Previous View.

In this section, you have learned how to page through a PDF document, change the magnification and page layout mode, and follow links. In later lessons, you'll learn how to create links and create and use other navigational features, such as bookmarks, page thumbnails, and articles.

Printing PDF files

When you print Adobe PDF files, you'll find that many of the options in the Acrobat Print dialog box are the same as those found in the Print dialog boxes of other popular applications. For example, the Acrobat Print dialog box, lets you print a page, a view, an entire file, or a range of pages within a PDF file. (On Windows, you can also choose Print from the context menu.)

Here's how you can print non-contiguous pages or portions of pages in Acrobat.

1 In the Illus_Excerpt1.pdf document, do one of the following:

• Click the Pages tab and click the page thumbnails corresponding to the pages you want to print. You can Ctrl-click (Windows) or Command-click (Mac OS) page thumbnails to select non-contiguous pages, or Shift-click to select contiguous pages.

• To print an area on a page (rather than the entire page) on Windows, select the Zoom In tool and drag on the page to select the area that you want to print.

2 If you have a printer attached to your system and turned on, choose File > Print. Make sure the name of the printer attached to your system is displayed.

• If you have selected pages in the Pages panel, the Selected Pages option will be selected automatically in the Print dialog box.

• If you have zoomed in on a view of a page on Windows, click the Current View option in the Print dialog box. The Preview window shows the print area.

3 Click OK or Print to print your selected pages. Click Cancel to abort the printing operation.

If you have an Internet connection and a Web browser installed on your system, you can click Printing Tips in the Print dialog box to go to the Adobe Web site for the latest troubleshooting help on printing.

For information on printing comments, see Lesson 8, "Using Acrobat Professional in a Document Review Cycle."

If your PDF file contains oddly sized pages, you can use the Page Scaling option in the Print dialog box. The Fit to Paper option scales each page to fit the printer page size. Pages in the PDF file are magnified or reduced as necessary. The Shrink Large Pages option shrinks large pages to fit the printer page size. Undersize pages are not enlarged. The Tiling options print oversize pages on several pages that can be assembled to reproduce the oversize image.

4 Choose File > Close. You don't need to save any changes to the file.

Printing over the Internet

You can open Adobe PDF documents to printers and fax machines in the PrintMe network using the third-party plug-in, PrintMe Internet Printing. You can also securely store PDF files online for on-demand printing.

To print over the Internet:

1. Save the document, and then choose File > PrintMe Internet Printing.

2. In the PrintMe Networks dialog box, follow the prompts to sign up for a PrintMe user account, or log into your existing account. If you need assistance, refer to the PrintMe Help system.

Note: On Windows, you can also choose Programs > PrintMe Internet Printing > Download Driver from the Start menu to download the universal PrintMe driver, and then sign up for a PrintMe user account. Using the universal PrintMe driver will allow you to print over the Internet from any application installed on your computer.

—From the Complete Acrobat 6.0 Help.

Using the Complete Acrobat 6.0 Help

This book and the lessons in this book focus on commonly used tools and features of Acrobat 6.0 Professional. You can get complete information on all the Acrobat Professional tools, commands, and features for both Windows and Mac OS systems from the Complete Acrobat 6.0 Professional Help, an accessible HTML-based help system. The Complete Acrobat 6.0 Help is easy to use because you can look for topics in several ways:

• Scan the table of contents.

• Search for keywords.

• Use the index.

• Jump from topic to topic using related topics links.

Opening the Complete Acrobat 6.0 Help

1 Choose Help > Complete Acrobat 6.0 Help, or press F1 to open the Acrobat 6.0 online Help.

Acrobat Help opens in your browser. The help content is displayed in the right panel—the Topic frame; the navigation information is displayed in the left panel—the Navigation frame.

2 Click the Using Online Help link in the navigation pane to see the topic pages on how to use the Complete Acrobat 6.0 Help in the right panel.

3 Click the Using Other Assistance Features link in the right panel to read about other sources of help.

4 Use the Zoom In button (⊕) at the top of the Navigation frame to enlarge the image area if necessary.

5 When you are finished reading the information, click the Back button (◀) in your browser as required to return to the first page of the help system.

6 Click the minus sign (Windows) or downward pointing arrow (Mac OS) next to the Using Online Help bookmark in the Contents panel to collapse the contents.

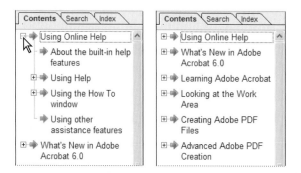

7 Use the scroll bar on the right of the Navigation frame to scroll through the headings. Click on any of these major topic headings to open a list of secondary topic headings in the Topic frame.

You can collapse or expand any topic listing in the Contents Navigation frame.

If you can't find the topic you need in the Contents, try using the index.

Using the index

1 Click the Index tab in the Navigation frame.

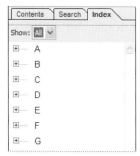

2 Click on any of the letters to see the entries under that letter. We clicked the letter **B**. As with the Contents list, you can expand any entry that is preceded by a plus sign (Windows) or an arrow (Mac OS). You can also use the scroll bar in the Navigation frame to move through the index.

3 Click the plus sign or arrow next to the backgrounds, watermarks" entry to expand the entry. Then click the entry "adding."

The Topic frame displays the information on adding watermarks and backgrounds.

💡 *You can also select the letter whose entries you want to review from the Show menu at the top of the Contents panel.*

Using the Search feature

If you can't find the information that you need using the Contents listing or the Index, you can use the Search feature.

1 Click the Search tab at the top of the Navigation frame to start a search.

2 Type in the word or words you want to search for. We typed in **Multiple Files** because we want to know more about the commands under the Create PDF button (📄).

Note: The search is not case-sensitive.

If you use multiple words in the search field, the search results will return all topics that contain one or all the search words. For this reason, you should be as precise as possible about the search word or phrase that you use.

3 Click the Search button.

The search results are listed in the Navigation frame.

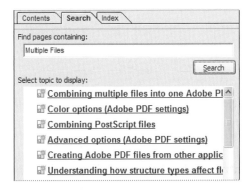

The search may take a few seconds to complete.

4 Move your pointer over the first topic listed, "Combining Multiple Files into One Adobe PDF File." The topic looks promising, so click the link to view the help topic. Occurrences of the search word or words are highlighted.

You can view the help topics on-screen, or you can print them.

Printing help topics

1 To print a help topic, simply click the Print Topic button (⬚) on the Help toolbar, and click the Print button in the Print dialog box.

2 Click the browser Close button to close the online Help.

3 Exit or quit Acrobat Professional.

Printing the complete online Help

Your Acrobat Professional application CD contains an Adobe PDF file of the complete online help in a printable format. Browse your application CD to find the Acrobat 6 Help.pdf file in the Help folder. You can print a page, a range of pages, or the entire file.

Now that you're familiar with the Acrobat work area, you can move through the lessons in this book and learn how to create and work with Adobe PDF files.

Review questions

1 How do you select a hidden tool?

2 Name several ways in which you can move to a different page.

3 Name several ways in which you can change the view magnification.

4 How do you reset the toolbars to their default configuration?

5 How would you find a topic in the Complete Acrobat 6.0 Help?

Review answers

1 Do one of the following:

• Select a hidden tool by holding down the mouse button on the arrow or triangle next to the related tool until the additional tools appear, and then drag to the tool you want.

• Choose Tools, and choose the appropriate category from the menu. Then choose the tool from the listing.

• Display the expanded toolbar by holding down the mouse button on the arrow or triangle next to the tool, and then choosing the command to show the toolbar.

2 You can move to a different page by clicking the Previous Page or Next Page button in the status bar; dragging the scroll box in the scroll bar; highlighting the page box in the status bar and entering a page number; or clicking a bookmark, page thumbnail, or link that jumps to a different page.

3 You can change the view magnification by clicking the Actual Size, Fit Page, or Fit Width buttons in the toolbar; marquee-zooming with the Zoom In or Zoom Out tool; choosing a preset magnification from the magnification menu in the Zoom toolbar; or highlighting the entry in the magnification box and entering a specific percentage.

4 Choose View > Toolbars > Reset Toolbars.

5 You can look for a topic using the Acrobat 6.0 online Help contents listing. You can also look in the index for keywords, and you can search for words in the Complete Acrobat 6.0 Help using the Search command.

Lesson 3w

3w Converting Microsoft Office Files (Windows)

Acrobat Professional is designed to work efficiently with your Microsoft Office applications. You can create Adobe PDF files and email them without ever leaving your Microsoft application. Friends and colleagues can open your documents reliably, regardless of whether they work on Mac OS, Windows, or UNIX. You can even convert Web pages to Adobe PDF from inside Internet Explorer and print them reliably—no more cut-off pages.

This lesson is designed for Windows users who have Microsoft Office applications—Microsoft Word, Microsoft PowerPoint, Microsoft Excel, Microsoft Outlook, and Internet Explorer—installed on their computer. You cannot complete this lesson if you do not have any of these Microsoft applications installed. If you do not use Microsoft Office applications, you should skip this lesson and move on to Lesson 4, "Converting Files to Adobe PDF."

In this lesson, you'll learn how to do the following:

- Convert a Microsoft Word file to Adobe PDF.

- Convert Word headings and styles to Adobe PDF bookmarks.

- Convert Word comments to Adobe PDF notes.

- Add password protection to your Adobe PDF files.

- Change the Adobe PDF conversion settings.

- Convert a Microsoft Excel file and send it for review online.

- Convert a file and attach it to an email in Microsoft Outlook.

This lesson will take about 60 minutes to complete.

If needed, remove the previous lesson folder from your hard drive, and copy the Lesson03\Win folder onto it.

Note: Windows users may need to unlock the lesson files before using them. For information, see "Copying the Classroom in a Book files" on page 3.

Getting started

PDFMaker, which is installed automatically when you install Acrobat Professional, is used to create Adobe PDF files from within Microsoft Office applications. Convert to Adobe PDF buttons and an Adobe PDF menu are added automatically to the toolbar and menu bar in the Microsoft Office applications. You also use this menu and buttons to control the settings used in the conversion to Adobe PDF, email your PDF file, and set up an email review process without ever leaving your Microsoft Office application. For complete information on which Microsoft applications are supported and which versions of the Microsoft applications are supported, visit the Adobe Web site (www.adobe.com).

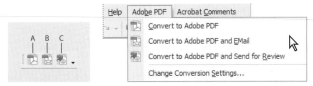

Acrobat adds buttons and a menu to your Office application that let you quickly convert a file to Adobe PDF.
A. Convert to Adobe PDF
B. Convert to Adobe PDF and Email
C. Convert to Adobe PDF and Send for Review

Note: *For the PDFMaker buttons and menu to be installed correctly, your Microsoft Office applications must be installed before you install Acrobat Professional. If you install a Microsoft Office application after installing Acrobat Professional, you can use the Help > Detect and Repair feature in Acrobat to retroactively install the PDFMaker buttons and menu. If you still don't see the Acrobat buttons and menu, choose View > Toolbars in your Office application, and make sure that PDFMaker 6.0 is checked.*

Acrobat installs essentially the same buttons and commands for creating PDF files, creating and emailing PDF files, and creating and emailing PDF files for review in Word, PowerPoint, and Excel. Although there are some application-specific differences in the Acrobat/Office interface—for example, PDFMaker for Excel offers the ability to convert an entire workbook, an option that isn't available in Word or PowerPoint—you should be able to complete all sections in this lesson, even if you have only one Microsoft Office application, such as Word, installed on your system. Just follow the steps in each section, avoiding application-specific steps, and use the lesson file that corresponds to the Microsoft Office application that you have. (You do need to have Microsoft Outlook and Internet Explorer installed to complete "Converting and attaching a file in Microsoft Outlook" on page 79 and "Converting Web pages from Internet Explorer" on page 81.)

Converting a Microsoft Word file to Adobe PDF

Word is a popular authoring program that makes it easy to create a variety of types of document. Very often, users of Word apply styles to create headings and create hyperlinks to make their documents more usable. In a review process, users may also add Word comments.

When you create an Adobe PDF document from your Word document, you can convert Word styles and headings to Acrobat bookmarks and convert comments to Acrobat notes. Hyperlinks in your Word document are preserved. Your Adobe PDF file will look just like your Word file and retain the same functionality, but it will be equally accessible to readers on all platforms (Mac OS, Windows, UNIX), regardless of whether or not they have the Word application.

About the Microsoft Word file

First you'll look at the Word file that you'll convert to Adobe PDF.

1 Start Microsoft Word.

2 Choose File > Open. Select the file Our_Wines.doc, located in the Lesson03\Win folder, and click Open. Then choose File > Save As, rename the file **Our_Wines1.doc**, and save it in the Lesson03\Win folder.

3 If necessary, choose Whole Page from the Zoom menu so that you can view the entire page.

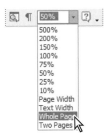

4 Place the pointer on the heading "Awards," and click to create an insertion point. Notice that the Word style is titled "Chamberg Title." (If necessary, open the Styles and Formatting panel by choosing Format > Styles and Formatting to view the styles and formatting options.)

*Click in the heading or select the heading to
display the name of the Word style.*

5 Now place the pointer on the heading "PinotNoir," and click to create an insertion point. Notice that the Word style is titled "Chamberg Heading."

You'll use this information to convert your Word styles to bookmarks in Adobe PDF.

Notice also that a Word comment has been added to the document, requesting that a spelling error be corrected. In the next section you'll verify that this comment converts to an Acrobat note in the PDF document.

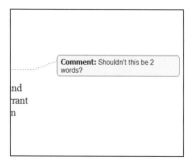

*Word comments are converted
automatically to Adobe PDF comments.*

Converting Word headings and styles to PDF bookmarks

If your Word document contains headings and styles that you want to convert to bookmarks in Adobe PDF, you must identify these headings and styles in the Acrobat PDFMaker dialog box. Word Heading 1 through Heading 9 styles are converted automatically and maintain their hierarchy. You do not need to change the Adobe PDF Conversion Settings to convert these nine styles to Adobe PDF bookmarks. Because the headings used in Our_Wines1.doc aren't formatted using Headings 1 through 9, you'll make sure that the styles used convert to bookmarks when you create the Adobe PDF file.

1 On the Word menu bar, choose Adobe PDF > Change Conversion Settings.

*The settings used in the conversion of a Word
document to an Adobe PDF document are made
in the Acrobat PDFMaker dialog box.*

The Acrobat PDFMaker dialog box is where you define the settings that control the conversion of your Microsoft application files to Adobe PDF. The tabs available in this dialog box vary with the Microsoft Office application that you are using. Because you are using Microsoft Word, the Word tab and the Bookmarks tabs are available in the Acrobat PDFMaker dialog box. Later in this lesson, you'll open the Acrobat PDFMaker dialog box from within PowerPoint and Excel. With these applications, you'll see only the Settings and Security tabs.

2 Click the Bookmarks tab.

This tab is where you determine which Word headings and styles are converted to Adobe PDF bookmarks. The author of Our_Wines1.doc used styles to format headings, and now you'll make sure that these Word styles are converted to PDF bookmarks.

3 Scroll down the list of bookmarks and styles, until you see the styles Chamberg Title and Chamberg Heading.

4 Move your pointer over the empty square in the Bookmarks column opposite Chamberg Title, and click in the empty box.

A cross appears indicating that a bookmark will be created for this style. Notice that the level is automatically set to 1. This is the hierarchical level of the PDF bookmark.

5 Move your pointer over the empty square in the Bookmarks column opposite Chamberg Heading, and click in the empty box.

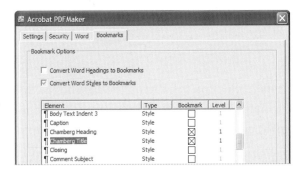

Again, a cross appears indicating that a bookmark will be created for this style. Notice again that the level is automatically set to 1. Because this level of heading is subordinate to the main heading, "About the Wines," you'll change the level setting so that the PDF bookmarks are nested to show the correct hierarchy.

6 Click on the number 1 in the Level column opposite Chamberg Heading, and select 2 from the menu. Changing the level to 2 nests these bookmarks under the first-level "About the Wines" bookmark.

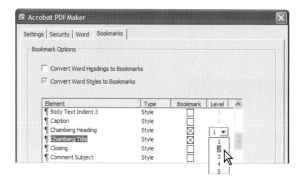

7 Click OK to accept the settings and close the dialog box.

Any settings that you make in the Bookmarks tab apply only to the conversion of Word documents.

Converting Word comments to PDF notes

You needn't lose any comments that have been added to your Word document when you convert the document to Adobe PDF, allowing your converted Word comments to become part of any Acrobat review process, as described in Lesson 8, "Using Acrobat Professional in a Document Review Cycle."

Now you'll make sure that the comment in your Word document is converted to a note in the Adobe PDF document.

First you'll hide the Word comments so they don't clutter up the page on the Adobe PDF document. (If you don't hide the comments, an image of the comment will appear on the PDF page, in addition to the Acrobat note that corresponds to the Word comment.)

1 In Word, choose View > Markup to hide the Word comment. (This option may not be available depending on your operating system.)

2 On the Word menu bar, choose Adobe PDF > Change Conversion Settings.

3 Click the Word tab in the Acrobat PDFMaker dialog box, and verify that the Convert Comments to Notes option is checked.

4 In the Comments window, you'll see one comment to be included. Make sure that the box in the Include column is checked.

5 To change the color of the note in the Adobe PDF document, click on the icon in the Color column to cycle through the available color choices. We chose blue.

6 To have the note automatically open in the PDF document, click in the box in the Notes Open column. You can always close the note in the PDF document later if you wish.

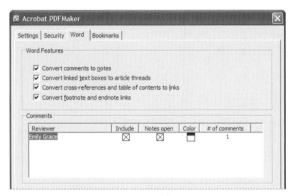

Set the color of your Adobe PDF notes and specify whether they are automatically opened.

Any settings that you make in the Word tab apply only to the conversion of Word documents.

Later in this lesson, you'll see the Adobe PDF note created from the Word comment. First though, you'll limit access to the PDF document in its review stage.

Adding security to your Adobe PDF file

There are several ways you can apply security to your Adobe PDF documents. You can add password security to prevent unauthorized users from opening, changing, or even printing your document, you can limit access to the PDF document to a predefined list of users, and you can certify the status of a document.

In this lesson, you'll add password security to your document to prevent unauthorized users from opening the document.

1 Click the Security tab in the Acrobat PDFMaker dialog box to review the security settings that you can apply to the PDF document that you create.

You'll see that no security is specified for the Adobe PDF document that you will create. However, since this is a copy for internal review only, you'll add password protection so that only users with the password can open the document, minimizing the chance that the document might be released to the public prematurely.

2 Click in the Require a Password to Open the Document box. The option is selected when the box contains a checkmark.

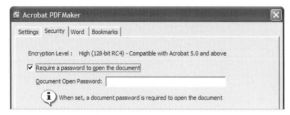

Set security options for your Adobe PDF document.

Now you'll set the password that opens the document.

3 In the Document Open Password text box, type in your password. We entered **wine123.** Be sure not to forget your password. You'll need to share this password with your colleagues, otherwise they won't be able to open your document.

Next you'll review the general conversion settings.

4 Click the Settings tab.

Before you can review the general conversion settings, you have to re-enter the password that you just set.

5 Re-enter your password. We entered **wine123.** Click OK to clear the confirmation dialog box.

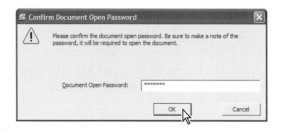

For more information on passwords and security, see Lesson 11, "Adding Signatures and Security."

About passwords and document security

When creating Adobe PDF documents, authors can use password security to add restrictions for opening, printing, or editing the document. PDF documents that include such security restrictions are called restricted documents. The following methods can enhance document security:

• Restricting opening, editing, and printing. (See "Adding passwords and setting security options" in the Complete Acrobat 6.0 Help.)

• Limiting the PDF document to a defined list of users. Determining which users can edit a PDF document is a process called encrypting. (See "Encrypting PDF files for a list of recipients" in the Complete Acrobat 6.0 Help.)

• Certifying a PDF document. When a document is certified, editing changes are restricted. (See "Certifying a document" in the Complete Acrobat 6.0 Help.)

• Changing permission settings for playing movies and sound clips. (See "Setting Trust Manager preferences" in the Complete Acrobat 6.0 Help.)

When someone sends you a restricted PDF document, you may need to enter a password to open it. If a document is encrypted, you may not be able to open it without permission from the person who created the document. In addition, restricted or certified documents may prevent you from printing your files or copying information to another application. If you're having trouble opening a PDF document, or if you're restricted from using certain features, contact the PDF document author.

—From the Complete Acrobat 6.0 Help.

Changing the conversion settings

Later in the lesson, you'll use a different set of conversion settings to create a smaller file that is more suitable to be emailed as an attachment. For this part of the lesson though, you'll use the default settings for the conversion.

Note: Conversion settings made in the Settings tab and the Security tab of the Acrobat PDFMaker dialog box remain in effect until you change them. If you apply password protection in the conversion process, for example, you should be sure to remove the password protection setting in the Acrobat PDFMaker dialog box unless you want that security to apply to subsequent conversions.

1 In the Acrobat PDFMaker dialog box, click the arrow next to the Conversion Settings menu.

This menu lists the predefined conversion settings used to create Adobe PDF files. For most users, these predefined settings—High Quality, Press Quality, Smallest File Size, and Standard—are sufficient. If you need to customize the conversion settings you can use the Advanced Settings button to access the Adobe PDF Settings dialog box. Lesson 5, "Customizing Adobe PDF Output Quality," describes how to customize the Adobe PDF Settings. Any customized settings that you have created are also listed in this menu.

To see an explanation of the default conversion settings, choose the name of a conversion set in the Conversion Settings menu. A description is displayed next to the information icon. Use the up and down scroll arrows to move through the text if the description exceeds two lines.

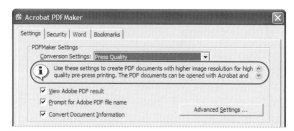

A description of each default conversion setting is displayed below the Conversion Setting menu.

2 Choose Standard from the Conversion Settings pop-up menu.

3 Verify that the View Adobe PDF Result option is checked. When this option is checked, Acrobat Professional is launched automatically and the Adobe PDF file that you create is displayed as soon as the conversion is complete.

Make sure that the Enable Accessibility and Reflow with Tagged PDF option is on (checked). Creating tagged PDF makes your files more accessible.

4 Click OK to apply your settings.

5 Now you've defined the settings to be used for the conversion, you're ready to convert your Word file to Adobe PDF, but first you'll save your file.

6 Choose File > Save to save your work in the Lesson03\Win folder.

Converting your Word file

1 Simply click the Convert to Adobe PDF button () on the Word toolbar.

2 In the Save Adobe PDF As dialog box, name and save your file. We named the file **Our_Wines1.pdf** and saved it in the Lesson03\Win folder.

Your file is converted to Adobe PDF. The status of the conversion is shown in the Acrobat PDFMaker message box. Because you applied password security to prevent unauthorized users from opening your document, the document does not open automatically. Instead, you have to enter the password that you set earlier in this section.

3 In the Password dialog box, enter your password and click OK. We entered **wine123**.

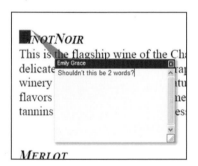

Acrobat displays your converted file. Notice that the Word comment has been converted to an open Adobe PDF note.

4 After you have read the note, click the close box on the note to close it.

5 Click the Bookmarks tab in the navigation pane, and notice that bookmarks have been created automatically and follow the hierarchy of the Word document. Click the Sparkling Wine bookmark to go to the associated text.

6 When you have finished reviewing the file, choose File > Close to save and close your work.

7 Choose File > Exit to close Acrobat Professional.

8 In Word, choose Adobe PDF > Change Conversion Settings.

9 In the Acrobat PDFMaker dialog box, click the Security tab and click in the Require a Password to Open the Document box to turn the option off, and click OK. If you don't turn this option off, all documents that you create using Acrobat PDFMaker will require entry of the password before you can open them.

10 Exit Microsoft Word.

For information on using the Convert to Adobe PDF and Email button (□), see "Converting and emailing a PowerPoint presentation" on page 72. For information on using the Convert to Adobe PDF and Send for Review button (□), see "Converting an Excel document and starting a review" on page 76.

You can convert multiple Office files of different file types and consolidate them into one PDF file using the Create From Multiple Files command in Acrobat. For more information, see Lesson 4, "Converting Files to Adobe PDF" and "Exploring on your own" at the end of this lesson.

Converting and emailing a PowerPoint presentation

PowerPoint presentations are an effective way to deliver your message, but not every place that you visit has a system available with Microsoft PowerPoint installed on it, nor does every person that you'd like to share your presentation with have this software. Converting your PowerPoint presentation to Adobe PDF allows you to show the presentation on any system that has the free Adobe Reader software installed. Similarly, you can email a PDF version of your presentation to anyone who has Adobe Reader. They'll see your presentation as you created it. All the page transitions are preserved.

In this section of the lesson, you'll convert a PowerPoint presentation to Adobe PDF and email it without ever leaving your PowerPoint application.

If you don't have PowerPoint installed on your system, you can use the Convert to Adobe PDF and Email button in Word to convert and email the Our_Wines.doc file. Open Our_Wines.doc in Word, skip the "About the PowerPoint file" section and go directly to the "Checking the conversion settings" section.

About the PowerPoint file

1 Start Microsoft PowerPoint.

2 Choose File > Open. Select the file Welcome.ppt, located in the Lesson03\Win folder, and click Open. Then choose File > Save As, rename the file **Welcome1.ppt**, and save it in the Lesson03\Win folder.

First you'll review the PowerPoint file.

3 Choose View > Slide Show.

4 Press Enter to move to the second page.

First you'll notice that a page transition has been applied to the presentation.

Also, on the second page, notice the fly-in bullets and the locators on the map. All these elements will appear in the Adobe PDF file that you create. (The fly-in animation is not preserved, but all the information is present.)

The fly-in information is preserved.

5 Press the Esc key to return to the normal PowerPoint view.

Checking the conversion settings

You'll check the default Adobe PDF Settings first to make sure they are appropriate for your needs.

1 Choose Adobe PDF > Change Conversion Settings.

2 In the earlier part of this lesson, when you converted a Word file, the Acrobat PDFMaker dialog box had four tabs—Settings, Security, Word, and Bookmarks. With PowerPoint, the dialog box has only the Settings and Security tabs.

3 In the Acrobat PDFMaker dialog box, click the Security tab.

No security is set for the conversion, which is correct because you want anyone to be able to open and view your PDF file. If you did want to add security, you would do so in the same way as described in "Adding security to your Adobe PDF file" on page 67.

4 Click the Settings tab.

Because you're going to email the file to various people, you want the file to be as small as possible.

5 Click the arrow next to the Conversion Settings to open the menu, and choose Smallest File Size.

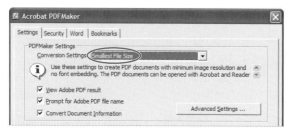

Choose the predefined Conversion Settings that give the smallest file size.

To customize the conversion settings, you would click the Advanced Settings button. For information on customizing the conversion settings, see Lesson 5, "Customizing Adobe PDF Output Quality."

You'll use the default settings for all the other conversion options.

Make sure that the Enable Accessibility and Reflow with Tagged PDF option is on (checked). Creating tagged PDF makes your files more accessible.

6 Click OK to apply the settings and close the dialog box.

Converting and emailing the presentation

Now you're ready to convert your PowerPoint presentation to Adobe PDF and email it in one easy step.

1 On the PowerPoint toolbar, click the Convert to Adobe PDF and Email button ().

2 In the Save Adobe PDF File As dialog box, click Save to save the file as **Welcome1.pdf** in the Lesson03\Win folder.

The conversion to Adobe PDF is shown in a progress window.

Your default email application is opened automatically, and your Adobe PDF document is attached. All you have to do is fill out recipient information and type a message.

3 In the newly opened email message window, type in recipient information, a subject line, and a message if you wish. We suggest that you send the message to yourself as a test.

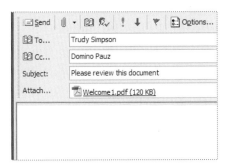

4 When you're ready to send the message, click Send or Send Message.

That's all there is to it. You've created a PDF version of your PowerPoint presentation and emailed it without ever leaving PowerPoint. The PDF version of your presentation is also saved on your hard drive. Now you'll check your PDF file.

5 If you emailed the PDF file to yourself, open your email application and open the PDF attachment. If you didn't email the PDF file to yourself, double-click the Welcome1.pdf file in the Lesson03\Win folder.

6 If necessary, click the Single Page button (▢) on the status bar to view the presentation one page at a time. Then use the Next Page button (▶) and the Previous Page button (◀) to navigate between the pages.

In a later lesson, you'll learn how to create a PDF file that opens in full-screen view so that your PDF files look just like PowerPoint presentations. (See Lesson 13, "Preparing Presentations.")

7 When you're finished reviewing the Welcome1.pdf file, close the file and exit Acrobat Professional.

8 Close the Welcome1.ppt file and exit PowerPoint.

Converting an Excel document and starting a review

In the prior section, you saw how easy it is to create a PDF file from a Microsoft Office application and email it to friends or colleagues without ever leaving your Microsoft Office application. In this section, you'll create a PDF file from an Excel document and start a formal review process in which the PDF file is emailed to selected reviewers. In addition to managing the email process, the Acrobat email review process also offers powerful file management and comment management tools to facilitate the review.

If you don't have Excel installed on your system, you can use the Convert to Adobe PDF and Email button in Word to convert and start an email review of the Our_Wines.doc file. Open Our_Wines.doc in Word, and go directly to the "Checking the conversion settings" section.

About the Excel file

1 Start Microsoft Excel.

2 Choose File > Open. Select the file Projections.xls, located in the Lesson03\Win folder, and click Open. Then choose File > Save As, rename the file **Projections1.xls**, and save it in the Lesson03\Win folder.

3 Change the Zoom value on Excel toolbar from 50% to 100%.

Now you'll review the Excel file. Notice that the first sheet has case-lot projections for red-wine sales.

4 Click the Sheet 2 button at the bottom of the Excel spreadsheet. The second sheet has case-lot projections for white wines. When you create your PDF file, you'll need to convert both these sheets.

Converting the entire workbook

If you convert an Excel file to Adobe PDF by simply clicking the Convert to Adobe PDF button on the Excel toolbar, you'll convert only the active worksheet. If you want to convert all the worksheets in a book, you must first select the Convert Entire Workbook option.

Note: Your Excel worksheet will be automatically sized for your printer page size. You don't need to worry about defining a custom page size.

Choose Adobe PDF > Convert Entire Workbook. The Convert Entire Workbook option is on when there is a checkmark; it is off when there is no checkmark. (The default is off.)

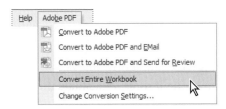

Checking the conversion settings

The settings used by Acrobat PDFMaker to convert Excel files are set in the same way as for Word and PowerPoint.

1 Choose Adobe PDF > Change Conversion Settings.

2 In the Acrobat PDFMaker dialog box, choose Smallest File Size from the Conversion Settings menu because you're going to be emailing the PDF file.

To customize the conversion settings, you would click the Advanced Settings button. For information on customizing the conversion settings, see Lesson 5, "Customizing Adobe PDF Output Quality."

You'll use the default values for all the other conversion settings.

Make sure that the Enable Accessibility and Reflow with Tagged PDF option is on (checked). When you create tagged PDF, you can more easily copy tabular data from PDF files back into spreadsheet applications. For more information, see "Exploring on your own" on page 81. Creating tagged PDF also makes your files more accessible.

Now you'll check that no security is specified for the file.

3 In the Acrobat PDFMaker dialog box, click the Security tab.

No security is set for the conversion, which is correct because you want anyone to be able to open and view your PDF file. If you did want to add security, you would do so in exactly the same way as described in "Adding security to your Adobe PDF file" on page 67.

4 Click OK to apply the conversion settings and close the dialog box.

Now you'll convert your Excel file and send it for review.

Starting an email-based review

When you send a file for review by email using the Convert to Adobe PDF and Send for Review button (🗐), you package your PDF file in an FDF setup file. When the recipient opens this setup file, the PDF file opens, together with instructions for adding and returning comments. When you in turn open comments returned by your reviewers, the comments are automatically added to a master copy of the PDF file.

You can also use the Review Tracker feature to invite additional reviewers to join the process or to send reminders to reviewers. For more information on using Acrobat in the reviewing and commenting process, see Lesson 8, "Using Acrobat Professional in a Document Review Cycle."

1 Click the Convert to Adobe PDF and Send for Review button (🗐).

First you'll be prompted to save the file.

2 In the Save Adobe PDF File As dialog box, and click Save to save the file as Projections1.pdf in the Lesson03\Win folder.

The conversion to Adobe PDF is shown in a progress window.

Acrobat launches automatically.

Your Adobe PDF document (in an FDF wrapper) is attached to a new email message window. All you have to do is fill out recipient information. Instructions for participating in the review are already included in the body of the email message. You can add further information to the review information if you wish. To add a personal note, click in the email message window to create an insertion point, and type your message.

3 If this is the first time you have used the Convert to Adobe PDF and Send for Review button, you will be asked to enter your own email address. Do so, and click OK. This is the address to which review comments are returned.

4 Enter the email address of a friend or colleague in the Send for Review by Email dialog box, and click OK. Acrobat uses this email address as the return address for comments submitted by reviewers.

Note: The Convert to Adobe PDF and Send for Review process requires that the sender and recipient be on two different systems. The process will not work correctly if you email the message to yourself.

5 When you're ready to send the message, click Send, and follow any on-screen prompts to complete the email process.

6 Close the Projections1.xls file, and exit Microsoft Excel.

You cannot experience the email review feature without at least one other participant. We encourage you to experiment with this feature when you have a document to review with colleagues.

Converting and attaching a file in Microsoft Outlook

Acrobat Professional adds an Attach as Adobe PDF button to Microsoft Outlook that allows you to convert files to Adobe PDF and attach the converted file to an email without leaving the Outlook application. You will only see the Attach as Adobe PDF button in a New Mail or New Discussion window.

1 Open Microsoft Outlook, and click the New button (or choose New > Mail Message) to open a new mail message.

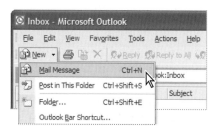

Note: Outlook 2000 is not supported if Microsoft Word is the email editor inside Outlook.

2 On the toolbar of the new mail message, click the Attach as Adobe PDF button to open the Choose File to Attach as Adobe PDF dialog box.

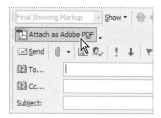

3 Choose the Memo.txt file in the Lesson03\Win folder, and click Open.

Note: If the file type cannot be converted to an Adobe PDF file, you will be asked if you want to attach the unconverted file. Supported file types include Microsoft Office files, PostScript, image format files, text files, and HTML files.

4 In the Save Adobe PDF Files As dialog box, name the file **Memo.pdf** and save it in the Lesson03\Win folder.

A message box shows the progress of the conversion, and depending on file type, the authoring application may launch in the background and close automatically when the conversion is complete.

The source file is converted to Adobe PDF, saved in the designated location on your system, and a copy of the PDF file is attached to the new mail message window in Microsoft Outlook. All you have to do is provide recipient information, write the text of your email message, and click Send.

5 When you're finished, exit Microsoft Outlook.

Converting Web pages from Internet Explorer

Acrobat adds a button and a menu to the toolbar of Internet Explorer 5.0.1 or later that allow you to convert the currently displayed Web page to an Adobe PDF file or convert and print it in one easy operation. When you print a Web page that you have converted to an Adobe PDF file, the page is reformatted to a standard printer page size and logical page breaks are added. You can be sure that your print copy will have all the information on the Web page that you see onscreen.

For complete information on converting Web pages from within Internet Explorer, see Lesson 6, "Creating Adobe PDF from Web Pages."

Exploring on your own

You can copy material out of PDF files for use in other applications almost as easily as you can convert an application file to Adobe PDF. In this optional section of the lesson, you can explore how easy it is to copy a table in a PDF file into an editable table in an Excel spreadsheet and how you can convert and combine Word, PowerPoint, and Excel files into one Adobe PDF file in one easy step.

Exporting tables from PDF files

You can easily copy and paste tables from a tagged PDF file into spreadsheet applications such as Excel. Earlier in this lesson ("Converting an Excel document and starting a review" on page 76), you converted an Excel workbook into a PDF file. You'll use that file to see how easy it is to copy and paste tables from PDF files back into spreadsheet applications.

1 Navigate to the Lesson03\Win folder, and double-click the Projections1.pdf file to open it in Acrobat Professional.

2 On the Acrobat toolbar, click the arrow next to the Select Text tool ( ), and choose the Select Table tool ( ).

3 Click anywhere in the table on the first page of the PDF file. The table is highlighted, and selected text is enclosed in a bounding box.

Note: If you can't select the table by clicking in it, right-click in the table, and make sure that the Select Table Uses Document Tags option is not selected. Then click in the table again.

4 Right-click in the selected table, and choose the Open Table in Spreadsheet command from the context menu.

Acrobat automatically launches Excel and copies and pastes the table into a new spreadsheet.

You can use the Save Selected Table As command in the context menu to save the table to a different file format. Supported file formats are listed in the Save As Type menu in the Acrobat Save As dialog box.

5 When you are finished close the new Excel spreadsheet and exit Excel. Then close Projections1.pdf.

Converting and combining multiple Office files

As you saw in this lesson, you can convert Office files to Adobe PDF from within the Office application that you used to author the files. However, if you have several Office files—for example, a Word file, a PowerPoint file, and an Excel file—you can also convert and consolidate the files in one easy step from within Acrobat.

1 In Acrobat, choose File > Create PDF > From Multiple Files.

2 In the dialog box, click the Browse button under Add Files, and navigate to the Lesson03\Win folder.

3 Make sure that All Supported Formats is selected for Files of Type, and then Ctrl-click to select the files, Our_Wines.doc, Projections.xls, and Welcome.ppt. Click Add.

You can rearrange the files in the Files to Add window, but for this exercise, you'll simply convert the files. You'll learn more about the Create PDF From Multiple Files command in Lesson 4, "Converting Files to Adobe PDF."

4 Click OK.

Acrobat opens and closes the authoring applications as necessary, and converts the files to Adobe PDF and consolidates them into one file. You have more control over the conversion process if you create individual PDF files and consolidate them separately, but if you have a number of similar and simple files, creating a PDF file from multiple source files in this one easy step is convenient.

5 Acrobat opens the consolidated PDF file. Notice that only one page of the Excel spreadsheet is converted.

6 When you have reviewed the file, close it without saving your work and exit Acrobat.

Review questions

1 How can you be sure that Word styles and headings are converted to Acrobat bookmarks when you convert Word documents to Adobe PDF using PDFMaker?

2 Can you convert an entire Excel workbook to Adobe PDF?

3 How can you add security to a PDF file that you create from a Microsoft Office application?

Review answers

1 If you want Word headings and styles to be converted to bookmarks in Acrobat, you must be sure that the headings and styles are identified for conversion in the Acrobat PDFMaker dialog box. In Microsoft Word, choose Adobe PDF > Change Conversion Settings, and click the Bookmarks tab. Make sure that the required headings and styles are checked.

2 Yes. Before you convert your Excel file to Adobe PDF, choose Adobe PDF > Convert Entire Workbook on the Excel toolbar. The option is selected when it has a check mark next to it.

3 You can add security in the Acrobat PDFMaker dialog box. Before you convert your Microsoft Office file to Adobe PDF, in your Microsoft Office application, choose Adobe PDF > Change Conversion Settings. Set the required security on the Security tab.

Lesson 3m

3m | Converting Microsoft Office Files (Mac OS)

Acrobat Professional is designed to work efficiently with your Microsoft Office applications. You can create Adobe PDF files and email them without ever leaving your Microsoft application. Friends and colleagues can open your documents reliably, regardless of whether they work on Mac OS, Windows, or UNIX.

This lesson is designed for Mac OS users who have Microsoft Office applications—Microsoft Word, Microsoft PowerPoint, and Microsoft Excel—installed on their computer. You cannot complete this lesson if you do not have any or all of these Microsoft applications installed. If you do not use Microsoft Office applications, you should skip this lesson and move on to Lesson 4, "Converting Files to Adobe PDF."

In this lesson, you'll learn how to do the following:

• Convert a Microsoft Word file to Adobe PDF.

• Change the conversion settings in Acrobat Distiller.

• Add password protection to your Adobe PDF files.

• Convert a Microsoft PowerPoint file and attach it to an email message.

This lesson will take about 30 minutes to complete.

If needed, remove the previous lesson folder from your hard drive, and copy the Lesson03:Mac folder onto it.

Getting started

PDFMaker, which is installed automatically when you install Acrobat Professional, is used to create Adobe PDF files from within Microsoft Office applications. Convert to Adobe PDF buttons are added automatically to the toolbar in the Microsoft Office applications so that you can easily convert your files to Adobe PDF and convert and email your files without leaving your Microsoft application. For complete information on which Microsoft applications and which versions of the Microsoft applications are supported, visit the Adobe Web site (www.adobe.com).

*Acrobat Professional
adds two buttons.*

Note: Your Microsoft Office applications must be installed before you install Acrobat Professional in order for the PDFMaker buttons to be installed correctly. You can use the Help > Detect and Repair feature in Acrobat to retroactively install the PDFMaker buttons if you install a Microsoft Office application after installing Acrobat Professional. If you don't see the Acrobat buttons on your Microsoft Office application toolbar, choose View > Toolbars in your Office application, and make sure that Adobe Acrobat PDFMaker is checked.

Acrobat installs essentially the same buttons for creating PDF files and creating and emailing PDF files in Word, PowerPoint, and Excel. As a result, you should be able to complete all sections in this lesson, even if you have only one Microsoft Office application, such as Word. Just follow the steps in each section, but use the lesson file for the application that you have.

Note: To convert a Mac OS X Office application file to Adobe PDF, you must have the Microsoft Office X Service Release 1, 2, or 3 installed.

Converting a Microsoft Word file to Adobe PDF

Word is a popular authoring program that makes it easy to create a variety of documents. When you convert your Word file to Adobe PDF, your Adobe PDF file will look just like your Word file and retain the same functionality, but it will be equally accessible to readers on all platforms (Mac OS, Windows, UNIX), regardless of whether or not they have the Word application.

About the Microsoft Word file

First you'll open the Word file that you'll convert to Adobe PDF.

1 Start Microsoft Word.

2 Choose File > Open. Select the file Our_Wines.doc, located in the Lesson03:Mac folder, and click Open. Then choose File > Save As, rename the file **Our_Wines1.doc**, and save it in the Lesson03:Mac folder.

Changing your conversion settings in Distiller

On Mac OS, PDFMaker uses the Distiller Adobe PDF Settings to convert Office files to Adobe PDF. In this part of the lesson, you'll use one of the predefined settings to create your PDF file, but you can also create custom settings.

First you'll open Distiller.

1 Start Acrobat, and choose Advanced > Acrobat Distiller.

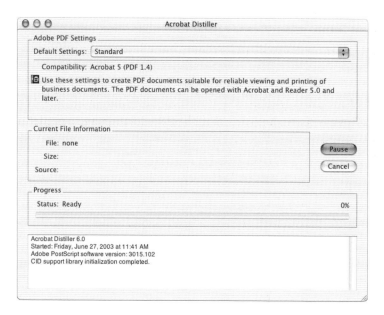

2 In the Acrobat Distiller dialog box, click the arrow to open the Default Settings pop-up menu.

You have several predefined settings to select from. For most users, these predefined settings—High Quality, Press Quality, Smallest File Size, and Standard—are sufficient. If you need to customize the conversion settings you can use the Settings > Edit Adobe PDF Settings command to access the Adobe PDF Settings dialog box. Lesson 5, "Customizing Adobe PDF Output Quality," describes how to customize the Adobe PDF settings. Any customized settings that you have created are also listed in this menu.

3 From the Default Settings menu, click Press Quality, and notice that the description under Compatibility changes.

If you have time, click each of the predefined Adobe PDF Settings and read the descriptions.

Later in the lesson, you'll use a different set of conversion settings to create a smaller file that is more suitable to be emailed as an attachment. For this part of the lesson though, you'll use the default settings for the conversion—the Standard set.

4 From the Default Settings pop-up menu, choose Standard.

You should check your Distiller conversion settings often. The settings do not revert to the default settings automatically.

Adding security to your Adobe PDF file

There are several ways you can apply security to your Adobe PDF documents. You can add password security to prevent unauthorized users from opening, changing, or even printing your document, you can limit access to the PDF document to a predefined list of users, and you can certify the status of a document.

In this lesson, you'll add password security to your document to prevent unauthorized users from opening the document.

1 In Distiller, choose Settings > Security.

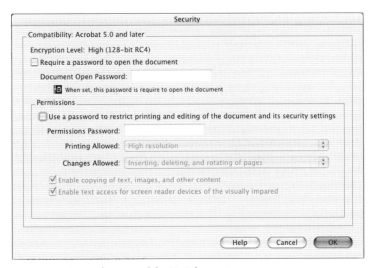

Set security options for your Adobe PDF document.

You'll see that no security is specified for opening, editing, or printing the Adobe PDF document that you will create. Since this is a copy for internal review only, you'll require that a password be used to open the document so that it isn't released to the public prematurely.

2 Click in the Require a Password to Open the Document box. The option is selected when the box contains a checkmark.

Now you'll set the password that opens the document.

3 In the Document Open Password text box, type in your password. We entered **wine123**. Be sure not to forget your password. You'll need to share this password with your colleagues, otherwise they won't be able to open your document. Passwords are case-sensitive, so if you use capital letters, be sure to remember that.

You could restrict the printing and editing of the document, but since this document is going to be circulated for inhouse review, you won't bother adding that level of security. You can learn more about restricting printing and editing in Lesson 11, "Adding Signatures and Security."

4 Click OK to apply your security settings.

Before you can finish the process, you have to re-enter the password that you just set.

5 Re-enter your password. We entered **wine123**. Click OK to clear the confirmation dialog box.

6 Choose Distiller > Quit Acrobat Distiller to quit Distiller.

You should remove your Distiller security setting as soon as you no longer need it to be applied. The security settings do not revert automatically to the default of no security.

Now that you've set the conversion settings and the security settings, you're ready to convert your Word file to Adobe PDF.

About passwords and document security

When creating Adobe PDF documents, authors can use password security to add restrictions for opening, printing, or editing the document. PDF documents that include such security restrictions are called restricted documents. The following methods can enhance document security:

• Restricting opening, editing, and printing. (See "Adding passwords and setting security options" in the Complete Acrobat 6.0 Help.)

• Limiting the PDF document to a defined list of users. Determining which users can edit a PDF document is a process called encrypting. (See "Encrypting PDF files for a list of recipients" in the Complete Acrobat 6.0 Help.)

• Certifying a PDF document. When a document is certified, editing changes are restricted. (See "Certifying a document" in the Complete Acrobat 6.0 Help.)

Changing permission settings for playing movies and sound clips. (See "Setting Trust Manager preferences" in the Complete Acrobat 6.0 Help.)

When someone sends you a restricted PDF document, you may need to enter a password to open it. If a document is encrypted, you may not be able to open it without permission from the person who created the document. In addition, restricted or certified documents may prevent you from printing your files or copying information to another application. If you're having trouble opening a PDF document, or if you're restricted from using certain features, contact the PDF document author.

—From the Complete Acrobat 6.0 Help.

Converting your Word file

1 In Word, simply click the Convert to Adobe PDF button (📄) on the Word toolbar.

2 In the Save dialog box, make sure that the PDF file will be named **Our_Wines1.pdf** and saved in the Lesson03:Mac folder. Click Save.

3 The Acrobat PDFMaker dialog box shows the status of the conversion.

4 When the conversion is complete, click the View File button.

Acrobat Professional launches automatically, but because you have applied password protection, you have to enter the password before Acrobat will open the file.

5 In the Enter Password text box, enter the password that you entered in Step 3, "Adding security to your Adobe PDF file" on page 91. We entered **wine123**. And then click OK.

Your Adobe PDF file opens in Acrobat Professional.

That's all there is to creating an Adobe PDF file from your Microsoft Office file.

6 When you're finished reviewing your PDF file, choose File > Close to close your work.

Note: If you aren't going to do any more of this lesson, be sure to reset your security settings in Distiller, otherwise all the PDF files you create will be password-protected.

7 Choose Acrobat > Quit Acrobat.

8 Choose Word > Quit Word to quit Microsoft Word.

Converting and emailing a PowerPoint presentation

PowerPoint presentations are an effective way to get your message across, but not every place that you visit has a system available with Microsoft PowerPoint installed on it, nor does every person that you'd like to share your presentation with have this software. Converting your PowerPoint presentation to Adobe PDF allows you to show the presentation on any system that has the free Adobe Reader software installed. Similarly, you can email a PDF version of your presentation to anyone who has Adobe Reader.

Note: Files created from PowerPoint files using the Convert to Adobe PDF button are not tagged Adobe PDF and the PowerPoint transitions are not preserved.

In this section of the lesson, you'll convert a PowerPoint presentation to Adobe PDF and email it without ever leaving your PowerPoint application.

If you don't have PowerPoint installed on your system, you can use the Convert to Adobe PDF and Email button in Word to convert and email the Our_Wines.doc file. Open Our_Wines.doc in Word, skip the "About the PowerPoint file" section, and go directly to the section on checking the conversion settings and security settings in Distiller.

About the PowerPoint file

1 Start Microsoft PowerPoint.

2 Choose File > Open. Select the file Welcome.ppt, located in the Lesson03:Mac folder, and click Open. Then choose File > Save As, rename the file **Welcome1.ppt**, and save it in the Lesson03:Mac folder.

First you'll review the PowerPoint file.

3 Choose View > Slide Show.

4 Press Return to move to the second page.

5 First you'll notice that a page transition has been applied to the presentation.

Also, on the second page, notice the fly-in bullets and the locators on the map. All these elements will appear in the Adobe PDF file that you create. (The fly-in animation is not preserved, but all the information is present.)

6 Press the Esc key to return to the normal PowerPoint view.

Checking your conversion settings and security settings in Distiller

You'll check the default Adobe PDF settings first to make sure they are appropriate for your needs.

1 Start Acrobat, and choose Advanced > Acrobat Distiller.

Because you're going to email the file to various people, you want the file to be as small as possible.

2 Click the arrow next to the Default Settings menu, and choose Smallest File Size.

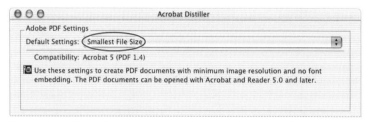

Choose the predefined conversion setting that gives the smallest file size.

For information on customizing the conversion settings, see Lesson 5, "Customizing Adobe PDF Output Quality."

Now you'll remove the security settings that you applied for the conversion of the Word document in the prior section.

3 In Distiller, choose Settings > Security.

4 Click in the Require a Password to Open the Document box. The option is deselected when the box is empty.

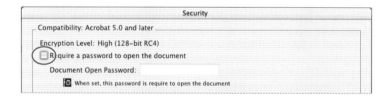

5 Click OK to remove the previously used security settings.

6 Choose Distiller > Quit Acrobat Distiller to quit Distiller.

You should check your Distiller conversion settings periodically. The settings do not revert to the default settings automatically.

Converting and emailing the presentation

Now you're ready to convert your PowerPoint presentation to Adobe PDF and email it in one easy step.

1 On the PowerPoint toolbar, click the Convert to Adobe PDF and Email button ( ).

First you'll be prompted to save the file.

2 Click Save, and save the file as Welcome1.pdf in the Lesson03:Mac folder.

The conversion to Adobe PDF is shown in a progress window.

Your default email application is opened automatically, and your Adobe PDF document is attached. All you have to do is fill out recipient information and type a message.

3 In the newly opened email message window, type in recipient information, a subject line, and a message if you wish. We suggest that you send the message to yourself as a test.

4 When you're ready to send the message, click Send or Send Message.

That's all there is to it. You've created a PDF version of your PowerPoint presentation and emailed it without ever leaving PowerPoint. The PDF version of your presentation is also saved on your hard drive. Now you'll check your PDF file.

5 If you emailed the PDF file to yourself, open your email application and open the PDF attachment. If you didn't email the PDF file to yourself, click the View File button in the Acrobat PDFMaker status box to open the file or double-click the Welcome1.pdf file in the Lesson03:Mac folder.

Notice that the page transitions are preserved, and although the animation of the fly-in bullets is lost, all the text is preserved.

In a later lesson, you'll learn how to create a PDF file that opens in full-screen view so that your PDF files look just like PowerPoint presentations. (See Lesson 13, "Preparing Presentations.")

6 When you're finished reviewing the Welcome1.pdf file, close the file and quit Acrobat Professional.

7 In PowerPoint, choose PowerPoint > Quit PowerPoint.

Tips on converting Excel files

In the prior section, you saw how easy it is to create a PDF file from a Microsoft Office application and email it to friends or colleagues without ever leaving your Microsoft Office application. You can equally easily convert Excel files to Adobe PDF or convert and email them without leaving Excel.

About the Excel file

1 Start Microsoft Excel.

2 Choose File > Open. Select the file Projections.xls, located in the Lesson03:Mac folder, and click Open. Then choose File > Save As, rename the file **Projections1.xls**, and save it in the Lesson03:Mac folder.

3 Change the Zoom value on Excel toolbar from 50% to 100%.

Now you'll review the Excel file. Notice that the first sheet has case-lot projections for red-wine sales.

4 Click the Sheet 2 tab at the bottom of the Excel spreadsheet. The second sheet has case-lot projections for white wines. When you create your PDF file, you'll need to convert both these sheets.

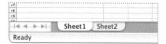

Converting the entire workbook

If you convert an Excel file to Adobe PDF by simply clicking the Convert to Adobe PDF button (📄) on the Excel toolbar, you'll convert only the active worksheet. If you want to convert all the worksheets in a book, you must convert each sheet individually and then use the Create PDF From Multiple Files command to consolidate the PDF files of the individual sheets. You will need to give each sheet a unique name as you convert the Excel spreadsheets to Adobe PDF.

Note: Your Excel worksheet will be automatically sized for your printer page size. You don't need to worry about defining a custom page size.

Checking the conversion settings

You'll use the same settings to convert Excel files to Adobe PDF as you used to convert PowerPoint files. If you need help, follow the steps in "Checking your conversion settings and security settings in Distiller" on page 95 to verify that Smallest File Size is selected for the Adobe PDF Setting and that no security will be applied to the document.

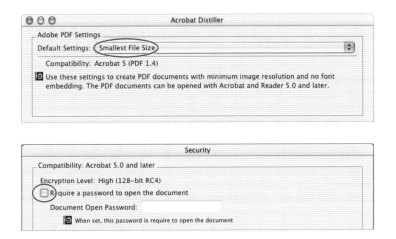

Creating an Adobe PDF file

You'll convert your Excel file to Adobe PDF in the same way as you converted the Word file to Adobe PDF.

1 Click the Sheet 1 tab at the bottom of the Excel window to return to the first page of the workbook.

2 Click the Convert to Adobe PDF button (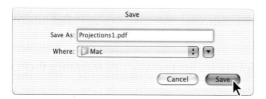) on the Excel toolbar.

3 Name and save your PDF file. We named Sheet 1, **Projections1.pdf**, and saved it in the Lesson03:Mac folder.

4 When the conversion is complete, click the View File button in the Acrobat PDFMaker status box to view your PDF file.

5 Repeat steps 1 through 3 for Sheet 2, naming the PDF file **Projections2.pdf**, and saving it in the Lesson03:Mac folder.

6 When you are finished, quit Excel and Distiller. Leave the two PDF files open.

Consolidating PDF files

Now you'll consolidate the two PDF files, Projections1.pdf and Projections2.pdf, into one PDF file.

1 In Acrobat Professional, choose File > Create PDF > From Multiple Files.

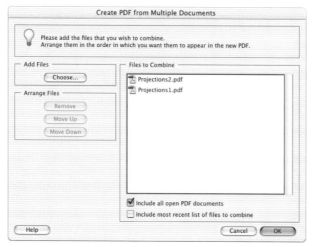

You can consolidate PDF files in Acrobat Professional.

The Create PDF From Multiple Documents dialog box is where you assemble PDF documents that you want to consolidate. You can also assemble documents that you want to convert to Adobe PDF and consolidate them in one step in this dialog box. (See Lesson 4, "Converting Files to Adobe PDF.")

2 The Files to Combine window should display both the file Projections2.pdf and the file Projections1.pdf.

It doesn't matter in what order the files are in, because you can rearrange them in the Create From Multiple Files dialog box

3 If the files are not in the correct order (Projections1.pdf first and Projections2.pdf second), select the Projections1.pdf file and click the Move Up button once.

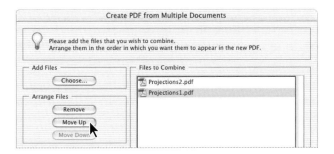

Now you're ready to create the consolidated Adobe PDF file.

4 Click OK to consolidate the listed files into one Adobe PDF file.

A dialog box shows the progression of the consolidation process.

The consolidated Adobe PDF file, called Binder1.pdf, opens automatically.

5 Choose File > Save As, and in the Save As dialog box, type in **Projections.pdf** as the file name. Click Save to save your work.

6 Use the Next Page (▶) and Previous Page (◀) buttons to page through your consolidated documents.

7 When you are finished, choose Acrobat > Quit Acrobat. Your saved PDF file closes also.

Review questions

1 Where do you select the Adobe PDF Settings used to convert Microsoft Office files to Adobe PDF on Mac OS?

2 How do you add security to a file created using PDFMaker on Mac OS?

3 Can you convert an entire Excel workbook to Adobe PDF?

Review answers

1 PDFMaker on Mac OS uses the Adobe PDF Settings from Distiller. You must open Distiller and change the Default Settings in Distiller to change the conversion settings used by PDFMaker. The Default Settings menu lists the predefined Adobe PDF Settings as well as any custom settings that you may have defined.

2 You change the security settings for Adobe PDF files created with PDFMaker in the Security dialog box of Distiller. In Distiller, choose Settings > Security to limit access to a file and to restrict printing and editing.

3 No. But you can convert each worksheet to an Adobe PDF file and then consolidate the PDF files using the Create PDF From Multiple Files command in Acrobat.

Lesson 4

4 Converting Files to Adobe PDF

You can convert a variety of file formats to Adobe PDF quickly and easily. You can even assemble files of different types, including Adobe PDF files, and consolidate and convert them to one Adobe PDF file in a single action. Once you've created your PDF file, you can add custom headers and footers to the pages and add watermarks or backgrounds. Creating and customizing Adobe PDF files has never been easier.

In this lesson, you'll learn how to do the following:

- Convert a TIFF file to Adobe PDF.

- Consolidate PDF files into one Adobe PDF file.

- Convert a file using the authoring application's Print command.

- Add headers and footers.

- Add a background.

- Search a PDF file.

This lesson will take about 45 minutes to complete.

If needed, remove the previous lesson folder from your hard drive, and copy the Lesson04 folder onto it.

Note: Windows users may need to unlock the lesson files before using them. For information, see "Copying the Classroom in a Book files" on page 3.

Getting started

You can convert a variety of file formats to Adobe PDF, preserving all the fonts, formatting, graphics, and color of the source file, regardless of the application and platform used to create it. In addition to creating Adobe PDF files from virtually any software application, you can also create PDF files by downloading and converting Web pages and by scanning and capturing paper documents.

The prior lesson, Lesson 3, "Converting Microsoft Office Files," describes how to create Adobe PDF files directly from Microsoft Office files. This lesson covers several ways of creating Adobe PDF files from image files and from application files other than Microsoft Office files. Lesson 6, "Creating Adobe PDF from Web Pages," describes how to create Adobe PDF files from Web pages. Converting paper documents by scanning is not covered in this book.

Increasingly the content of Adobe PDF files is being reused when the security settings applied by the creator of the document allow reuse of the PDF file content. Either content is extracted for use in another authoring application or the content is reflowed for use with handheld devices or screen readers. The success with which content can be repurposed or reused depends very much on the structural information in the PDF file. The more structural information a PDF document contains the more opportunities you have for successfully reusing the content and the more reliably a document can be used with screen readers. For complete information, see "Building flexibility into Adobe PDF files" in the Complete Acrobat 6.0 Help.

Creating an Adobe PDF file from a TIFF file

If you receive faxes electronically (rather than as paper), you may receive the fax as a TIFF file. You can easily convert the TIFF file to an Adobe PDF file. In this lesson, you'll convert a faxed vendor agreement—a TIFF file—to Adobe PDF, add a comment, and email the agreement to an associate.

You can use this method to convert a variety of image and non-image file types to Adobe PDF.

1 Open Acrobat Professional.

2 Click the Create PDF button on the Acrobat toolbar, and choose From File.

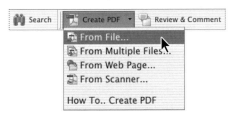

*The Create PDF button gives you easy access to
the commands for creating Adobe PDF files.*

3 In the Open dialog box, click the arrow to open the Files of Type (Windows) or Show (Mac OS) pop-up menu, and choose TIFF for the file type.

The pop-up menu lists all the file types that can be converted using this method.

4 Click the Settings button to open the Adobe PDF Setting dialog box.

This is where you set the compression that will be applied to color, grayscale, and monochrome images, and where you select the color management options used when the file is converted to Adobe PDF.

5 Click Cancel to leave the options unchanged. You'll learn more about these settings in later lessons.

Resolution is determined automatically.

6 In the Open dialog box, navigate to the Lesson04 folder, select the file GC_VendAgree.tif, and click Open.

7 Click OK to close the Adobe Picture Tasks dialog box.

You'll learn more about the Picture Tasks button in Lesson 14, "Working with Pictures and Images."

Acrobat Professional converts the TIFF file to Adobe PDF and opens the PDF file automatically.

8 Scroll down the page to view the hand-written note "And Section 2875" that the signer of the agreement has added.

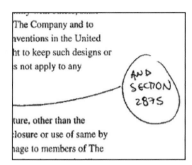

You'll add your own Acrobat note, asking that the agreement be redone to include the information in this hand-written note and that the revised agreement be re-signed. But first you'll save your Adobe PDF file.

9 Choose File > Save As, name the file **GCVend_Agree1.pdf**, and save it in the Lesson04 folder.

Adding a note

1 Click the Review & Comment button on the Acrobat Professional toolbar to open the Commenting toolbar.

2 Click the Note tool (). Position the pointer close to the hand-written note, and click to add an empty note. You may have to scroll down in the document pane to see the handwritten note.

An empty note is added to the PDF document, and an insertion point is created automatically so that you're ready to type the text of your note. In Lesson 8, "Using Acrobat Professional in a Document Review Cycle," you'll learn how to change the color and author information for these notes.

3 We typed in the text, "Emily Grace, can you get this retyped and re-signed, please. Alternatively, we need to get this addition initialed and dated. Thanks."

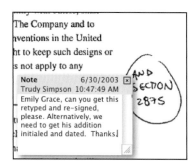

4 Click the Close button on the Commenting toolbar to hide the toolbar.

5 Choose File > Save to save your work.

You've added a note asking your colleague to follow up with finalizing the agreement. Now you can simply email the document to your colleague without leaving Acrobat Professional.

Emailing an Adobe PDF file

1 Click the Email button ( ) on the Acrobat Professional toolbar.

Acrobat Professional launches your email program and automatically attaches your PDF file to a new email message window. Acrobat Professional also inserts the file name in the subject line.

You'll add recipient information and change the subject line information. You can send the email to yourself if you have an email address and are connected to the Internet. If you don't have email capability, skip the next steps and move on to "Converting and combining different types of files" on page 111.

2 In the "To:" text box, type in your own email address.

3 In the "Subject:" text box, select the file name, and replace it with your preferred information. We typed in "**Please fix this vendor agreement.**"

If you wish, you can type a message in the email message area.

Your PDF file is automatically attached to a new email message window.

4 When you're finished, email your message. The steps for sending a message vary with your email application.

5 Close your email application.

That's all there is to adding notes and emailing an annotated file. You'll leave your PDF file open for the next part of the lesson.

Converting and combining different types of files

You can convert a variety of file formats to Adobe PDF and consolidate them into one Adobe PDF file without leaving Acrobat Professional.

In this part of the lesson, you'll use the Create PDF From Multiple Files command to assemble several documents related to a network upgrade project for the Global Corp. The files that you'll consolidate include PDF files and JPEG image files.

In the past, if you needed to archive these project documents, you'd need to generate paper copies that you could file, or you'd need to be sure that you always had the necessary software to open and view the files. Similarly, if you need to circulate the project documents for review, each of your colleagues would have to have the necessary software to open and view the files, or you'd have to create and distribute paper copies. With Adobe PDF you don't have these problems. When you convert your application files to Adobe PDF, they can be opened on any platform using the free Adobe Reader.

Assembling the files

1 In Acrobat Professional, click the Create PDF button on the toolbar and choose From Multiple Files.

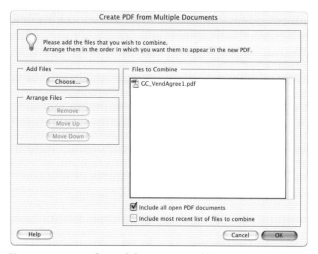

You can convert and consolidate a variety of file types without leaving Acrobat.

The Create PDF From Multiple Documents dialog box is where you assemble PDF documents that you want to consolidate or where you assemble the documents that you want to convert to Adobe PDF and consolidate. Notice that the document GCVend_Agree1.pdf is already listed. This is because the Include All Open PDF Documents option is checked. (The option is on if the box is checked.) If you deselect the Include All Open PDF Documents option in this dialog box, the file is automatically removed from the window. For this lesson, leave the option selected.

Now you'll add the other project documents to the dialog box.

2 Click the Browse (Windows) or Choose (Mac OS) button under Add Files.

3 In the Open dialog box, click the arrow next to the Files of Type (Windows) or Show (Mac OS) text box to show the pop-up menu. This menu lists the types of files that you can convert and consolidate using this dialog box. Make sure that All Supported Formats is selected.

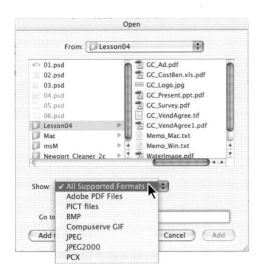

Note: *The types of files that you can convert varies depending on whether you are working on Windows or Mac OS.*

4 Still in the Open dialog box, navigate to the Lesson04 folder and select the file GC_Logo.jpg, and click Add to add the file to the Files to Combine list in the Create PDF From Multiple Documents dialog box.

5 Click Browse or Choose, and repeat step 4 to add the following files:

• GC_CostBen.xls.pdf

• GC_Ad.pdf

• GC_Survey.pdf

• GC_Present.ppt.pdf

• GC_VendAgree.tif

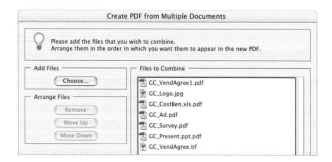

It doesn't matter in what order you add these files, because you'll rearrange them in the Create From Multiple Files dialog box. But first you'll remove the GCVend_Agree1.pdf file because that is an annotated version of the vendor agreement.

6 In the Create PDF From Multiple Documents dialog box, select the file GCVend_Agree1.pdf, and click the Remove button to remove the file from the list.

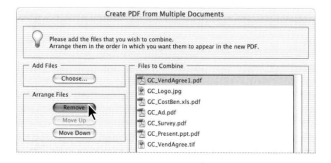

7 Select each of the remaining files in turn, and use the Move Up and Move Down button to arrange the files in the following order:

- GC_VendAgree.tif

- GC_Ad.pdf

- GC_Present.ppt.pdf

- GC_Survey.pdf

- GC_CostBen.xls.pdf

- GC_Logo.jpg

Note: You can also drag files up and down in the list.

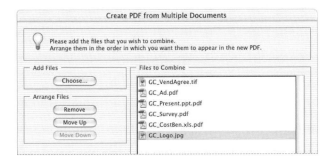

Now you're ready to create the Adobe PDF file.

Converting and consolidating the files

1 Click OK to convert and consolidate the listed files into one Adobe PDF file.

A dialog box shows the progression of the conversion and consolidation process. Depending on the files you convert and your operating system, some of the authoring programs may open and close automatically.

The consolidated Adobe PDF file, called Binder1.pdf, opens automatically.

2 Choose File > Save As, and in the Save As dialog box, type in **GC_Presentation.pdf** as the file name. Click Save and save your work in the Lesson04 folder.

3 Click the Fit Page button, and use the Next Page (▶) and Previous Page (◀) buttons to page through your consolidated documents.

Without leaving Acrobat Professional, you have converted a JPEG file and a TIFF file to Adobe PDF and combined them with several other PDF files.

When you convert files to Adobe PDF using the Create PDF From Multiple Files command, Acrobat Professional determines the conversion method to be used for each file and the conversion settings. If you want more control over the conversion settings, you can convert the files individually, using your preferred conversion settings for each file, and then consolidate the resulting PDF files.

Now you'll add project-related text, page numbers, and a background image to each page to identify the pages as being part of one project.

Adding header text and page numbers

1 Click the First Page button (|◀) to go to the first page of the consolidated document.

2 Choose Document > Add Headers & Footers to open the dialog box that lets you add page numbers and text to each of your PDF pages.

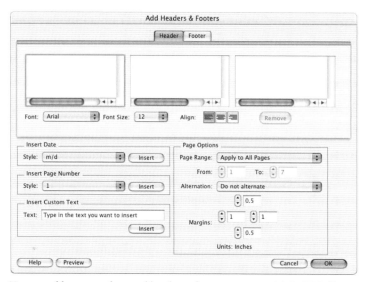

You can add page numbers and header or footer text to any Adobe PDF file.

3 In the Add Headers & Footers dialog box, click the Footer tab to bring it to the front.

You'll add a page number to the bottom of each page.

4 Under Insert Page Number, click the down arrow next to the Style text box to open the pop-up menu. Choose Page 1 from the menu. Then click the Insert button.

By default, the page number is added to the bottom left of the page (the left panel in the dialog box). You can change the position of the page number by using the Align buttons in the dialog box in the dialog box.

5 Click the center align button (▤) to center the page number on the page.

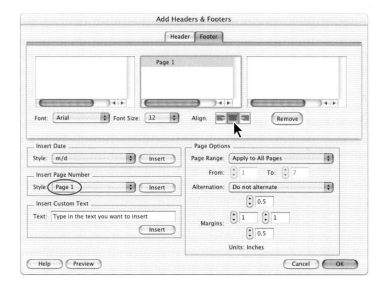

You can use the Font and the Font Size menus to change the type style of the page numbers, but for this lesson, you'll use the default values.

6 Click the Preview button at the bottom of the dialog box to preview your page numbering style. When you're finished, click OK to close the Preview pane.

Now you'll add a header to identify the project that the documents relate to.

7 In the Add Headers & Footers dialog box, click the Header tab.

8 Under Insert Custom Text, select the sample text, "Type in the text you want to insert," and replace it with text to add as a header for this document. We typed in **Red Dot Project**. Click the Insert button. (If your text isn't inserted in the middle panel, click the center align button.)

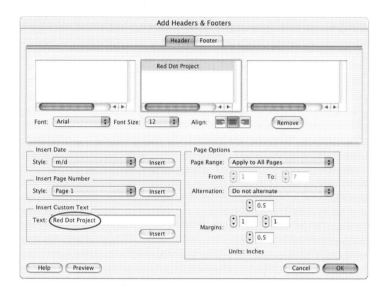

Now you'll add a date.

9 In the Insert Date area, click the down arrow next to the Style text box to open the menu. Select a style for the date. We used mm/dd/yy. Click the Insert button.

The date is centered under the header, but you want it to be at the top left of the pages, so you'll realign it now.

10 With the date still highlighted, click the left align button (▤). The date moves to the left panel.

11 Click Preview to preview the header information.

The header is a little low on the page, so now you'll adjust the margins to move the added text higher on the page.

12 Click OK to close the Preview and return to the Add Headers & Footers dialog box.

13 In the Page Options area, select the top value for Margins, and replace 0.5 with 0.25. The units are in inches. For information on changing the page units, see Lesson 7, "Modifying PDF Files."

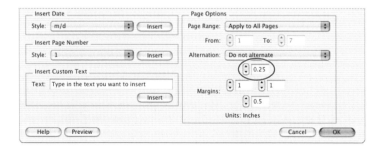

Notice that you can also choose whether to add the header and footer information to all or selected pages. For this project, you'll add the information to all pages (the default value).

14 When you are satisfied with your header and footer information, click OK.

15 Use the Next Page (▶) and Previous Page (◀) buttons to page through the document and view your work.

As you page through the document, you notice that the header and footer do not look good on page 7, the last page of the combined document. You'll remove the header and footer from this page, but first you'll save your work.

16 Choose File > Save.

Editing headers and footers

First you'll remove all the headers and footers.

1 If necessary, click the First Page button (◀) to go to the first page of the PDF file.

2 Choose Edit > Undo Headers/Footers.

All the header and footer information is removed from all pages.

3 Choose Document > Add Headers & Footers.

Notice that your header and footer information is preserved. Now you'll reapply the information, but only to the first six pages.

4 Click the Header tab, and click the down arrow to open the Page Range menu. Choose Apply to Page Range.

5 Leave the 1 in the From text box, but click the down arrow of the To text box to change the value from 7 to 6.

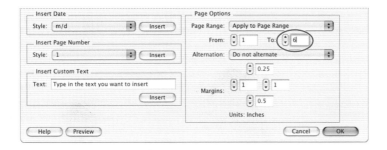

6 Click the Footer tab and verify that the page range for the footer has been changed also.

7 Click OK to apply the changes.

8 Use the Next Page (▶) and Previous Page (◀) buttons to page through the document to make sure your changes have been made. When you're sure the changes are satisfactory, choose File > Save to save your work.

Adding a watermark image

Now that you've consolidated the project files, you want to be sure that anyone who opens and reviews this PDF file understands that this is the archive copy of the project documentation. To do this, you'll add a watermark image to each page.

1 Choose Document > Add Watermark & Background.

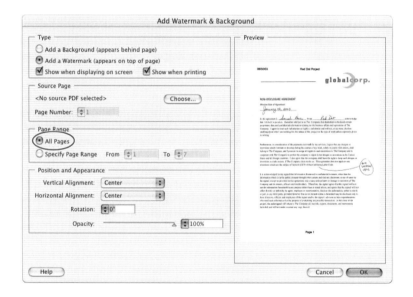

2 For Type, make sure that the option Add a Watermark is selected. Verify that the options Show When Displaying On Screen and Show When Printing are selected.

3 For Page Range, make sure that the option All Pages is selected.

Now you'll locate the file that contains the watermark image. The file in which you keep this watermark image may contain multiple images, but each image must be on a separate page.

4 For Source Page, click Browse (Windows) or Choose (Mac OS).

5 In the Open dialog box, select WaterImage.pdf in the Lesson04 folder, and click Open.

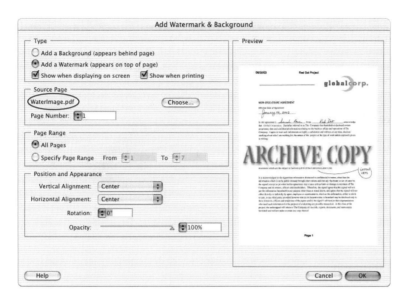

The Preview pane shows the composite effect.

Now you'll rotate the watermark image and set the opacity.

6 For Position and Appearance, make sure that Center is selected for Vertical Alignment and for Horizontal Alignment. This centers the image on the page.

7 For Rotation, enter the degree of rotation for the image. We entered 45 degrees. You can type in a value or use the up and down arrows to change the value. Then drag the opacity slider to 25%. This sets the opacity of the watermark image.

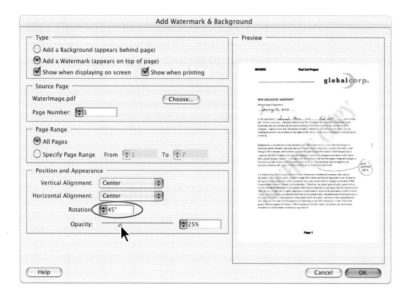

8 When you're satisfied with the appearance, as shown in the preview panel of the dialog box, click OK.

9 Use the Next Page (▶) and Previous Page (◀) buttons to browse through the file.

10 Choose File > Save, and save the GC_Presentation.pdf file when you are finished reviewing your work. Do not close the file.

11 Choose Window and select the GC_VendAgree1.pdf file to make the file active. Choose File > Close to close the file.

Searching a PDF file

You can easily search any PDF file that you have open in Acrobat using the Search PDF pane, and if you have an active Internet connection, you can also search the Web for Adobe PDF files that meet your search criteria.

In this lesson, you'll search the document that you just assembled for a word that may need to be replaced. Your marketing department would like to replace the term "program" with "application" when program is used to refer to a software product. You'll search the GC_Presentation.pdf file to see how often the word is used.

1 Click the Search button (🐾) on the Acrobat toolbar to open the Search PDF pane to the right of the document pane.

2 Enter **program** in the text box labeled "What word or phrase would you like to search for?" You can enter a word, several words, or a word fragment.

Notice that you can search the active document, or you can search all documents in a specified folder or location. You can also refine your search by using the search criteria options. Additional search criteria are available if you click the Use Advanced Search Options link at the bottom of the Search PDF pane. You can restore the limited search criteria by clicking the Use Basic Search Options link at the bottom of the Search PDF pane.

For now, you'll search the current PDF document for the one word.

3 Make sure that the In the Current PDF Document option is checked and that the Search in Bookmarks option is not checked, and then click Search.

4 The search results are listed in the Results window. The icon next to the search result indicates that the occurrences of the word are in the document. In a moment, you'll search for terms in bookmarks.

5 Click on each occurrence of the search term to go to that word in the document pane.

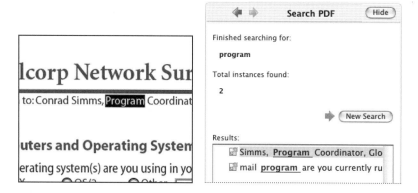

You can also extend your search to include bookmarks and comments.

6 Click the New Search button in the Search PDF pane.

7 Type **Global Corp.** in the search text box.

8 Click the Search in Bookmarks option so that the box contains a check mark.

9 Click the Search button.

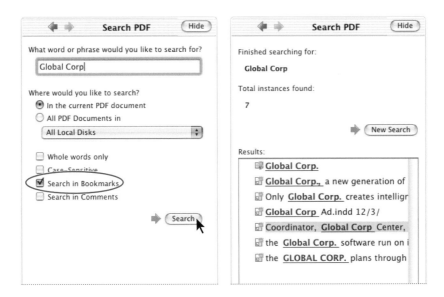

Notice that the first occurrence of Global Corp. is preceded by a different icon. This icon indicates that the search term is found in a bookmark.

10 Click the search result marked with the bookmark icon. The Bookmarks panel opens automatically if it isn't already open, and the bookmark label containing the search term is highlighted.

11 When you are finished, choose File > Close, and close the GC_Presentation.pdf file.

12 Choose File > Exit (Windows) or Acrobat > Quit Acrobat (Mac OS) to exit or quit Acrobat Professional.

Using the Print command to create Adobe PDF files

Microsoft Office applications such as Word, PowerPoint, and Excel, include Convert to Adobe PDF buttons that allow you to convert a Microsoft Office file to Adobe PDF quickly and easily without leaving your authoring program. Other authoring applications, such as Adobe InDesign®, Adobe Photoshop, and Adobe PageMaker®, have special commands such as the Export command and the Save As command that allow you to convert a file to Adobe PDF. To make full use of these commands, you should consult the documentation that came with your application.

While not all authoring applications have special buttons or commands for converting files, you can still create an Adobe PDF file from these application files by using the application's Print command in conjunction with the Adobe PDF printer.

Note: The Adobe PDF printer isn't a physical printer like the one sitting in your office or on your desk. Rather, it is a printer driver that converts your file to Adobe PDF instead of printing it to paper.

Finding your Adobe PDF printer

On both Windows and Mac OS, the Adobe PDF printer is installed and added to the printer menu automatically.

1 To verify that the Adobe PDF printer is installed, do one of the following:

• On Windows 2000, click the Start menu, and choose Settings> Printers.

• On Windows XP, click the Start menu, and choose Printers and Faxes.

• On Mac OS, navigate to Applications:Utilities:Print Center.

You'll see the Adobe PDF printer listed with the other printers present on your system.

2 Close the dialog box when you're finished.

Printing to the Adobe PDF printer

In this part of the lesson, you'll convert a text file to Adobe PDF using the File > Print command in conjunction with the Adobe PDF printer. You can use this technique from almost any application, including the Microsoft and Adobe applications that have built-in Convert to Adobe PDF buttons and Export or Save As Adobe PDF commands.

Navigate to the Lesson04 folder, and double-click the Memo_Win.txt file (Windows) or Memo_Mac.txt file (Mac OS).

The text file should open in NotePad (or equivalent) on Windows and in TextEdit (or equivalent) on Mac OS. Follow the steps for your platform, Windows or Mac OS, to convert the file to Adobe PDF.

On Windows:

Note: Steps may vary depending on whether you are using Windows 98, 2000, or XP. These steps assume that you are using Windows XP Pro.

1 Choose File > Page Setup.

2 In the Page Setup dialog box, click the Printer button.

3 Click the arrow next to the Name text box to open the list of available printers. Select Adobe PDF, click OK, and click OK again to return to the memo.

If you want to change the settings used in the conversion of the text file to Adobe PDF, you would do so by clicking the Properties button in the Page Setup dialog box. Lesson 5, "Customizing Adobe PDF Output Quality" describes how to change these Adobe PDF Settings. For this lesson, you'll use the default values.

4 Choose File > Print, make sure that the Adobe PDF printer is selected, and click Print.

5 Click Save in the Save PDF File As dialog box. You can name the PDF file and choose where it is saved in the Save dialog box. For this lesson, save the file using the default name (Memo_Win.pdf) in the default location (My Documents).

A dialog box shows the progression of the conversion.

6 If the PDF file doesn't open automatically, navigate to the My Documents directory, and double-click the Memo_Win.pdf file to open it in Acrobat. When you have reviewed the file, close it and exit Acrobat Professional. Exit NotePad (or equivalent).

On Mac OS:

1 Choose File > Print, and make sure that the Adobe PDF printer is selected.

If you want to change the settings used in the conversion of the text file to Adobe PDF, you would do so by choosing PDF Options from the pop-up menu. Lesson 5, "Customizing Adobe PDF Output Quality" describes how to change the Adobe PDF Settings. For this lesson, you'll use the default values.

2 Click Print.

3 In the Save to File dialog box, you can rename the PDF file and choose where to save it. For this lesson, save the file as **Memo_Mac.pdf** in the Lesson04 folder.

4 Click Save.

A dialog box shows the progression of the conversion.

5 If the PDF file doesn't open automatically, navigate to the Lesson04 folder, and double-click the Memo_Mac.pdf file to open it in Acrobat. When you have reviewed the file, close it and quit Acrobat.

You have just converted a simple text document to an Adobe PDF document using the Print command.

Exploring on your own (Windows)

On Windows, you can also create and consolidate Adobe PDF files using the context menu.

Using the Convert to Adobe PDF command

1 Navigate to the Lesson04 folder, and right-click on the file Memo_Win.txt.

2 From the context menu, choose Convert to Adobe PDF.

Text files are converted to Adobe PDF using Web Capture and opened in Acrobat Professional. Different conversion methods are used for other file types, but the conversion method is always determined automatically by Acrobat.

3 Choose File > Save. Name the file and choose where to save it in the Save As dialog box.

When you are finished, close any open Adobe PDF files and exit Acrobat Professional.

Using the Combine in Adobe Acrobat command

1 Navigate to the Lesson04 folder, and select the file GC_Logo.jpg.

2 Ctrl-click to add more files to the selection. We added GCVend_Agree.tif.

3 Right-click, and from the context menu, choose Combine in Adobe Acrobat.

Acrobat Professional opens and displays the Create PDF From Multiple Files, with the target files listed in the Files to Combine list. You can add to the list of files, rearrange files, delete files, and convert and consolidate files as described in "Converting and combining different types of files" on page 111.

When you are finished, close any open PDF files and exit Acrobat Professional.

Review questions

1 How can you find out which file types can be converted to Adobe PDF using the Create PDF From File or Create PDF From Multiple Files commands?

2 If you're working with a file type that isn't supported by the Create PDF From File or From Multiple Files command, how can you create a PDF file?

3 How can you add a "confidential" image or text to some or all pages in an Adobe PDF file?

4 After you have added a header or footer to an Adobe PDF document, can you change the header or footer?

Review answers

1 Do one of the following:

• Choose File > Create PDF > From File. Open the Files of Type (Windows) or Show (Mac OS) menu in the Open dialog box to view the supported file types.

• Choose File > Create PDF > From Multiple Files. Click the Browse or Choose button, and open the Files of Type (Windows) or Show (Mac OS) menu in the Open dialog box to view the supported file types.

2 Simply "print" your file using the Adobe PDF printer. In your authoring application, choose File > Print, and choose the Adobe PDF printer in the Print or Page Setup dialog box. When you click the Print button, Acrobat creates an Adobe PDF file rather than sending your file to a desktop printer.

3 First you need to create the image or text that you want to add to each page and convert the image or text to Adobe PDF. Then you can add this image or text file as a background or watermark using the Document > Add Watermark & Background command.

4 Yes. You can undo any header or footer operation using the Edit > Undo Headers/Footers command.

Lesson 5

5 | Customizing Adobe PDF Output Quality

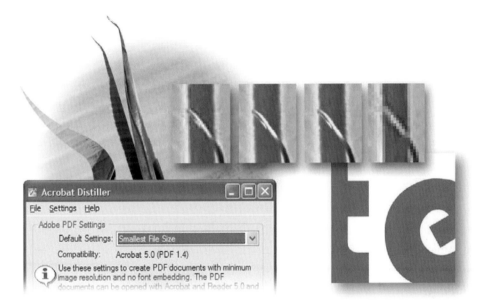

You control the output quality of your files by specifying appropriate Adobe PDF Settings for converting the files to PDF. In addition to the default Adobe PDF Settings designed to produce satisfactory results for the more common output needs, you can customize the Adobe PDF Settings to produce the best balance of file size and quality for your specific needs.

In this lesson, you'll learn how to do the following:

• Explore the different ways of changing the Adobe PDF settings used to convert files to Adobe PDF.

• Compare the quality and file size of Adobe PDF files converted with different Adobe PDF Settings.

• Choose compression, sampling, and image quality settings.

• Explore the color management options.

This lesson will take approximately 60 minutes to complete.

If needed, remove the previous lesson folder from your hard drive, and copy the Lesson05 folder onto it.

Note: Windows users may need to unlock the lesson files before using them. For information, see "Copying the Classroom in a Book files" on page 3.

Getting started

Acrobat Professional produces Adobe PDF files that accurately preserve the look and content of the original document. When creating Adobe PDF files, Acrobat Professional uses various methods to compress text, line art, and bitmap images so that they use less file space. In this lesson, you'll learn how to choose Adobe PDF conversion settings to create the Adobe PDF quality and file size appropriate to your output needs.

First you'll look at the default settings that are available for converting your application files to Adobe PDF and where you change these settings.

About the Adobe PDF Settings

The Adobe PDF Settings—the settings that control the conversion of files to Adobe PDF—can be accessed and set from a number of different places. You can access the Adobe PDF Settings from Distiller, from the Adobe PDF printer, from the Adobe PDF menu in Microsoft Office applications, from the Print dialog box in many authoring applications, and from the Start menu on Windows. Regardless of where you access the settings from, the Adobe PDF Settings dialog box and the options it contains are the same.

In this first part of the lesson, you'll look at where you change the predefined (or default) Adobe PDF Settings and where you define custom Adobe PDF Settings. Since the options vary by platform (Windows or Mac OS), you should skip the sections that don't apply to your platform.

In the later part of this lesson, you'll look at the results of using the different Adobe PDF Settings.

Changing the Adobe PDF Settings in Distiller

Distiller is available on both Windows and Mac OS.

1 Open Acrobat Professional.

2 Choose Advanced > Acrobat Distiller to open Distiller.

You can choose one of the predefined Adobe PDF Settings, or you can customize the settings.

3 To choose one of the predefined Adobe PDF Settings, click the arrow next to the Default Settings menu, and choose High Quality, Press Quality, Smallest File Size, or Standard. We chose **Smallest File Size.**

Choosing a default Adobe PDF Setting for converting files to Adobe PDF

These are the predefined Adobe PDF settings. A brief explanation of each setting is given in the information box below the Default Settings menu. For most beginning users of Acrobat, these predefined settings are sufficient. You'll examine the difference in quality and file size produced by the different settings later in this lesson.

Note: Any customized Adobe PDF Settings that you may have created are also displayed in this menu.

4 To examine the settings for the Smallest File Size conversion settings or to customize the Adobe PDF Settings based on the selected default setting, choose Settings > Edit Adobe PDF Settings to open the Adobe PDF Settings dialog box.

The settings on the General, Images, Fonts, Color, and Advanced tabs are those for the Smallest File Size Adobe PDF Settings. For information on customizing the options on these tabs, see "Creating custom Adobe PDF Settings" in the Complete Acrobat 6.0 Help.

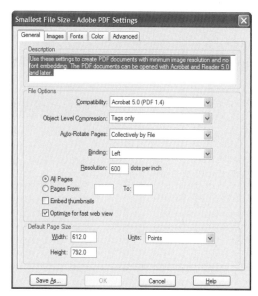

Customizing the Adobe PDF Settings

5 After you have reviewed the settings on the various tabs, click Cancel to leave the settings unchanged, and exit or quit Distiller.

Later in this lesson you'll customize the settings on the Images tab of the Adobe PDF Settings dialog box.

Changing the Adobe PDF Settings in PDFMaker

On Windows, you can change the settings used to convert Microsoft Office documents to Adobe PDF without leaving your Microsoft Office application.

Note: On Mac OS, you set the conversion settings used by PDFMaker in Acrobat Distiller, as described in "Changing the Adobe PDF Settings in Distiller" on page 137.

1 On Windows, open a Microsoft Office application, such as Word.

2 Click the Adobe PDF button on the menu bar, and choose Change Conversion Settings from the menu.

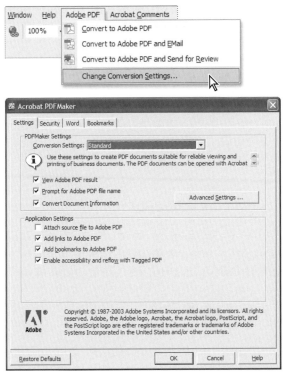

Choosing a default Adobe PDF Setting for converting files to Adobe PDF

You can choose one of the predefined Adobe PDF Settings, or you can customize the settings.

3 To choose one of the predefined Adobe PDF Settings, click the arrow next to the Conversion Settings menu, and choose High Quality, Press Quality, Smallest File Size, or Standard. We chose **Smallest File Size.**

These are the predefined Adobe PDF settings. A brief explanation of each setting is given in the information box below the Default Settings menu. Use the scroll bars to view the entire explanation if the text exceeds two lines. For most beginning users of Acrobat, these predefined settings are sufficient.

Note: Any customized Adobe PDF Settings that you may have created are also displayed in this menu.

For additional information on setting the PDFMaker settings, see Lesson 3, "Converting Microsoft Office Files (Windows)."

4 To customize the Adobe PDF Settings, click the Advanced Settings button. Notice that the dialog box that opens has the same tabs and settings as the Adobe PDF Settings dialog box that you accessed using Distiller in the prior section of this lesson.

5 After you have reviewed the settings on the various tabs, click Cancel to leave the settings unchanged, and click Cancel to close the Acrobat PDFMaker dialog box.

6 Exit your Microsoft Office application.

Changing the Adobe PDF Settings in the Adobe PDF printer

You can create a PDF file from many source application files by "printing" your file using the Adobe PDF printer. In this case, you simply use the File > Print command in your source application, and select Adobe PDF as your printer in the application's print dialog box. When you click the Print button, you create or "print" an Adobe PDF file rather than send a document to be printed on your printer.

On Windows:

1 Open an authoring application such as Adobe FrameMaker or Microsoft Word.

2 Choose File > Print, and choose Adobe PDF from the printer menu.

Depending on your application, Click the Properties or Preferences button. (In some applications, you may need to click Setup in the Print dialog box to access the list of printers and the Properties or Preferences button.)

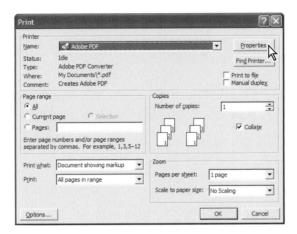

3 In the Adobe PDF Settings tab of the Adobe PDF Document Properties dialog box, choose one of the predefined Adobe PDF Settings from the Default Settings menu.

Note: Any customized Adobe PDF Settings that you may have created are also displayed in this menu.

4 To customize the conversion settings, click the Edit button next to the Default Settings menu. Notice again that this Adobe PDF Settings dialog box has the same tabs and settings as the dialog box accessed from Distiller.

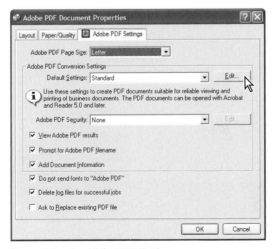

Customizing the Adobe PDF Settings

5 After you have reviewed the settings on the various tabs, click Cancel to leave the settings unchanged, and click Cancel to return to the Print or Print Setup dialog box.

If you wanted to convert the file you have open to Adobe PDF, you would click the Print button in the Print dialog box.

6 For this lesson, close the Print dialog box without printing.

7 Close your authoring application.

Changing the Adobe PDF Settings from the Print dialog box, changes the settings for that application only. To change the Adobe PDF Settings for all applications, change the settings from the Printers or Printers and Faxes Control Panel. For more information, see "Setting the Adobe PDF Printer Properties" in the Complete Acrobat 6.0 Help.

On Mac OS:

1 Open an authoring application such as Microsoft Word or TextEdit.

2 Choose File > Print, and choose Adobe PDF from the Printer menu.

3 Select PDF Options from the pop-up menu to access the Adobe PDF Settings.

4 Choose a setting from the Adobe PDF Settings menu. If you want to use a custom setting, you must first create the custom setting in Distiller. Any custom settings created in Distiller are available in the Adobe PDF Settings menu in this Print dialog box.

5 From the After PDF Creation menu, choose whether to save the Adobe PDF file or launch Acrobat and display the PDF file.

6 Choose Cancel to close the Print dialog box without creating a PDF file. If you wanted to convert your open file to Adobe PDF, you would click the Print button in the Print dialog box.

7 Quit your authoring application.

Regardless of how you access the Adobe PDF Settings, you should check your settings periodically. Acrobat uses the last settings defined; the settings do not revert to the default values.

Predefined Adobe PDF settings

You can choose a predefined settings file for creating Adobe PDF files. These settings are designed to balance file size with quality, depending on how the Adobe PDF file is to be used.

You can choose from the following sets of predefined Adobe PDF settings:

- *High Quality creates PDF files for high-quality output. This set of options downsamples color and grayscale images at 300 dpi and monochrome images at 1200 dpi, does not embed subsets of fonts used in the document, prints to a higher image resolution, and uses other settings to preserve the maximum amount of information about the original document. These PDF files can be opened in Acrobat 5.0 and Acrobat Reader 5.0 and later.*

- *Press Quality creates PDF files for high-quality print production, for example, on an imagesetter or platesetter. In this case, file size is not a consideration. The objective is to maintain all the information in a PDF file that a commercial printer or prepress service provider needs to print the document correctly. This set of options downsamples color and grayscale images at 300 dpi and monochrome images at 1200 dpi, embeds subsets of all fonts used in the document, prints to a higher image resolution, does not automatically rotate pages based on the orientation of the text or DSC comments, and uses other settings to preserve the maximum amount of information about the original document. Print jobs with fonts that cannot be embedded will fail. These PDF files can be opened in Acrobat 5.0 and Acrobat Reader 5.0 and later.*

Note: Before creating an Adobe PDF file to send to a commercial printer or prepress service provider, find out what the output resolution and other settings should be, or ask for a .joboptions file with the recommended settings. You may need to customize the Adobe PDF settings for a particular provider and then provide a .joboptions file of your own.

- *Smallest File Size creates PDF files for displaying on the Web or an intranet, or for distribution through an email system for on-screen viewing. This set of options uses compression, downsampling, and a relatively low image resolution. It converts all colors to sRGB, and does not embed fonts unless absolutely necessary. It also optimizes files for byte serving. These PDF files can be opened in Acrobat 5.0 and Acrobat Reader 5.0 and later.*

• *Standard* creates PDF files to be printed to desktop printers or digital copiers, published on a CD, or sent to a client as a publishing proof. This set of options uses compression and downsampling to keep the file size down, but it also embeds subsets of all fonts used in the file, converts all colors to sRGB, and prints to a medium resolution to create a reasonably accurate rendition of the original document. Note that Windows font subsets are not embedded by default. These PDF files can be opened in Acrobat 5.0 and Acrobat Reader 5.0 and later.

Note: (Windows only) The five default job options files from Acrobat 5.0 (Screen, Print, Press, CJKScreen, and eBook) are available to Adobe PageMaker and Adobe FrameMaker users for backward compatibility.

—From Adobe Acrobat 6.0 online Help.

Using the default Adobe PDF Settings

In this section, you'll compare the image quality and file size of three different PDF files prepared by converting a sample PostScript file to Adobe PDF three times, using a different predefined set of Adobe PDF Settings each time. To save time, we've created the PDF files for you.

1 In Acrobat Professional, choose File > Open, and select the three Adobe PDF files— Color1.pdf, Color2.pdf, and Color3.pdf—in the PDF folder in the Lesson05 folder. (You can Shift-click to select contiguous files.) Click Open.

Color1.pdf was created using the Standard Adobe PDF Settings, Color2.pdf was created using the High Quality Adobe PDF Settings, and Color3.pdf was created using the Smallest File Size Adobe PDF Settings.

Note: The difference between Press Quality and High Quality is primarily in font embedding. Since this lesson addresses differences in image quality, you'll use only the High Quality setting.

2 Choose Window > Tile > Vertically to display all the files in the document pane. If needed, use the scroll bars to display the same area in each of the files.

At the default magnification, all three images look very similar.

Color1.pdf   *Color2.pdf*   *Color3.pdf*

3 Click in each image several times with the Zoom-In tool (🔍) or use the magnification pop-up menu to display each image at 400% magnification. Scroll as needed so that you can see the same area in each of the files.

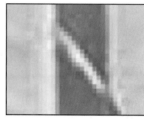

Color1.pdf   *Color2.pdf*   *Color3.pdf*

In comparison with the other images, Color3.pdf (the smallest file size) has a more jagged display quality. Since Color3.pdf is intended for low-resolution, on-screen use, for emailing, and especially for Web use where download time is important, it does not require as detailed a display quality.

4 Select the Hand tool (✋).

5 With the Color3.pdf window active, choose File > Close, and close the Color3.pdf file without saving any changes.

6 Choose Window > Tile > Vertically to resize the remaining two images.

7 Select the Zoom-In tool and click twice in each document pane to display Color1.pdf and Color2.pdf at 800% magnification. Scroll as needed to display the same area in the two files.

Color1.pdf (the Standard file) has the coarser display quality of the two. The Standard Adobe PDF Settings are chosen to balance image quality with a reasonable file size. The conversion settings are designed to produce a file that is suitable for printing to desktop printers or digital copiers, distributed on a CD, or used as a publishing proof. The display quality of Color2.pdf (the High Quality file) is much better. The image resolution is higher for improved print quality.

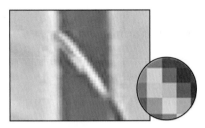
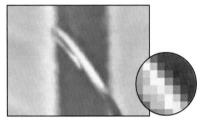

Color1.pdf 76KB   *Color2.pdf 960KB*

8 Choose Window > Close All to close both files without saving them.

9 Select the Hand tool, and then click the Minimize button to minimize the Acrobat window.

Now you'll compare the file sizes of the three Adobe PDF files.

10 On Windows, use Windows Explorer to open the Lesson05 folder, and note the sizes of the three files. On Mac OS, open the PDF folder in the Lesson05 folder, select the file Color1.pdf, and view the files in list view. (If necessary, choose File > Get Info to determine the file size on Mac OS.) Do the same for the Color2.pdf, and Color3.pdf files and note the comparative file sizes.

Color3.pdf has the lowest image quality and the smallest file size, while Color2.pdf has the highest image quality and the largest file size. Note that the significantly smaller Color1.pdf file does indeed balance image quality with small file size.

Note: File sizes may vary slightly depending on whether you are using a Windows or Mac OS system.

11 Close all open windows.

PDF creation often involves a trade-off between image quality and file compression. More compression means smaller file sizes but also coarser image quality, while finer image quality is achieved at the expense of larger file sizes.

About compression and resampling

Many factors affect file size and file quality, but when you're working with image-intensive files, compression and resampling are important.

You can choose from a variety of file compression methods designed to reduce the file space used by color, grayscale, and monochrome images in your document. Which method you choose depends on the kind of images you are compressing. The default Adobe PDF Settings use Automatic (JPEG) compression for color and grayscale images and CCITT Group 4 compression for monochrome images.

In addition to choosing a compression method, you can *resample* bitmap images in your file to reduce the file size. A bitmap image consists of digital units called *pixels,* whose total number determines the file size. When you resample a bitmap image, the information represented by several pixels in the image is combined to make a single larger pixel. This process is also called *downsampling* because it reduces the number of pixels in the image. The Adobe PDF Settings use bicubic downsampling ranging from 100 to 1200 pixels per inch.

Using custom compression settings

The default Adobe PDF Settings are designed to produce optimum results in most cases. However, you can customize the Adobe PDF Settings if you want to fine-tune the compression methods used. In this part of the lesson, you'll practice applying custom compression and resampling settings to a color PostScript file.

Note: Compression and resampling do not affect the quality of either text or line art.

Changing the Adobe PDF Settings

By combining the appropriate compression and downsampling Adobe PDF Settings, you can greatly reduce the file size of a PDF document without losing noticeable detail in an image. You'll apply your custom settings to the original high-resolution PostScript file Color.ps.

1 Maximize the Acrobat Professional window.

2 In Acrobat, choose Advanced > Acrobat Distiller.

First you'll change the Distiller preferences.

3 On Windows, choose File > Preferences, and on Mac OS, choose Distiller > Preferences.

4 Select the Ask for PDF File Destination option, and click OK.

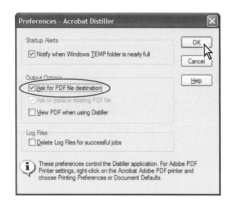
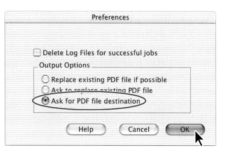

5 In Acrobat Distiller, choose Smallest File Size from the Default Settings pop-up menu.

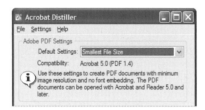

6 Choose Settings > Edit Adobe PDF Settings, and click the Images tab.

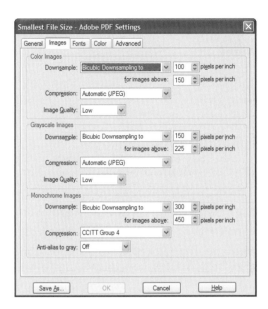

The default compression values associated with the Smallest File Size settings are displayed. You'll now adjust several options to produce your own custom setting (using the Smallest File Size settings as your base) for optimizing on-screen PDF display.

7 In the Color Images area, choose Average Downsampling To from the Downsample (Windows) or Sampling (Mac OS) pop-up menu.

Average downsampling averages the pixels in a sample area and replaces the entire area with the average pixel color at the specified resolution. A slower but more precise approach is to use bicubic downsampling, which uses a weighted average to determine pixel color. Bicubic downsampling yields the smoothest tonal gradations. Subsampling, which chooses a pixel in the center of the sample area and replaces the entire area with that pixel at the specified resolution, significantly reduces the conversion time but results in images that are less smooth and less continuous.

8 Enter 72 ppi for the Downsample (Windows) or Sampling (Mac OS) value and for the For Images Above option. (These are much lower values than you would normally use.)

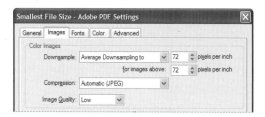

This will downsample the original PostScript color image file (assuming the image resolution is above 72 ppi) to a resolution of 72 ppi. Values that you enter in the Color Images section of the dialog box affect only color images. Any changes you make to the grayscale or monochrome options have no effect on color images. Distiller recognizes the type of PostScript image file, and applies the appropriate color, grayscale, or monochrome compression settings.

Resampling resolution and printer resolution

The following table shows common types of printers and their resolution measured in dpi, their default screen ruling measured in lines per inch (lpi), and a resampling resolution for images measured in pixels per inch (ppi). For example, if you were printing to a 600-dpi laser printer, you would enter 170 for the resolution at which to resample images.

Printer resolution	Default line screen	Image resolution
300 dpi (laser printer)	60 lpi	120 ppi
600 dpi (laser printer)	85 lpi	170 ppi
1200 dpi (image setter)	120 lpi	240 ppi
2400 dpi (image setter)	150 lpi	300 ppi

—From the Complete Acrobat 6.0 Help.

Note: The minimum resolution of images that will be downsampled is determined by the sampling value you choose.

9 Leave the Compression set to Automatic (JPEG) to allow Acrobat Professional to determine the best compression method for color and grayscale images, and leave the Image Quality set to Low.

Note: JPEG2000 is a new international standard for the compression and packaging of image data.

10 Since the Color.ps file you'll be converting contains no grayscale or monochrome images, you'll leave the default values in these sections.

Now you'll save the custom setting that you have specified so that you can use it again in the future.

11 Click Save As. Save the custom setting using the default name **SmallestFileSize**(1). Click Save to complete the Save process. (You cannot overwrite the default Adobe PDF Settings.)

Your custom setting will now be available from the Adobe PDF Settings menu, along with the default settings.

12 If necessary, click OK.

13 Leave the Distiller window open.

Methods of compression

Distiller applies ZIP compression to text and line art, ZIP or JPEG compression to color and grayscale images, and ZIP, CCITT Group 3 or 4, or Run Length compression to monochrome images.

You can choose from the following compression methods:

• ZIP works well on images with large areas of single colors or repeating patterns, such as screen shots and simple images created with paint programs, and for black-and-white images that contain repeating patterns. Acrobat provides 4-bit and 8-bit ZIP compression options. If you use 4-bit ZIP compression with 4-bit images, or 8-bit ZIP with 4-bit or 8-bit images, the ZIP method is lossless, which means it does not remove data to reduce file size and so does not affect an image's quality. However, using 4-bit ZIP compression with 8-bit data can affect the quality, since data is lost.

Note: The Adobe implementation of the ZIP filter is derived from the zlib package of Jean-loup Gailly and Mark Adler, whose generous assistance we gratefully acknowledge.

• JPEG (Joint Photographic Experts Group) is suitable for grayscale or color images, such as continuous-tone photographs that contain more detail than can be reproduced on-screen or in print. JPEG is lossy, which means that it removes image data and may reduce image quality, but it attempts to reduce file size with the minimum loss of information. Because JPEG eliminates data, it can achieve much smaller file sizes than ZIP compression.

Acrobat provides six JPEG options, ranging from Maximum quality (the least compression and the smallest loss of data) to Minimum quality (the most compression and the greatest loss of data). The loss of detail that results from the Maximum and High quality settings are so slight that most people cannot tell an image has been compressed. At Minimum and Low, however, the image may become blocky and acquire a mosaic look. The Medium quality setting usually strikes the best balance in creating a compact file while still maintaining enough information to produce high-quality images.

• CCITT (International Coordinating Committee for Telephony and Telegraphy) is appropriate for black-and-white images made by paint programs and any images scanned with an image depth of 1 bit. CCITT is a lossless method.

Acrobat provides the CCITT Group 3 and Group 4 compression options. CCITT Group 4 is a general-purpose method that produces good compression for most types of monochrome images. CCITT Group 3, used by most fax machines, compresses monochrome images one row at a time.

• Run Length is a lossless compression option that produces the best results for images that contain large areas of solid white or black.

—From the Complete Acrobat 6.0 Help.

Processing the color file with custom settings

Now you're ready to try out your customized Adobe PDF Settings.

1 In Distiller, make sure that Smallest File Size (1) is selected in the Default Settings menu.

2 Choose File > Open. Select Color.ps in the Lesson05 folder, and click Open.

3 Save the Adobe PDF file **Color.pdf** in the PDF folder in the Lesson05 folder.

The conversion of the PostScript file is shown in the Distiller window.

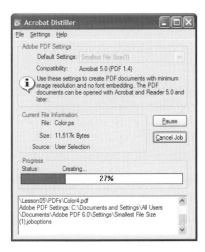

4 In Acrobat Professional, choose File > Open. Select Color.pdf and Color3.pdf (the other PDF file created with the smallest file size setting) in the PDF folder in the Lesson05 folder, and click Open.

5 Choose Window > Tile > Vertically to display the files side-by-side, and use the Zoom-In tool to view both files at 200% magnification. If needed, use the scroll bars to display the same area in each of the files.

Color3.pdf is smoother than Color.pdf. Because Color3.pdf has a higher resolution (100 ppi rather than 72 ppi), it contains more pixel detail and finer image quality.

Color3.pdf 33KB   *Color.pdf 23KB*

6 Select the Hand tool.

7 Choose Window > Close All to close the files without saving them.

8 Minimize the Acrobat window.

9 Compare the file size of the two images. On Windows use Windows Explorer; in Mac OS, use the list view in the Finder or choose Get Info from the File menu. Color3.pdf is significantly larger than Color.pdf.

Processing grayscale and monochrome images

You can experiment with applying default compression and resampling settings to a grayscale and a monochrome PostScript image file. This part of the lesson is optional.

You'll convert the sample PostScript files Gray.ps and Mono.ps, located in the Lesson05 folder to Adobe PDF using the Smallest File Size Adobe PDF Settings. (We converted the two PostScript files (Gray.ps and Mono.ps) using both the High Quality and Standard Adobe PDF Settings for you; however, you can experiment with creating the files yourself using these Adobe PDF Settings if you have time. You can also customize the Adobe PDF Settings as you did in the previous section.)

1 Maximize the Distiller window if necessary.

2 In Distiller, choose Smallest File Size from the Default Settings menu.

The Smallest File Size setting creates output appropriate for on-screen display, such as desktop computers, laptops, and eBook reading devices.

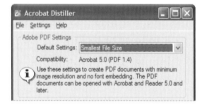

3 Choose File > Open. Select Gray.ps in the Lesson05 folder on your hard drive, and click Open.

4 Save the Adobe PDF file **Gray.pdf** in the PDF folder in the Lesson05 folder. Distiller shows the status of the conversion process to Adobe PDF.

5 Repeat steps 1 through 3 for the Mono.ps file to obtain the Adobe PDF file Mono.pdf.

Note: If you don't want to convert the PostScript file to Adobe PDF, you can use the Gray1.pdf and the Mono1.pdf files that we provided for you in place of Color.pdf and Mono.pdf.

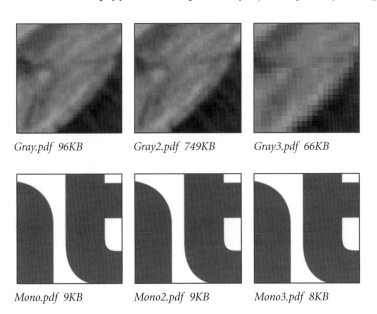

Gray.pdf 96KB   Gray2.pdf 749KB   Gray3.pdf 66KB

Mono.pdf 9KB   Mono2.pdf 9KB   Mono3.pdf 8KB

6 In Acrobat Professional, open the "Gray" series of files (Gray.pdf that you created and Gray2.pdf and Gray3.pdf that we created for you) and the "Mono" series of files (Mono.pdf that you created and Mono2.pdf and Mono3.pdf that we created for you). Compare the image quality and file size as you did for the Color1.pdf, Color2.pdf, and Color3.pdf files in "Using the default Adobe PDF Settings" on page 144.

You'll notice that images with larger file sizes do not necessarily yield better display quality. Downsampling a monochrome file may not significantly reduce its size. When converting your images to Adobe PDF, choose compression and resampling options that will give you adequate quality at the smallest file size possible.

7 When you've finished comparing image quality and file size, choose Window > Close All to close all the files without saving them.

Managing color

You can manage color when you create an Adobe PDF file, and you can manage color when you view an Adobe PDF file.

Managing color in Distiller or PDFMaker

When you use Distiller or PDFMaker to convert a file to Adobe PDF, you can choose to use the color management information contained in the source file, or you can modify any embedded color management information using the color settings in the Adobe PDF Settings file.

Take a few minutes to explore the color management settings in the Adobe PDF Settings dialog box.

1 Do one of the following:

• In the Acrobat Distiller window, select Standard from the Default Settings pop-up menu, and then choose Settings > Edit Adobe PDF Settings.

• In a Microsoft Office application, choose Adobe PDF > Change Conversion Settings, select Standard from the Default Settings pop-up menu, and click Advanced Settings.

• On Windows, choose Printers or Printers and Faxes from the Start menu, right-click on the Adobe PDF printer, and choose Printing Preferences. Select Standard from the Default Settings pop-up menu, and click the Edit button next to the Default Settings menu.

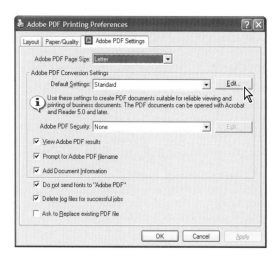

2 In the Adobe PDF Settings dialog box, click the Color tab.

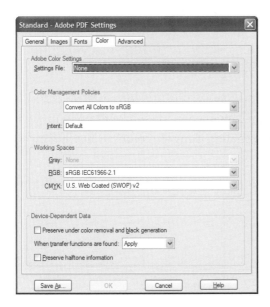

For each of the default Adobe PDF Settings (Standard, Smallest File Size, High Quality, and Press Quality), the Settings File is set to None—that is, Distiller or PDFMaker uses color management information contained in the file. If the file contains unmanaged color spaces, however, Distiller or PDFMaker converts or tags those spaces based on the color management policy and working spaces settings set in this dialog box.

3 Open the Settings File menu.

If you are working in a well-defined color workflow, you can select a color settings file (CSF) from the Settings File pop-up menu. Notice that these color settings files mirror those used in Photoshop and Illustrator.

4 Choose U.S. Prepress Defaults.

Notice that the Color Management Policies and Working Spaces options cannot be edited for these predefined color settings files. These options are dimmed whenever a specific Settings File is selected.

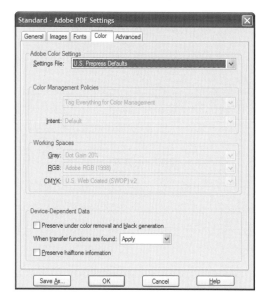

5 Click Cancel and Cancel again to close the Adobe PDF Settings dialog box without making any changes.

6 Close Distiller or your Microsoft Office application.

For more information on these color settings, see "Using predefined color management settings" in the Complete Acrobat 6.0 Help.

Managing color in Acrobat

Colors must often be converted when they are displayed to a monitor or sent to a printer. Any image in a file created by an ICC-compliant application such as Photoshop or Illustrator may have an ICC profile—a description of a device's color space—attached. Acrobat can interpret embedded ICC profiles to automatically manage color, and it can also assign ICC profiles to unmanaged color spaces. The Color Management preferences in Acrobat provide profiles for converting unmanaged color spaces.

Any color management embedded in a PDF file always takes precedence over the CSF setting.

Now you'll look at the Color Management preferences.

1 In Acrobat, choose Edit > Preferences (Windows) or Acrobat > Preferences (Mac OS), and select Color Management in the left pane.

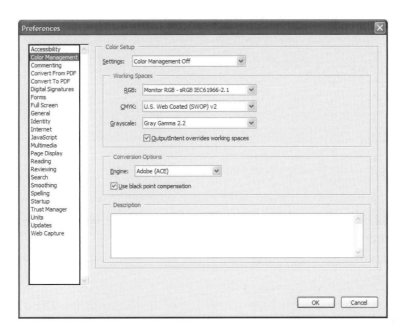

The Settings menu lists the predefined color management settings files (CSFs) available in Acrobat. You can use any of these predefined settings or use any one of them as a starting point for a customized CSF. The Web Graphics Defaults are the settings best suited for content that will be published on the Web.

Color Management Off, the default Settings value, is commonly used for content that is to be displayed on-screen or for video presentations. It uses minimal color management settings to simulate the behavior of applications that do not support color management.

2 From the Settings menu, choose Web Graphics Defaults.

3 Under Working Spaces, choose Wide Gamut RGB from the RGB menu. Notice that the Settings entry changes from Web Graphics Defaults to Custom. You cannot change the predefined CSF settings.

Lastly you'll select a color management engine.

Color matching problems occur when different devices and different software use different color spaces—that is, they speak a different color "language." The color management engine compares the color space in which a color was created with the color space in which the color will be output and adjusts the color so that the two are as consistent as possible.

4 Under Conversion Options, click the arrow to open the Engine menu. These are the color management engines that specify the system and color matching method used to convert colors between color spaces. The choice of engines varies with the platform that you are working on, but the default is the Adobe color management system and color engine.

Note: Because there is no standard technique for how ICC profiles map pure black from the source to the destination, the pure black of a source profile could be different from the pure black of the destination profile. Black point compensation examines the black points of both profiles to see if they are compatible.

5 Choose Cancel to exit the Color Management preferences dialog box and leave the settings unchanged.

6 Exit or quit Acrobat.

Review questions

1 Which of the default Adobe PDF Settings best balances file size with image quality?

2 What is sampling? What is downsampling?

3 Where can you change the Adobe PDF Settings?

Review answers

1 The Standard Adobe PDF Settings give the best balance of image quality with file size.

2 Sampling refers to reducing the number of pixels in an image to minimize the file size. Multiple pixels in the original image are combined to make a single, larger pixel that represents approximately the same image area. Downsampling is the same as sampling.

3 You can change the Adobe PDF Settings in a variety of places, including in Distiller, from the Start menu on Windows, from the Adobe PDF menu in Microsoft Office applications, and in the Properties dialog box accessed from the Print or Print Setup box of a number of authoring applications.

Lesson 6

6 Creating Adobe PDF from Web Pages

Acrobat Professional lets you create editable and searchable files by converting Web pages to Adobe PDF files. You can use the resulting PDF files for a variety of archival, presentation, and distribution needs. On Windows, you can convert Web pages directly from Internet Explorer.

In this lesson, you'll learn how to do the following:

• Convert a Web page to Adobe PDF using Web Capture.

• Download and convert web links from a PDF version of a Web page.

• Build a PDF file of favorite Web pages.

• Update or refresh your PDF version of a Web site.

• Convert Web pages to Adobe PDF and print them directly from Internet Explorer (Windows).

This lesson will take about 30 minutes to complete.

Copy the Lesson06 folder to your desktop, or create a Lesson06 folder on your desktop. This is where you'll save your converted Web pages.

Getting started

You can use Acrobat Professional to download or "capture" pages from the World Wide Web and convert them to Adobe PDF. You can define a page layout, set display options for fonts and other visual elements, and create bookmarks for Web pages that you convert to Adobe PDF.

Because captured Web pages are in Adobe PDF, you can easily save, distribute, and print them for shared or future use and review. Acrobat Professional gives you the power to convert remote, minimally formatted files into local, fully formatted PDF documents that you can access at any time.

Web Capture is especially useful for people who make presentations that include Web pages and those who travel a lot. If you need to include a Web site in a presentation, you can convert the Web site to a PDF file so that you have no concern about Web access during your presentation. If you have downloaded all the linked pages, links will behave in the same way as if you were on the actual Web site. Similarly, if you travel extensively, you can create one PDF file containing all of your most visited Web sites. Whenever you have convenient Web access, you can refresh all pages on the site in one simple action. Regardless of the quality or cost of the Web access in your remote location, you can browse your updated PDF versions of the Web sites at your leisure.

Connecting to the Web

Before you can use Web Capture, you must be able to access the World Wide Web. If you need help with setting up an Internet connection, talk to your Internet Provider.

When you have a connection to the Internet, you can set your Acrobat preferences for handling Adobe PDF files.

1 Start Acrobat Professional.

2 In Acrobat Professional, choose Edit > Preferences (Windows) or Acrobat > Preferences (Mac OS), and select Internet in the left pane of the Preferences dialog box.

3 In the Preferences dialog box, make sure that the option for checking your browser settings when starting Acrobat is checked. Having this option checked, ensures that your settings are checked automatically whenever you launch Acrobat.

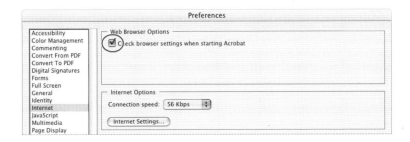

4 Click the Internet Settings button to check your network settings. On Windows, your settings are on the Connections tab

5 Click OK in the Preferences dialog box to apply any changes you have made.

Setting options for converting Web pages

You set options for capturing Web pages before you download the pages. In this section of the lesson, you'll set options that determine the structure and appearance of your captured pages.

1 Choose File > Create PDF > From Web Page.

2 Click Settings.

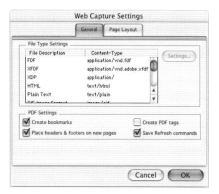

3 In the dialog box, click the General tab.

4 Under File Type Settings, in the File Description column, select HTML and click Settings.

5 Click the General tab and look at the options available.

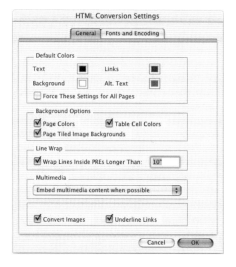

You can select colors for text, page backgrounds, links, and Alt text (the text that replaces an image on a Web page when the image is unavailable). You can also select background display options. For this lesson, you'll leave these options unchanged and proceed to selecting font and encoding options.

6 Click the Fonts and Encodings tab.

You see that Times-Roman is used for body text, Helvetica for headings, and Courier for pre-formatted text. You'll change these defaults.

7 Click the Change button under Language Specific Font Settings.

This opens the Select Fonts dialog box that allows you to reset the fonts used for body, heading and pre-formatted text in converted Web pages.

8 Under Font for Body Text, choose a font from the pop-up menu. (We chose **Helvetica.**)

9 Under Font for Headings, choose a thick sans serif font from the menu. (We chose **Arial Black.**)

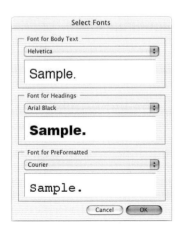

10 Click OK to accept the new font settings.

11 For the Base Font Size menu, choose a size for the body text. We used **14**. Heading text will be proportionately larger, as determined by the HTML coding.

Be sure to leave the Embed Platform Fonts When Possible option unchecked (blank). The embedding platform fonts option stores the font used on the pages in the PDF file so that the text always appears in the original fonts. Embedding fonts in this way increases the size of the file.

12 Click OK to return to the General tab of the Web Capture Settings dialog box.

13 On the General tab, under PDF Settings, make sure that the following options are selected (checked):

• Create Bookmarks to create a tagged bookmark for each downloaded Web page, using the page's HTML title tag as the bookmark name. Tagged bookmarks help you organize and navigate your captured pages.

• Create PDF Tags to store structure in the PDF file that corresponds to the HTML structure of the original Web pages.

• Place Headers and Footers on New Pages to place a header with the Web page's title and place a footer with the page's URL, page number in the downloaded set, and the date and time of download.

• Save Refresh Commands to save a list of all URLs in the PDF file for the purpose of refreshing pages.

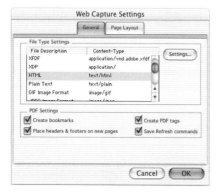

14 Click the Page Layout tab.

On Windows, a sample page with the current settings applied appears in the dialog box. You can choose from standard page sizes in the Page Size menu, or you can define a custom page size. You can also define margins and choose page orientation.

15 Under Margins, enter **0.5** for Left and Right, Top and Bottom.

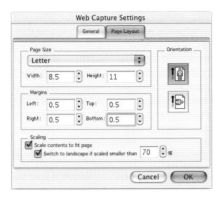

16 Click OK to accept the settings and return to the Create PDF from Web Page dialog box.

After you have some experience converting Web pages to Adobe PDF, you can experiment with the conversion settings to customize the look and feel of your converted Web pages.

About pages on Web sites

Keep in mind that a Web site can have more than one level of pages. The opening page is the top level of the site, and any links on that page go to other pages at a second level. Links on second-level pages go to pages at a third level, and so on. In addition, links may go to external sites (for example, a link at a Web site on tourism may connect to a Web site for a travel agency). Most Web sites can be represented as a tree diagram that becomes broader as you move down the levels.

Important: You need to be aware of the number and complexity of pages you may encounter when downloading more than one level of a Web site at a time. It is possible to select a complex site that will take a very long time to download. Use the Get Entire Site option with great caution. In addition, downloading pages over a modem connection will usually take much longer than downloading them over a high-speed connection.

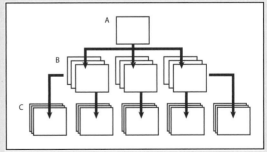

Web site tree diagram. A First level, B. Second level, C. Third level

Creating an Adobe PDF file from a Web page

Important: Because Web pages are updated on a regular basis, when you visit the Web pages described in this lesson, the content of the pages may have changed. You may have to use links other than those described in this section, though we have tried to use links that we think will be relatively stable. You should be able to apply the steps in this lesson to virtually any links on any Web site. If you are working inside a corporate firewall, for example, you might find it easier to do this lesson substituting an internal site for the Adobe Press site or the Peachpit site.

Now you'll enter a URL in the Create PDF from Web Page dialog box and capture some Web pages.

1 If the Create PDF from Web Page dialog box is not open, choose File > Create PDF > From Web Page.

2 For URL, enter the address of the Web site you'd like to capture. (We used the Adobe Press Web site at http://www.adobepress.com.)

3 You control the number of captured pages by specifying the levels of site hierarchy you wish to capture, starting from your entered URL. For example, the top level consists of the page corresponding to the specified URL; the second level consists of pages linked from the top-level page, and so on.

4 Make sure that the Get Only option is selected, and that 1 is selected for the number of levels.

5 Select Stay on Same Path to capture only pages that are subordinate to the URL you entered.

6 Select Stay On Same Server to download only pages on the same server as the URL you entered.

7 Click Create. The Web Capture Status dialog box displays the status of the download in progress. When downloading and conversion are complete, the captured Web site appears in the Acrobat Professional document window, with bookmarks in the Bookmarks panel. Tagged bookmark icons differ from the icons for regular bookmarks.

If any linked material is not downloadable you will get an error message. Click OK to clear the error message.

8 Use the Next Page button (▶) and the Previous Page button (◀) to review the two PDF pages. The single home page of the AdobePress.com Web site has been converted into two Web pages to preserve the integrity of the page content.

Note: On Windows, if you're downloading more than one level of pages, the Download Status dialog box moves to the background after the first level is downloaded. The globe in the Create PDF from Web Page button in the toolbar continues spinning to show that pages are being downloaded. Choose Advanced > Web Capture > Bring Status Dialogs to Foreground to see the dialog box again. (On Mac OS, the Download Status dialog box stays in the foreground.)

The captured Web site is navigable and editable just like any other PDF document. Acrobat Professional formats the pages to reflect your page-layout conversion settings, as well as the look of the original Web site.

Downloading and converting links in a converted Web page

When you click a web link in the Adobe PDF version of the Web page and the web link links to an unconverted page, Acrobat Professional downloads and converts that page to Adobe PDF. In order to convert linked pages to Adobe PDF, you must set Web Capture preferences to open web links in Acrobat Professional (the default setting) rather than in your default browser.

1 In Acrobat Professional, choose Edit > Preferences (Windows) or Acrobat > Preferences (Mac OS), and select Web Capture in the left pane of the Preferences dialog box.

2 For Open Web Links, make sure that In Acrobat is selected. Then click OK.

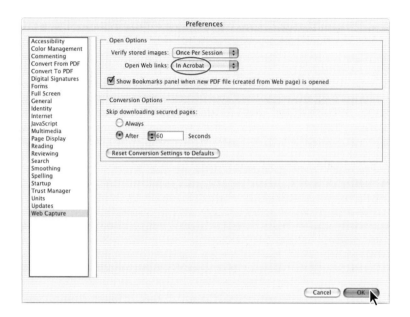

3 Navigate through the captured Web site until you find a web link to an unconverted page (we used the "About" link under the heading "Adobe Press"), and click the link. (The pointer changes to a pointing finger with a plus sign when positioned over a web link and the URL of the link is displayed.)

Note: If the Specify Web Link Behavior dialog box appears, make sure that Open Web Link in Acrobat Professional is selected, and click OK.

The Download Status dialog box again displays the status of the download. When download and conversion are complete, the linked page appears in the Acrobat Professional window. A bookmark for the page is added to the Bookmarks list.

4 Choose File > Save As, rename the file **Web1.pdf**, and save it in the Lesson06 folder.

5 Click the Previous View () button to return to the first page of the converted Adobe Press page.

You also think you might like to see what's involved in registering as a member.

6 Click the Register link under the "Save! Join Now!" heading.

Notice again, that the Web page has been converted into two PDF pages (pages 4 and 5).

The Download Status dialog box again displays the status of the download, and another bookmark for the page is added to the Bookmarks list.

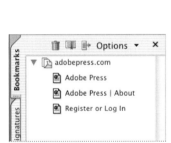

Deleting converted Web pages

After reading the membership information, you decide not to register at this moment. Rather than keep the unwanted form in your file, you'll delete the unwanted page.

1 In the Bookmarks panel, click the bookmark Register or Log-In to view the related page.

This is the page you'll delete.

2 Right-click (Windows) or Control-click (Mac OS) the bookmark, and choose Delete Page(s) from the context menu. Click Yes in the alert box.

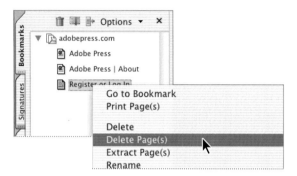

3 Both page 4 and page 5 of the PDF file are deleted.

The bookmark represents one HTML page, so when you delete a page using the bookmark, you delete all the Adobe PDF pages that correspond to that bookmark.

Note: If you click Delete in the context menu, you delete the bookmark only.

Now you'll use the Bookmarks panel to navigate to another captured page.

4 Click the Adobe Press bookmark in the Bookmarks panel to return to the first page of your PDF file.

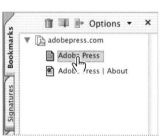

Clicking a tagged bookmark . . .   *. . . takes you to the corresponding page.*

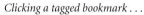

Updating converted Web pages

Because you selected the Save Refresh Commands option when you first converted the Web pages to Adobe PDF, you can refresh or update all pages from one or multiple sites from one Acrobat Professional dialog box.

You can refresh Web pages in a PDF document to retrieve the most up-to-date version from the Web site. Whenever you use the Refresh command, you download the entire Web site or link again and build a new PDF file. Any pages where components have changed—for example, text, web links, embedded filenames, and formatting—are listed as bookmarks in the Bookmarks panel under the New and Changed Pages bookmark. Any new pages that have been added to the site are also downloaded.

Note: The Refresh command may not update converted Web pages that contain forms data. In this case, you will get an error message identifying the pages.

1 With an internet connection open, choose Advanced > Web Capture > Refresh Pages.

2 Select Create Bookmarks for New and Changed Pages.

You specify whether Acrobat Professional looks only for text changes or all changes, including text, images, web links, embedded files, etc. (We used Compare All Page Components to Detect Changed Pages.)

3 Click Edit Refresh Commands List.

This window displays the URLs of all the Web sites that have been converted to Adobe PDF in this file. You can deselect any URLs for pages that you don't want to refresh.

4 Click OK to accept the default selection, and click Refresh to update your converted PDF pages.

Note: If you have difficulty here, you may need to open your browser and repeat the above steps from step 1 on.

Earlier in the lesson, you deleted a page from the PDF file of the converted Web site. Notice that the page you deleted in the earlier version is present in the refreshed file and is also listed in the Bookmarks panel under the New and Changed Pages bookmark. Any reorganization or deletion of pages in the PDF file is lost when you refresh.

5 Click the Window command on the Acrobat menu bar, and notice that you have two windows open. Because you want to keep the Web1.pdf file, you'll save the new file under a different name.

6 Choose File > Save As, and save the new file as **Web2.pdf**. Close the Web2.pdf file.

Building an Adobe PDF file of favorite Web pages

You've created a PDF file containing Web pages from the Adobe Press Web site. In addition to surfing this site, suppose you also like to check the Adobe home page.

In this section, you'll start to build an Adobe PDF file of your favorite Web pages by appending the Adobe home page to the Adobe Press PDF pages that you have already created.

1 With the Web1.pdf file open, choose Advanced > Web Capture > Append Web Page.

2 In the Add to PDF from Web Page dialog box, enter the URL for your favorite Web site. (We used **http://www.adobe.com**.)

3 For Get Only, select 1. Select the Stay on Same Path option and the Stay on Same Server option.

4 Click Create.

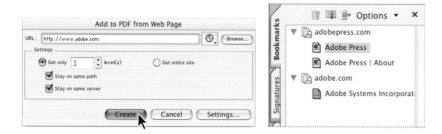

Acrobat Professional appends a PDF version of the Adobe home page to the Adobe Press pages. You can download any linked pages on this site as described in "Downloading and converting links in a converted Web page" on page 173.

You can repeat this process to build up a file of your favorite Web sites that you can keep on your system, share with friends, and refresh at your convenience.

When you are finished, choose Window > Close All to close any open files. Choose Save if you wish to save your work.

Converting Web pages in Internet Explorer (Windows)

If you've ever had the frustrating experience of printing a Web page from your browser only to discover text missing at the end of each line, you'll love the Acrobat Professional feature that allows you to create and print Adobe PDF without ever leaving your browser.

On Windows, Acrobat adds a button with a menu to the toolbar of Internet Explorer 5.0.1 or later, which allows you to convert the currently displayed Web page to an Adobe PDF file or convert and print it in one easy operation. When you print a Web page that you have converted to an Adobe PDF file, the page is reformatted to a standard page size and logical page breaks are added.

Button on PDF toolbar
provides easy conversion
and print options.

First you'll set the preferences used to create Adobe PDF pages from your Web pages.

Setting the conversion preferences

You set preferences from Internet Explorer to determine what happens to converted Web pages in Acrobat Professional.

1 Open Internet Explorer, and navigate to a favorite Web page. We opened the Peachpit Press home page at http://www.peachpit.com.

2 In Internet Explorer, click the arrow next to the Convert Current Web Page to an Adobe PDF file button ( ), and choose Preferences from the menu.

💡 *On Windows XP, if you don't see the button in Internet Explorer, choose View >
Toolbars > Adobe PDF.*

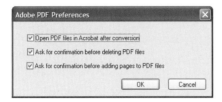

3 For this part of the lesson, you'll use the default values for the preferences. When you've
reviewed the options, click Cancel to close the dialog box without making any changes.

Opening the Adobe PDF pane

Acrobat Professional also adds an Adobe PDF pane to Internet Explorer where you can
manage your converted Web pages. Folders and PDF files are organized under the root
directory Desktop. You can create, rename, and delete folders in this window, as well as
rename and delete files. Only PDF files and folders containing PDF files are listed.

*Note: The files and folders displayed in the Adobe PDF pane are the same files and folders on
your system. Because only PDF files are displayed in the Adobe PDF pane, if you attempt to
delete a folder that contains files other than PDF files (files that are not visible in the Adobe
PDF pane), you will be asked to confirm the deletion.*

1 In Internet Explorer, click the arrow next to the Convert Current Web Page to an Adobe
PDF File button (🔁), and choose Adobe PDF Explorer Bar from the menu.

Before you convert the Peachpit Web page to Adobe PDF, you'll create a folder at the
desktop level in which to save the file.

2 Select the desktop icon in the Adobe PDF pane, and click the New Folder button (📂)
at the top of the Adobe PDF pane.

The new folder is automatically called New Folder.

💡 *If you want to add a new folder under an existing folder, select the folder in the Adobe PDF pane and click the New Folder button, or right-click the folder and choose New Folder.*

Now you'll rename the folder you created.

3 Click in the New folder text label to select the text, and type in your new label. We typed in **Peachpit**.

Now you'll convert the Peachpit home page to Adobe PDF and save it in the folder that you just created.

Converting Web pages to Adobe PDF

1 In the Adobe PDF pane, select the Peachpit folder that you just created.

2 Click the Convert button (⬚) at the top of the Adobe PDF pane.

3 In the Convert Web Page to Adobe PDF dialog box, your Peachpit folder should be selected automatically. You just need to rename the PDF file if necessary. We typed in the name **PeachpitHome.pdf**. Click Save.

The default filename used by Acrobat is the text used in the HTML tag <TITLE>. Any invalid characters in the Web page filename are converted to an underscore when the file is downloaded and saved.

4 If your Adobe PDF version of the Peachpit home page didn't open automatically, double-click the file name (PeachPitHome.pdf) to launch Acrobat and display the converted file.

Converting linked pages

You can convert linked pages to Adobe PDF and add them to your current PDF file, just as you did in "Downloading and converting links in a converted Web page" on page 173.

Remember that in order to convert linked pages to Adobe PDF, you must set Web Capture preferences to open web links in Acrobat Professional rather than in your default browser.

In this section, you'll convert and add the Adobe Press pages to your PDF version of the Peachpit home page.

1 In Acrobat, scroll through the Adobe PDF file until you see the Book Catalog listing. (Ours was on page 4 of the PDF file.)

2 Click the Adobe Press link. The Download Status dialog box shows the progress of the conversion.

The PDF pages are automatically added to the end of the current file.

3 Choose File > Save to save your work, and then close any open files.

Now you'll see how converting a Web page to PDF before printing it avoids unpleasant surprises. First you'll try printing a Web page.

Converting and printing Web pages

1 In Internet Explorer, navigate to the Federal Emergency Management home page at http://www.fema.gov/.

2 If you have a printer connected to your system, click the Print button ( ) on the Internet Explorer toolbar.

Your printed copy of the Web page will probably be missing a word or so at the end of each line of text. In this next section, you'll convert the Web page to Adobe PDF and print it without leaving Internet Explorer. With an Adobe PDF version of the page, you'll see *all* the text. Acrobat automatically resizes the Web page to standard printer page sizes to avoid disappointing print results.

3 In Internet Explorer, click the arrow next to the Convert Current Web Page to an Adobe PDF file button ( ), and choose Print Web Page from the menu.

The progress of the conversion is shown in the Printing Status dialog box. When the conversion is complete, the Print dialog box for your default system printer opens automatically.

4 In the Print dialog box, select any required print options and click Print.

Take a look at the printed copy and notice that all the text is included and readable. Converting Web pages to Adobe PDF before printing is an easy way to avoid unpleasant print results.

5 Close Internet Explorer, Acrobat Professional, and close any open PDF files.

Review questions

1 How do you control the number of Web pages captured by Acrobat Professional?

2 How do you convert destinations of web links to PDF automatically?

3 How do you update your PDF file to show the latest version of a captured Web site?

Review answers

1 You can control the number of captured Web pages by specifying the following options:

• The Levels option lets you specify how many levels in the site hierarchy you want to capture.

• The Stay on Same Path option lets you download only pages that are subordinate to the specified URL.

• The Stay on Same Server option lets you download only pages that are stored on the same server as the specified URL.

2 To convert the destination of a web link to PDF, first choose Edit > Preferences (Windows) or Acrobat > Preferences (Mac OS), and then choose Web Capture in the left pane. Choose In Acrobat for the Open Web Links option. After you have set this preference, clicking the web link in the PDF file will convert the link's destination to PDF.

3 With an Internet connection open, choose Advanced > Web Capture > Refresh Pages to build a new PDF file using the same URLs and links. Select the Create Bookmarks for New and Changed Pages option if you want Acrobat Professional to create bookmarks for pages that have been modified or added to the Web site since you last converted the Web site and its links. You also specify whether Acrobat Professional looks only for text changes or for all changes. (You cannot refresh pages unless you selected the Save Refresh Commands option in the Web Capture Settings dialog box to save a list of all URLs in the PDF file for the purpose of refreshing pages.)

Lesson 7

7 Modifying PDF Files

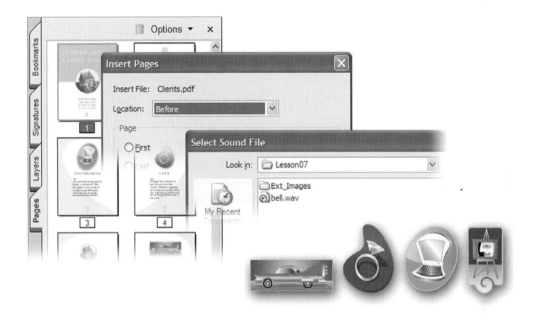

Once you have converted your document to Adobe PDF, you can use Acrobat Professional to make final edits and modifications. In addition to adding links and bookmarks, you can edit text and insert, reorder, and extract pages. Powerful tools let you repurpose Adobe PDF content. You can save text in other file formats, and you can save images in a variety of image formats.

In this lesson, you'll learn how to do the following:

• Convert a TIFF image file to Adobe PDF.

• Rotate and crop pages.

• Use page thumbnails to rearrange pages in a document and navigate through a document.

• Insert and extract pages from a document.

• Copy small amounts of text, and then copy all the text from a document in rich text format.

• Copy both individual images and all the art from a document.

• Renumber pages.

• Create links and bookmarks.

• Create an image file from a PDF file.

This lesson will take about 90 minutes to complete.

If needed, remove the previous lesson folder from your hard drive, and copy the Lesson07 folder onto it.

Note: Windows users may need to unlock the lesson files before using them. For information, see "Copying the Classroom in a Book files" on page 3.

Getting started

You'll work with a brochure that offers in-home services to busy families and professionals. The brochure has been designed both for print and for online viewing as an Adobe PDF file. Because this online brochure is in the developmental phase, it contains a number of mistakes. In this lesson you'll use Acrobat Professional to correct the problems in this PDF document and optimize the brochure for online viewing.

Later in the lesson, you'll copy all the text out of the file in rich text format (RTF) so that you can use it in the development of a Web page, and then you'll copy all the art into individual TIFF files ready for re-use in your authoring applications.

1 Start Acrobat Professional.

2 Choose File > Open. Select CustCare.pdf, located in the Lesson07 folder, and click Open. Then choose File > Save As, rename the file **CustCare1.pdf**, and save it in the Lesson07 folder.

Notice that the document opens with the Bookmarks panel open and that bookmarks for the pages in the brochure have already been created.

3 Use the Next Page button (▶) on the status bar to page through the brochure.

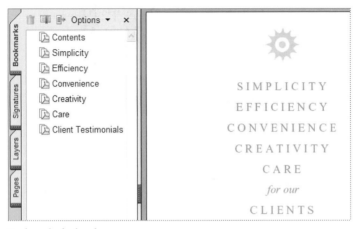

Bookmarks for brochure

4 With the Hand tool (🖐), click the Contents bookmark to return to the first page of the brochure, which acts as the list of contents of the brochure.

5 Move the pointer into the document pane. Notice that the titles in the list have already been linked, as shown by the hand changing to a pointing finger.

Move pointer into document.

When the file was converted to Adobe PDF, the entries in the formatted table of contents were converted to PDF bookmarks and linked automatically.

Certain page-layout and book-publishing programs, such as Adobe InDesign, Adobe PageMaker, and Adobe FrameMaker, work in conjunction with Acrobat Professional to automate the creation of links and bookmarks during the conversion to Adobe PDF. On Windows, you can also preserve links created in Microsoft Office applications.

6 Click the Simplicity entry in the contents to follow its link.

Notice that the page number in the document pane is 1, whereas the page number in the status bar shows the page as being page 4 of 6. Clearly the page is out of order.

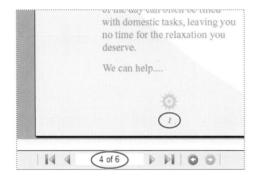

7 Click the Previous View button (○) to return to the contents.

You'll continue exploring this brochure.

Editing pages

Use the Next Page button (▶) and the Previous Page button (◀) to page through the brochure. When you've finished examining the brochure, go back to the first page (page 1 of 6). You'll notice that the first page, the contents page, is rather plain. To make the brochure more attractive, we've created a new cover page for you by scanning a printed image into a computer and saving the image as a TIFF file.

Converting and adding an image file

To add a title page to the brochure, you'll convert the TIFF image that we created for you, add it to the PDF file for the brochure, and then crop the new page to match the rest of the book. You'll convert the TIFF file to Adobe PDF and place it at the beginning of the brochure without leaving Acrobat Professional.

1 Choose File > Create PDF > From Multiple Files, or click the arrow next to the Create PDF task button on the Acrobat toolbar, and choose From Multiple Files from the menu.

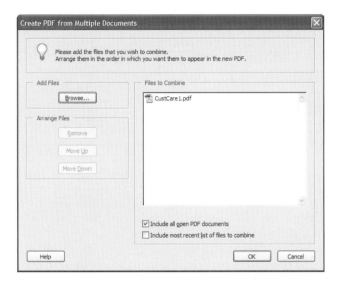

Because the file CustCare1.pdf is open, and because the option to include all open PDF documents is selected, the CustCare1.pdf file is already listed in the Files to Combine window.

2 Click the Browse button (Windows) or Choose (Mac OS) button under Add Files.

3 Select the file Cover.tif in the Lesson07 folder, and click Add.

The TIFF file is added to the Files to Combine window, but it follows the CustCare1.pdf file, and you want it to be the first page in the document. You'll rearrange the files in the Files to Combine window.

4 Click the Cover.tif file in the Files to Combine window to select the file, and then click the Move Up button under Arrange Files.

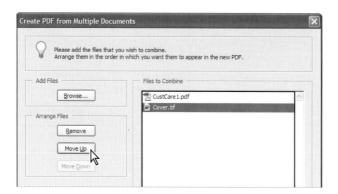

Your files are now in the desired order so you're ready to convert the TIFF file to Adobe PDF and combine it with the existing PDF file.

5 Click OK. A progress dialog box shows the conversion and combination of files.

By default, the resulting file is named Binder1.pdf.

6 Choose File > Save As, name the file **CustCare2.pdf**, and save the file in the Lesson07 folder.

You now have a cover page, but the cover page is incorrectly oriented and sized compared to the rest of the book. Now you'll rotate the page and crop it to match the other pages in the book. But first you'll close the CustCare1.pdf file.

Choose Window > CustCare1.pdf to return to the original PDF file, and then choose File > Close.

Converting image, HTML, and text files

You can convert a variety of file types to Adobe PDF by opening the files in Acrobat Professional using the Create PDF From File command or by dragging the file onto the Acrobat Professional icon or window.

Files are converted to an image only format—images and text are bitmaps, and therefore text cannot be edited. If your converted image has text, you may want to "capture" the image to change the bitmap text to PDF text that can be edited and searched.

An imported image can be saved in a new PDF file or appended to an existing file.

Rotating a page

Now you'll rotate the title page to the correct orientation.

1 Click the Fit Page button (▢) so that you can view the whole page that you imported.

2 Click the Pages tab to open the Pages panel, and click the page thumbnail corresponding to page 1, the new cover page, to select it.

3 Click the Options button at the top of the Pages panel, and choose Rotate Pages.

4 For Direction, choose Clockwise 90 degrees. Make sure that the Selection option is selected, and click OK.

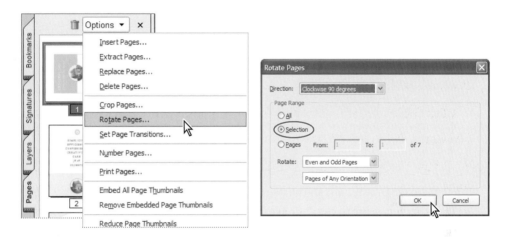

The page is rotated by 90° in the specified direction.

5 Choose File > Save to save your work.

💡 *If you want to rotate all the pages in a file for viewing purposes only, click the Rotate Clockwise button (⤵) or Rotate Counterclockwise button (⤴) on the toolbar. If the Rotate View toolbar is hidden, choose View > Toolbars > Rotate View to display the toolbar. You can also choose View > Rotate View > Clockwise or Counterclockwise. When you close the file, however, the pages revert to their original rotation.*

Rotating multiple pages

You can rotate one page or multiple pages within an Adobe PDF document using the Options menu of the Pages tab.

To rotate multiple pages in an Adobe PDF document:

__1.__ Click the Pages tab to show the page thumbnails for the document.

__2.__ Select the page thumbnails corresponding to the pages you want to rotate. Click a page thumbnail to select it; Control-click (Windows) or Command-click (Mac OS) to add more page thumbnails to the selection.

__3.__ Click the Options button at the top of the Pages pane to open the Options menu, and choose Rotate Pages.

__4.__ For Direction, select Clockwise 90 degrees, Counterclockwise 90 degrees, or 180 degrees to specify the degree and direction of rotation.

If you select page thumbnails corresponding to the pages you want to rotate, the Selection button is highlighted. If you do not select page thumbnails in the Pages tab, you can choose to rotate all pages or a range of pages.

You can choose to rotate only odd or even pages, or you can choose to rotate both.

You can choose to rotate only landscape pages or portrait pages, or you can choose to rotate both.
When you have chosen which pages to rotate and the direction and degree of rotation, click OK to complete the task.

View the page thumbnails in the pages tab. Although the new cover page is the same size as the other pages in the book, the image area is smaller. The cover image has a significant white margin around it. Now you'll crop the page so that the image fills the page.

Cropping a page

You'll use the Crop Pages dialog box to enter dimensions for the imported page so that it matches the other pages in the document. But first you'll change the page units from inches to points, which will give you more control over the crop operation.

1 Choose Edit > Preferences (Windows) or Acrobat > Preferences (Mac OS), and select Units in the left pane of the Preferences dialog box.

2 From the Page Units menu, chose Points. Click OK to apply the change.

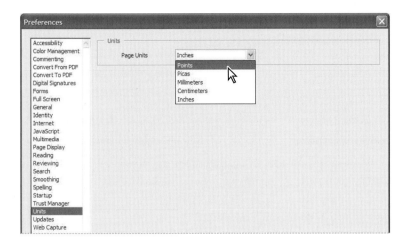

Now you'll crop the page.

3 With the Page 1 thumbnail still selected in the Pages panel, click the Options button at the top of the Pages tab and choose Crop Pages.

The Crop Pages dialog box appears, which lets you specify the margins.

4 For Left, enter **71.8** pt. Click outside the text box. (Don't press Enter or Return or you'll apply the crop operation and close the Crop Pages dialog box.)

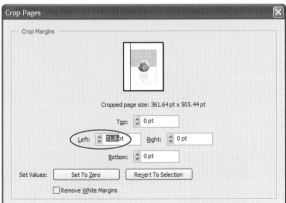

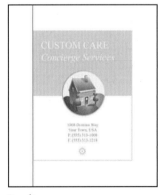

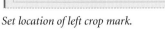

Set location of left crop mark.   *Result*

A line representing the crop location appears both in the preview in the dialog box and in the document. You may need to drag the Crop Pages dialog box out of the way to view the crop line in the document. You can drag the dialog box by its title bar.

5 If needed, use the up and down arrows next to the value for the Left margin in the Crop Pages dialog box to fine-tune the location of the crop line so that it aligns with the left edge of the title border.

6 For Top, enter **71.6** pt and click outside the box to apply the change. If needed, use the up and down arrows to align the crop line with the top edge of the title border.

7 Enter the following values for the remaining crop text boxes: **71.8** for Right and **72.5** for Bottom. Press Enter. Then use the up and down arrows to fine-tune the crop lines.

Add crop marks to remaining image edges.

Result

8 For Page Range, make sure that you are cropping only the selected page, page 1 of the document, and click OK.

9 Select the Hand tool, and repeat Steps 1 and 2, changing the page units back to inches.

10 Choose File > Save to save the CustCare2.pdf file.

💡 *You can also use the Crop tool ( ) to crop the page. Choose Tools > Advanced Editing > Crop Tool. Drag in the document pane to define the crop area, and then double-click in the crop area to open the Crop Pages dialog box and follow the steps above to complete the crop operation. Because Acrobat automatically enters your top and bottom, right and left crop margins when you use this method, all you have to do is fine-tune the settings.*

Moving pages with page thumbnails

Now that you have corrected the size and page orientation of the cover, you'll use page thumbnails to rearrange pages in the PDF document. Page thumbnails offer convenient previews of your pages. You can use them for navigation—they are especially useful if you are looking for a page that has a distinctive appearance. You can also drag them in the Pages panel to alter the pagination.

1 If the page thumbnails aren't stacked side-by-side in two columns, move your pointer over the margin between the navigation pane and the document pane. When the pointer changes shape (+||+), drag to the right to widen the navigation pane. Adjust the width of the navigation pane so that you have two columns of page thumbnails.

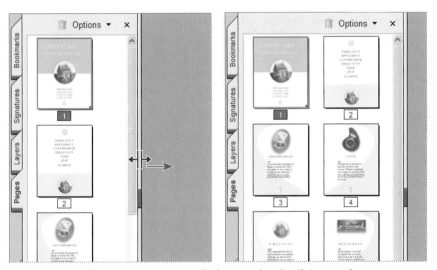

Drag the margin of the navigation pane to display page thumbnails in two columns.

Now you'll move two pages of the brochure that were incorrectly placed. As you noticed earlier, the page that is titled Simplicity is out of place. It should be the first page after the contents page. Because the Efficiency page should follow the Simplicity page, you'll move the two pages together.

💡 *If the page thumbnails are too small to read, click the Options button in the Pages panel, and choose Enlarge Page Thumbnails.*

2 Click the page 5 thumbnail to go to the Simplicity page.

3 Hold down Control (Windows) or Shift (Mac OS) and click the page 6 thumbnail to select it also. Release the Control or Shift key.

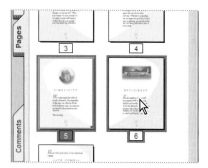

4 Drag the page 5 thumbnail image up until the insertion bar appears to the right of the page 2 thumbnail. The page 2 thumbnail represents the contents page. Because the page 6 thumbnail image is part of the selection, you're also moving that thumbnail image.

5 Release the mouse button to insert the page thumbnails into their new position.

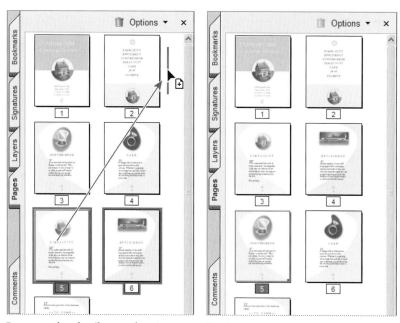

Drag page thumbnail to new location.   *Result*

The Simplicity page now follows the contents page, and the Efficiency page still follows the Simplicity page.

6 To check the sequence of pages, click the First Page button ( ) to go to the first page of the brochure, and then use the Next Page button to page through the brochure.

7 When you're satisfied that the pages are in the correct order, choose File > Save to save your work.

Inserting a page from another file

Next you'll insert a page from a different file to complete the brochure. You can use page thumbnails to insert pages into a document. First you'll resize the Pages panel.

1 To stack the page thumbnails vertically in one column, move your pointer over the margin between the navigation pane and the document pane. When the pointer changes shape ( ), drag to the left to make the navigation pane narrower.

2 Click the page thumbnail for page 2 to view the contents page.

3 In the document pane, click the Creativity link. Notice that you jump to the wrong page. The Creativity link incorrectly links to the Care page.

But if you look at the page thumbnails, you see that the Creativity page is missing. First you'll add the missing page, and then you'll correct the links.

4 Choose File > Open. Select Creativity.pdf in the Lesson07 folder, and click Open.

5 Click the Fit Page button ( ) so that you can see the entire page.

6 Choose Window > Tile > Vertically to arrange the two document windows side-by-side.

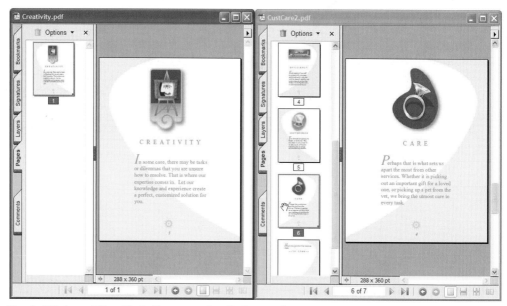

Use the Window > Tile > Vertically command to display two document windows side-by-side.

You can insert pages by dragging page thumbnails between document windows.

7 If necessary, scroll down the pages panel in the CustCare2.pdf window so that you can see the page thumbnails for pages 6 and 7.

8 Select the page thumbnail for the Creativity page in the Page panel of the Creativity.pdf window, and drag the selected page thumbnail into the Pages tab for the CustCare2.pdf window. When the insertion bar appears between the page 6 and page 7 thumbnails, release the mouse button.

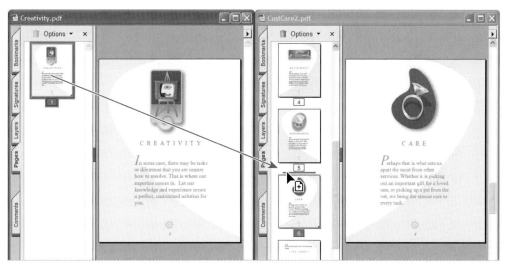

Dragging page thumbnail between documents

The Creativity page is inserted into the brochure in the correct location.

9 Close the Creativity.pdf file, and resize the CustCare2.pdf window to fill your desktop.

10 If necessary, click the page 7 thumbnail to view your newly inserted page.

11 Choose File > Save to save your work.

Now you'll edit the links to make sure that online viewers navigate to the correct pages.

Editing links

1 Click in the page number area of the status bar to select the page number, type 2, and press Enter or Return to return to the contents page.

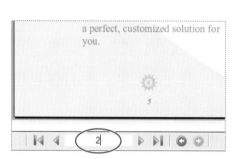

Enter a page number and press Enter or Return to move to that page.

2 On the contents page, click the Care link. Nothing happens. The Care link is not working.

3 Scroll down the page thumbnails in the Pages panel and notice that the Care page is page 6 in the brochure. You'll use this information to set the link correctly.

4 Choose Tools > Advanced Editing > Show Advanced Editing Toolbar to display the Advanced Editing toolbar.

5 Select the Link tool (🔗). Notice that all the links on the page are outlined in black when the Link tool is active.

6 Move the pointer over the broken Care link. The link is selected when red handles appear on the link box. Right-click (Windows) or Control-click (Mac OS) in the link box, and choose Properties from the context menu.

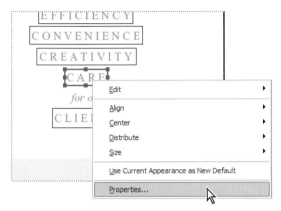

Red handles indicate that the link is selected.

7 Click the Actions tab to set the correct destination for the link.

8 Choose Go To a Page in This Document from the Select Action menu, and click Add.

9 Make sure that the Use Page Number option is selected, and enter **6** in the Page text box.

10 Select Fit Page from the Zoom menu, and click OK.

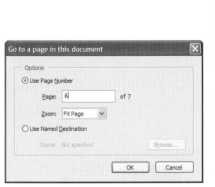

11 Click Close to apply your changes to the link.

12 Select the Hand tool and test your link. When you are finished, click the Previous View button (⊙) to return to the contents page.

Earlier in this lesson, you noticed that the Creativity link incorrectly took you to the Care page. Now you'll correct the Creativity link.

13 Select the Link tool, and move the pointer over the Creativity link. When the red handles appear on the link box, double-click in the link box to open the Link Properties dialog box.

14 Click the Actions tab to correct the destination for the broken link.

The Actions window in the Link Properties dialog box shows that the link is to page 6, which is the Care page. You'll edit the link so that it goes to the Creativity page, page 7 in the brochure.

15 Make sure that Go To a Page in This Document is selected in the Actions window, and click Edit.

16 Make sure that the Use Page Number option is selected, and change the entry in the Page text box from 6 to 7.

17 Select Fit Page from the Zoom menu, and click OK.

18 Click Close to apply your changes to the link.

19 Select the Hand tool and test your link. When you are finished, click the Previous View button to return to the contents page.

20 Choose File > Save to save your work.

21 Click the Close button to close the Advanced Editing toolbar.

Inserting PDF files

In Acrobat Professional, you can insert a page, a specified range of pages, or all pages from one PDF document into another. In the previous section, you used page thumbnails to insert a page from one PDF document into another. Now you'll add client testimonials to the CustCare2.pdf file by inserting all the pages of another file (Clients.pdf). You can insert an entire file easily by using the Insert command.

1 Click the Bookmarks tab in the navigation pane to display the bookmarks. If needed, resize the navigation pane to view the entire bookmark text.

Although the Client Testimonials bookmark appears in the list, the brochure contains only a placeholder for the client testimonials. You'll insert the testimonials from another document.

2 Drag in the scroll bar in the document pane to go to the last page 8 (8 of 8) in the document, or click the Client Testimonials bookmark in the Bookmarks panel.

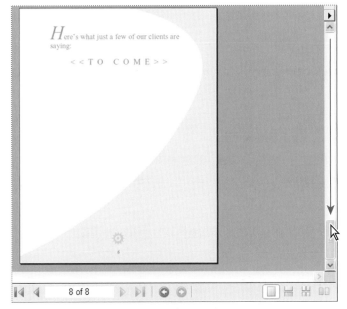

Drag the scroll bar to move through the PDF document.

3 Choose Document > Pages > Insert.

4 In the Select Files to Insert dialog box, select Clients.pdf in the Lesson07 folder, and click Select.

The Insert Pages dialog box appears.

5 For Location, choose Before.

6 Select Page, and enter **8** in the Page text box. Then click OK.

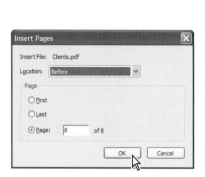

The client testimonials are inserted where they belong.

7 Page through the document to verify that the testimonials have been inserted in the correct location.

8 Choose File > Save to save your work.

You'll need to delete the placeholder page, but first you'll update the link for the Client Testimonials bookmark.

Updating a bookmark destination

1 In the Bookmarks tab, click the Client Testimonials bookmark. The document pane displays the place holder page.

2 In the Acrobat status bar, click the Previous Page button (◀) twice to go to page 8 (8 of 10) of the document, which is the page you want the bookmark to link to—the first page of the testimonials that you added.

3 Click the Options button at the top of the Bookmarks panel, and choose Set Bookmark Destination from the menu. Click Yes to the confirmation message to update the bookmark destination.

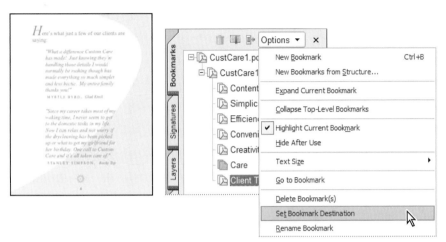

Go to page 8 in the document.   *Choose Set Bookmark Destination from the Options menu in the Bookmarks panel.*

4 Choose File > Save to save the CustCare2.pdf file.

Deleting a page

Now you'll delete the customer testimonials placeholder page from the brochure.

1 Click the Last Page button (▶│) to go to the last page of the brochure, page 10 of 10, the customer testimonial placeholder.

2 Choose Document > Pages > Delete.

3 Make sure that you are deleting page 10 to 10 of the brochure. Click OK. Click Yes to clear the confirmation box.

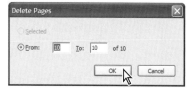

Go to page 10.   *Delete page 10.*

The page is deleted from the CustCare2.pdf file.

4 Choose File > Save, and save your work.

You can page through the brochure to check that the placeholder page has been deleted from the book.

Note: Because you have deleted the placeholder page and replaced it with two new pages, the Clients link from the contents page no longer works. If you wish, you can edit the link as described in "Editing links" on page 204. However, you can complete the remainder of the lesson without resetting the destination for this link.

Renumbering pages

You may have noticed that the page numbers on the document pages do not always match the page numbers that appear below the page thumbnails and in the status bar. Acrobat automatically numbers pages with arabic numerals, starting with page 1 for the first page in the document, and so on.

1 Click the Pages tab in the navigation pane to display the page thumbnails.

2 Click the page 2 thumbnail to go to the contents page.

The first two pages of the document contain front matter—the cover and the contents. You'll renumber these pages using lowercase roman numerals.

3 Click the Options button at the top of the Pages tab, and choose Number Pages.

4 For Pages, select From and enter pages from 1 to 2. For Numbering, select Begin New Section, choose "i, ii, iii" from the Style menu, and enter 1 in the Start text box. Click OK.

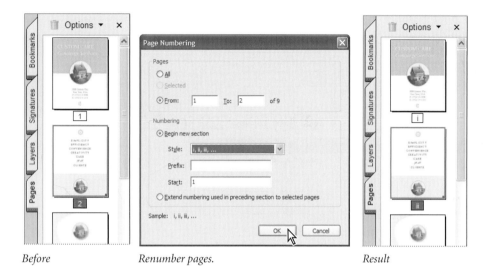

Before *Renumber pages.* *Result*

5 Choose View > Go To > Page. Enter 1, and click OK.

Notice that the number 1 in the status bar is now assigned to the first page of the brochure, the Simplicity page, matching the page number appearing at the center bottom of the page.

 You can physically add page numbers to the pages of your Adobe PDF document using the Add Headers & Footers command. See "Adding a personal message" in Lesson 14.

Editing text

You use the TouchUp Text tool to make last-minute corrections to text in a PDF document. You can edit text and change text attributes such as spacing, point size, and color. In order to edit text, you must have a licensed copy of the font installed on your system; you can change text attributes without having a licensed copy of the font installed.

You'll use the TouchUp Text tool to change the color of a heading.

1 Click the Bookmarks tab.

2 If needed, click the Contents bookmark to display the list of contents.

3 Choose Tools > Advanced Editing > TouchUp Text Tool, and click in the text "for our."

A bounding box encloses the text that can be edited.

4 Drag through the two lines of text, "for our" and "CLIENTS" to highlight them.

5 Right-click (Windows) or Control-click (Mac OS), and choose Properties from the context menu.

6 In the TouchUp Properties dialog box, click the Fill box, and choose a color for the two lines of text to distinguish them from the linked headings. (We used Burgundy.)

7 Click Close to close the dialog box, and click outside the text selection to view the result.

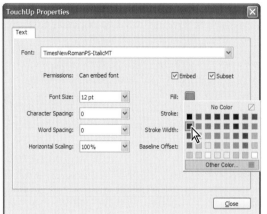 

You can experiment with changing other text attributes, such as the font and the font size.

8 Choose File > Save to save the file in the Lesson07 folder.

Copying and pasting tables

You can select and copy a table by dragging it to a spreadsheet application, such as Microsoft Excel, copying it to the clipboard, or saving it to a file that can then be loaded or imported to another application. If you have a CSV-compliant application on your system, such as Excel, you can open the selected table directly in the application.

To copy a table using the Select Table tool:

1. Select the Select Table tool. The tool is accessible via the Selection toolbar.

2. Click in the table to select the entire table, or drag a box around the rows and columns to be copied.

3. Do one of the following:

• To copy the table to an open document in another authoring application, Ctrl-click (Windows) or Command-click (Mac OS), and choose Copy Selected Table. Then paste the table into the open document.

• To copy the table to a file, Ctrl-click (Windows) or Control-click (Mac OS), and choose Save Selected Table As. Name the table, select a location and the format, and click Save.

• To copy the table to a spreadsheet, Ctrl-click (Windows) or Control-click (Mac OS), and choose Open Table in Spreadsheet. Your CSV-compliant application, such as Excel, opens to a new spreadsheet displaying the imported table.

• To use a document's tag information during table selection, Ctrl-click (Windows) or Control-click (Mac OS), and choose Select Table Uses Document Tags. This option is on by default in tagged PDF documents. The option is grayed out if the document is not a tagged PDF document. You can turn the option off (if a document is poorly tagged, for example), to override a document's tag information during table selection.

• To copy a table in RTF, drag the selected table into an open document in the target application.

Note: Copying tables containing Asian languages is supported.

–From the Complete Acrobat 6.0 Help.

Adding a bookmark

In most cases, you use links and bookmarks to jump to different views of a document. However, you can also use links and bookmarks to execute commands from the Acrobat menus and to play movies, sound clips, or perform other actions.

In this section of the lesson, you'll simply add a bookmark for the front cover of the brochure. First you'll display the page you want to bookmark.

1 Click the First Page button (▮◀) on the status bar to display the front cover of the brochure.

2 Click in a blank area of the Bookmarks panel to make sure that no bookmark is selected, and then click the Create New Bookmark icon (▤). A new, untitled bookmark is added at the bottom of the Bookmarks panel.

If a bookmark is selected when you click the Create New Bookmark icon, the new bookmark is added below the selected bookmark.

3 Click in the text box of the new bookmark to select the text "Untitled," and type in the bookmark label that you want. We typed in **Front Cover**. Click outside of the bookmark to deselect it.

Next you'll move the bookmark into the correct location in the bookmark hierarchy.

4 Drag the bookmark icon directly up and under the CustCare1.pdf bookmark. Release the bookmark when you see the red arrow directly under the parent bookmark icon.

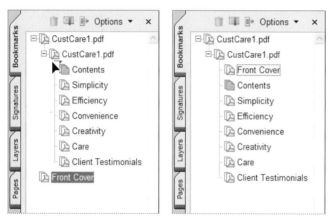

Drag the new bookmark to its correct location.

5 Choose File > Save to save your work.

Test your new bookmark by selecting another bookmark to change the document window view and then selecting the Front Cover bookmark again.

💡 *You can reset the destination of any bookmark using the Set Bookmark Destination command in the Options menu of the Bookmarks panel. To reset the Creativity bookmark, navigate to the Creativity page in the document pane, select the Creativity bookmark in the Bookmarks panel, and choose Set Bookmark Destination from the Options menu. Click OK to clear the message box.*

Adding sound

Now you'll add a page action. You'll add a sound that plays when the first page of the PDF file opens.

First you'll set the initial view of the brochure to make sure that your brochure always opens at the cover page with the entire page displayed.

1 If necessary, click the First Page button (◀) to go to the first page of the brochure.

2 Choose File > Document Properties, and select Initial View in the left pane.

3 For Show, choose Page Only from the menu.

4 For Page Layout, choose Single Page from the menu.

5 For Magnification, choose Fit Page so that the user will see the entire front cover.

6 Make sure that the open to page option is set to "i", and click OK to apply the changes.

The changes will be applied after you close the file. But first you'll add the page action that will play a door bell sound when the page is opened.

7 Click the Pages tab to open the Pages panel. The first page thumbnail, the page i thumbnail, should be selected.

8 With the page thumbnail selected, right-click (Windows) or Control-click (Mac OS) and choose Page Properties from the context menu.

9 In the Page Properties dialog box, click the Actions tab.

10 Choose Page Open from the Select Trigger menu.

11 Choose Play a Sound from the Select Actions menu, and click Add. (You may need to scroll down the Select Actions menu to see all the options available.)

12 In the Select Sound File dialog box, select the bell.wav file and click Select.

13 Click Close to apply the action to the page.

The bell will chime every time you return to the cover page in the PDF file.

14 Choose File > Save to save your work, and then choose File > Close to close the file.

You can check your sound effect and opening view settings by re-opening the file.

15 Choose File > Open, and open the CustCare2.pdf file. If your system is configured correctly, you should hear the door bell as the brochure opens.

For more information on sound system requirements and the types of sound file formats you can use with Acrobat Professional, see "Using actions for special effects" in the Complete Acrobat 6.0 Help.

Copying text and images from a PDF file

Now that the brochure is edited and assembled to your satisfaction, you can reuse the text and images in other applications. For example, you might want to prepare a Web page or a public relations release using the same text. If you no longer have the source file, you can copy the text out of the PDF file in rich text format so you can import it into your authoring application for reuse. You can save images in the file in JPEG or PNG format.

If you want to reuse only small amounts of text or one or two images, you can copy and paste text from a PDF file using the Select Text tool, and you can copy images to the clipboard or to an image format file using the Select Image tool.

For information on using the Snapshot tool to copy text and images, see Lesson 14, "Working with Pictures and Images."

Copying all the text and images

1 Choose File > Save As, and for Save as Type (Windows) or Format (Mac OS), choose Rich Text Format (*.rtf).

2 Click the Settings button to open the Save As RTF Settings dialog box.

3 In the Save As RTF dialog box, make sure that the Include Images option is checked if you want to save images in the RTF file. (If you wanted only the text in the file, you would uncheck this option.)

4 For Output Format, click JPG.

You'll let Acrobat determine the colorspace automatically.

5 Select the Change Resolution option, and choose 300 dpi from the menu. Images that are less than 300 dpi will not be downsampled. (If you do not select the Change Resolution option, images are created at the same resolution as in the PDF file.)

6 Select the Generate Tags for Untagged Files, and click OK. (This option temporarily tags untagged files for the conversion process. Untagged files cannot be converted.)

7 Click Save to complete the export of text and images.

The RTF file is saved as CustCare2.rtf in the Lesson07 folder.

8 Choose File > Close to close the CustCare2.pdf file.

9 Open the text file (CustCare2.rtf) using a text editing or authoring application, such as Microsoft Word. Notice that all the text is copied and that much of the spacing and formatting is retained to simplify re-use of the text. Images are included. Close the RTF file and the authoring application when you are finished.

💡 *You can export all the images in a PDF file in JPEG, PNG, TIFF, or JPEG2000 format using the Advanced > Export All Images command. Each image is saved in a separate file. (See "Converting PDF images to image files" on page 221.)*

Copying and pasting small amounts of text

As you saw in the prior section, copying all the text and images from a PDF file for use in another application is very easy. And it's equally easy to copy and paste a word, sentence, or paragraph into a document in another application using the Select Text tool.

1 Choose File > Open, and open the CustCare.pdf file in the Lesson07 folder.

2 Click the Convenience bookmark in the Bookmarks panel to go to that page in the document window.

3 Click the Select Text tool (🔠) and move the pointer over the text that you want to copy. Notice that the pointer changes when it is in the text-selection mode.

4 Drag through the text that you want to copy. We copied the second sentence of the paragraph.

5 Choose Edit > Copy.

6 Open a new or existing document in an authoring application such as Microsoft Word, and choose Edit > Paste.

Your sentence is copied into the document in your authoring application. You can edit and format the text as you wish.

Copying individual images

You can also copy individual images for use in another application using the Select Image tool.

1 Click the arrow next to the Select Text tool on the toolbar and choose the Select Image tool ( ) from the menu. Notice that the pointer changes when it is in the image-selection mode.

2 Click in the computer image at the top of the page. The image is highlighted.

3 Right-click (Windows) or Control-click (Mac OS), and choose Copy Image to Clipboard to copy the image to your clipboard.

You can also use the Save Image As command in the context menu to save the image in a bitmap (Windows), PICT (Mac OS), or JPEG format file.

4 When you're finished, close your clipboard viewer, and choose File > Close and close the CustCare.pdf file without saving any changes.

On Windows, you can easily convert any clipboard image to Adobe PDF using the File > Create PDF > From Clipboard Image command.

Converting a PDF page to an image format file

Earlier in this lesson, you copied the text and images in the brochure so that you can repurpose the content for your Web page or press release, but you may also want to include sample pages of the brochure. You could extract a PDF page from the file and use that, but it may be easier to create a JPEG version of a complete page.

Converting PDF pages to image files

To be able to use the testimonials in other situations, you'll create a JPEG version of the two testimonial pages.

1 In Acrobat, choose File > Open, and select Clients.pdf in the Lesson07 folder. Click Open.

2 Choose File > Save As, and choose JPEG for Save as Type (Windows) or Format (Mac OS). Rename the file **Testimonials.jpg**.

3 Click Settings to select the compression, format, and color management options. (For information on these Settings options, see "Copying images from a PDF file" in the Complete Acrobat 6.0 Help. We used JPEG (Quality:Medium) for Grayscale and Color, and Baseline (Standard) for Format. We used the default color management settings.) Click OK to accept your settings.

4 Click Save to convert the two pages to JPEG format.

You can experiment with different Settings values and compare file size and image quality for the Settings you choose.

5 Choose File > Close to close the Clients.pdf file.

You can open and view the two Testimonials.jpg files if you have Photoshop or an equivalent application, such as Preview (Mac OS) or Windows Picture and Fax Viewer (Windows). When you are finished, close the JPEG files and the associated viewing application.

Converting PDF images to image files

If you want to use the art from the brochure, it would be useful to have all the art in image file format. In this last section, you'll extract all the art into separate PNG files. You can also extract art into TIFF, JPEG, and JPEG2000 file formats.

1 Choose File > Open, and open the file CustCare2.pdf in the Lesson07 folder.

2 Choose Advanced > Export All Images.

3 Choose PNG for Save as Type (Windows) or Format (Mac OS).

4 Click Settings, and look at the options. For information on these Settings options, see "Copying images from a PDF file" in the Complete Acrobat 6.0 Help. We used the default values.

5 Click Cancel to return to the Export All Images As dialog box without making any changes.

6 For Save In (Windows) or Where (Mac OS), select the Ext_Images folder in the Lesson07 folder.

7 Click Save to save the files to the Extracted folder.

8 Choose File > Close to close the CustCare2.pdf file.

Each piece of art is saved in a separate file. Open one or more of the files using Photoshop or an equivalent application, such as Preview (Mac OS) or Windows Picture and Fax Viewer (Windows). When you are finished, close the PNG files and the associated viewing application.

Review questions

1 How can you change the order of pages in a PDF document?

2 What kinds of text attributes can you change from within Acrobat Professional?

3 How do you select multiple page thumbnails?

4 How do you insert an entire PDF file into another PDF file?

5 How do you copy text from a PDF file?

Review answers

1 You can change the page order by selecting the page thumbnails corresponding to the pages you want to move, and dragging them to their new locations.

2 You can use the TouchUp Text tool to change text formatting—font, size, color, letter spacing, and alignment—or to change the text itself.

3 To select more than one page thumbnail, click the first page thumbnail. Hold down Control (Windows) or Command (Mac OS) and click additional page thumbnails to add them to the selection.

4 To insert all the pages from a PDF file before or after any page in another PDF file, choose Document > Pages > Insert, and select the file you wish to insert. If you want to combine two PDF files—that is, add one file to the beginning or end of another PDF file, you can use the Create PDF From Multiple Files command.

5 If you're copying a couple of words or sentences, you use the Select Text tool to copy and paste the text into another application. If you want to copy all the text from a PDF document, you use the File > Save As command and save the PDF file in a text format.

Lesson 8

8 | Using Acrobat Professional in a Document Review Cycle

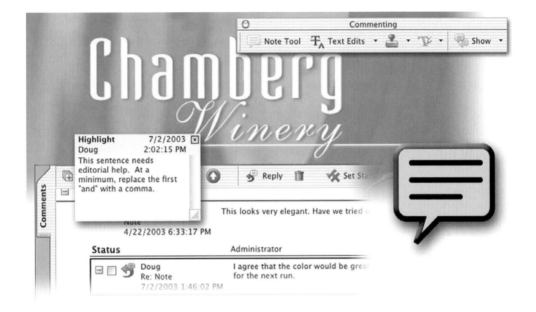

Acrobat Professional can play an effective role in streamlining your document review cycle. You can distribute a PDF document to an audience of reviewers, and you can receive comments back in the form of notes, text, sound files, stamps, files, drawing markups, and text markups added to the file. You can track the review process and then collate the comments and compile them in a single file for easier viewing.

In this lesson, you'll learn how to do the following:

- Manage, create, and respond to comments.
- Change the appearance of comments.
- Summarize and print comments.
- Export and import comments.
- Create custom stamps to apply to your PDF documents.

This lesson will take about 60 minutes to complete.

If needed, remove the previous lesson folder from your hard drive, and copy the Lesson08 folder onto it.

Note: Windows users may need to unlock the lesson files before using them. For information, see "Copying the Classroom in a Book files" on page 3.

Getting started

There are several ways to use Acrobat Professional in a review process depending on the formality of the review, the number of people involved, the interactivity of the review process, and the access of reviewers to a common server.

The simplest and least formal way to send a PDF document for review is to open the document that you want to have reviewed and click the Email button ( ) on the Acrobat toolbar. Acrobat automatically launches a new message window in your default email application and attaches the PDF document that you have open. All you have to do is provide the email addresses of the recipients and type a message for your reviewers. Reviewers receive the entire PDF file and can return comments to you as an FDF file (see "Exporting and importing comments" on page 236), or they can return the complete, annotated PDF file. You'll look at this review process in this lesson.

On Windows, you set your default email application in the Programs tab of the Internet Options panel or the Internet Properties panel of the Windows Control Panel. On Mac OS, you set your default email application in the Email tab of the Internet System Preferences.

If you want more control over the review process—for example, if you want to track several documents that are being reviewed, send reminder messages to reviewers, or invite additional reviewers to join the process—you can use the File > Send by Email for Review command to set up an email-based review. While an email-based review is easy to set up, the management tools it offers are powerful. With this process, the PDF file is packaged in a way that automatically opens the commenting toolbars for the recipients, opens the How To window on commenting topics, and provides instructions for returning comments. You'll see this process in action if you have time to work through the "Exploring on your own" section at the end of this lesson. This process is particularly helpful if you are working with reviewers who are new to the commenting process. For more information, see "Setting up an email-based review" on page 254.

If all your reviewers have access to a shared server, you can set up a browser-based review in which reviewers can review and respond to each other's comments interactively. The browser-based review process is available only to Windows users. For more information, see "Setting up a browser-based review (Windows only)" in the Complete Acrobat 6.0 Help.

Opening the work file

First you'll work with a poster for the Chamberg winery. This poster, which is ready for a final review, was sent as a simple email attachment to just a few colleagues. You'll examine comments that reviewers have added to the poster and add several of your own comments before sending the annotated poster off to the designer.

1 Start Acrobat Professional.

2 Choose File > Open. Select Poster.pdf in the Lesson08 folder, and click Open. Then choose File > Save As, rename the file **Poster1.pdf**, and save it in the Lesson08 folder.

Working with comments

Acrobat Professional's comment feature lets you attach comments to an existing document. These comments can be in the form of notes, text, sound files, stamps, application files, drawing markups, and text markups. Multiple reviewers can comment on and incorporate their comments into the same review version. And if you put your document on a shared server, your colleagues on Windows can simultaneously review and add comments from within their Web browsers.

Opening the commenting toolbars

You add comments to a PDF document using tools on the Commenting toolbar and the Advanced Commenting toolbar. The Commenting toolbar contains the Note tool, the text editing tools, the Stamp tool, and the text markup tools. The Advanced Commenting toolbar contains the drawing tools, the Text Box tool, the Pencil tool, the Pencil Eraser tool, and the file attachment tools.

1 Click the Review & Comment button on the Acrobat toolbar to open the Commenting toolbar. Be sure to click the Review & Comment button and not the arrow next to the button.

2 Now click the arrow next to the Review & Comment button, and choose Advanced Commenting Toolbar from the menu to open the Advanced Commenting toolbar.

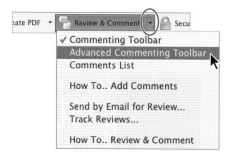

You can leave the two toolbars floating or you can dock them in the toolbar area. For help with moving the toolbars, see Lesson 2, "Getting to Know the Work Area."

Looking at other reviewer's comments

1 Click the Comments tab to display the Comments window. The Comments tab is at the bottom left of the Acrobat window.

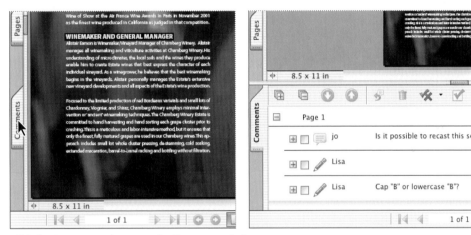

Click the Comments tab to open the Comments window.

A list of comments associated with the open document appears. By default, the list is sorted by page. You can sort the list by a variety of criteria, including type, author, and date. You'll resort the list by author.

2 Click the Sort By button ($\begin{smallmatrix}A\diamond\\2\diamond\end{smallmatrix}$) on the Comments window toolbar, and choose Author. Click OK to close the Showing and Sorting Comments message box.

3 Click the plus sign next to the author jo to expand the comments for that reviewer. Then click the plus sign next to the author Lisa to expand the comments for that reviewer.

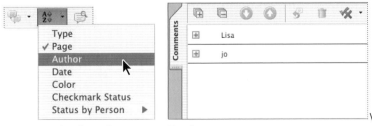

Sort annotations by author.   *Result*

4 Use the scroll bar at the right of the Comments window to scroll down the Comments window, and click the first yellow note listed under jo to highlight that comment on the page. You can read the comment in the Comments window. You can also display the contents of a comment automatically when your mouse rolls over the comment icon in the document pane.

5 Move your pointer into the document pane and position it over the highlighted comment. The text of the comment should be visible.

If you edit the text associated with a comment in the Comments window, the text in the comment in the document pane is updated automatically.

Now you'll look at the preferences that control how comments behave.

6 Choose Edit > Preferences (Windows) or Acrobat > Preferences (Mac OS), and select Commenting in the left pane. You can also open the Preferences dialog box by clicking the Show button ( ) on the Commenting toolbar, and choosing Commenting Preferences.

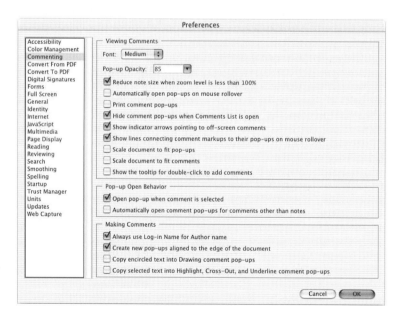

These Commenting preferences control how comments appear, whether pop-ups open automatically, and authoring options.

7 When you have finished reviewing the options, click Cancel to exit the Preferences dialog box without making any changes.

Now you'll examine the different types of comments that appear on the page and the different colored notes.

8 Double-click the blue note on the page to open the note.

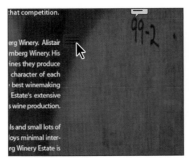
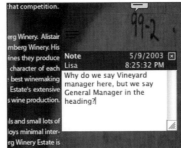

Double-click the blue note to open it.   *Result*

Reviewers can easily customize the appearance of their comments.

9 Click the close box at the top of the note window when you have finished reading the note.

Comments in the form of stamps, drawing markups, and text markups can also have notes associated with them. As with notes, double-clicking the comment opens the associated note window.

Except for text markups (highlighting, underlining, and cross-outs), comments can be easily moved around on a page. Drag any comment and release it when it is in the desired location.

Now you'll look at some text mark-ups.

10 Use the right scroll bar in the Comments window to scroll down until you see the last two comments from jo. Both are text insertions. Click the plus sign for the first text insertion. (You can also click in the text of the comment in the Comments window to select a comment in the document pane.) The comment is highlighted with a contrasting square on the poster, but it is difficult to read in the Fit Page view that the document opened in.

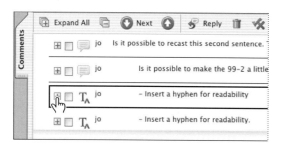

11 Select the Zoom-In tool ($\oplus$) and drag around the last paragraph of text in the document pane to enlarge it. Now you can clearly see the text insertions.

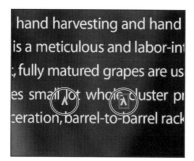

12 Select the Hand tool ($\langle^{\textrm{\fontsize{6pt}{6pt}\selectfont ▪}} \rangle$), and double-click the insertion carat to open the associated note.

Take a few minutes to review the rest of the comments. Double-click on any comment or annotation to open it. When you're finished, close all the note windows and click the Fit Page button.

$\overset{\bigcirc}{}$ *You can search for text in a comment using the Search Comment command on the toolbar of the Comments window. Clicking the Search Comments button ($\rlap{}$), opens the Search PDF window where you can enter your search string. Any comments containing the search string are highlighted in the Results window. The first search result is highlighted in the document window and in the Comments window.*

Soon you'll add a variety of your own comments to this document and respond to the existing comments, but first you'll customize your note style.

Setting the appearance of notes

You set the appearance of notes in either the Appearance tab of the Properties dialog box or in the Properties toolbar. The Properties toolbar is unusual in that its contents change depending on the tool selected. The name of the toolbar also changes to reflect the name of the tool selected. In this section, you'll use the Properties toolbar to change the appearance of your notes.

1 Choose View > Toolbars > Properties Bar.

If you didn't dock or move the Commenting and Advanced Commenting toolbars, you may need to reposition the Properties toolbar so that it doesn't hide either of the other toolbars.

2 Drag the Properties toolbar by its title bar so that it doesn't hide either of the commenting toolbars.

3 Click the Note tool ($\rlap{}$) on the Commenting toolbar to show the properties in the Note Tool Properties toolbar that you can change for notes.

When the Note tool is selected, the Properties toolbar shows the properties that can be set for notes.

Now you'll change the color of your notes.

4 On the Note Tool Properties toolbar, click the arrow next to the color square and choose a color from the color palette. We chose teal.

💡 *Reviewers often use the same color for all their annotations, mark-up, and drawing tools.*

Now you'll change the icon associated with the Note tool.

5 Click the Icon button (🖻) on the Note Tool Properties toolbar, and select an image to associate with the Note tool. We chose the Star.

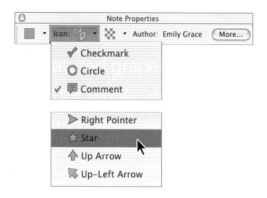

6 Click the Opacity button (▦) on the Note Tool Properties toolbar, and set the opacity of the note icons. We chose 60%.

7 If you want to keep the current tool selected after you have added a comment, click the check box next to the Keep Tool Selected option. (The option is on when the check box contains a check mark.) Because we're adding different types of comments, we chose not to select this option.

💡 *You can change the color associated with any text edit tools, any markup tools, or any drawing tools using the Properties toolbar. Select the tool whose color you want to change and then use the Properties toolbar to change the color. You must change the color associated with the tool before using the tool. To apply the color change to all subsequent uses of the tool, use the tool in the document pane and then right-click (Windows) or Control-click (Mac OS) on the tool or mark-up and choose Make Current Properties Default from the context menu.*

Changing the author name for comments

You cannot change the author name from the Properties toolbar. You can only change the author name in the General tab of the Properties dialog box, but first you must change the Commenting preferences to turn off the option to use the log-in name as the author name.

1 Click the Show button ( ) on the Commenting toolbar, and choose Commenting Preferences.

2 In the Making Comments section of the Commenting Preferences dialog box, click the check box to turn off the Always Use Log-In Name for Author Name option in the commenting preferences. (The option is off when the box is empty.) Then click OK to close the Preferences dialog box and apply your change.

Now you'll change the author name.

3 With the Note tool ( ) selected, click anywhere on the poster to add a note.

4 Right-click (Windows) or Control-click (Mac OS) on the title bar of the note, and choose Properties from the context menu.

5 Click the General tab, and enter your author name. We entered **Doug** as the author.

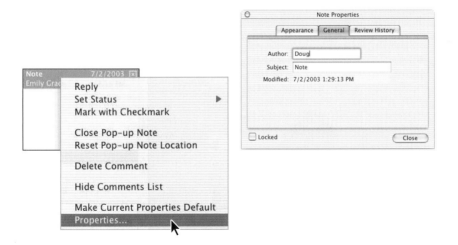

6 Click Close.

Now that you've set the color, opacity, icon, and author name for your notes, you'll make these the default properties. If you don't make these the default properties, your new setting will apply only to the current note and not to any subsequent notes that you add.

7 Right-click (Windows) or Control-click (Mac OS) on the note icon or on the title bar if the note is open, and choose Make Current Properties Default from the context menu.

8 Choose File > Save to save your work.

When you are finished with this lesson, you should be sure to reset the appearance and author information for your notes to better suit your needs.

To change the properties of any object, Right-click (Windows) or Control-click (Mac OS) the object, and choose Properties from the context menu.

Exporting and importing comments

As you have seen, the poster has been reviewed by several different reviewers. One reviewer, however, has placed comments in a separate copy of the poster. You'll export this reviewer's comments from a separate copy of the poster and place them in a Forms Data Format (FDF) file. You'll then combine the comments in the FDF file with the existing comments in the poster.

If you review a document and need to email the review comments to someone, it is usually easier to export your review comments to an FDF file and simply email the FDF file. Because the FDF file contains just the comments, it is much smaller then the annotated PDF file.

1 Choose File > Open. Select Review.pdf, located inside the Lesson08 folder, and click Open.

This file contains an orange note adjacent to the poster title.

2 Choose Document > Export Comments.

3 Name the file **Comments.fdf**, and save it in the Lesson08 folder.

4 Choose File > Close to close the Review.pdf file without saving any changes.

Now you'll import the comments from the Comments.fdf file into the Poster1.pdf file, so that you have all the comments in a single document. First take a moment to compare the size of the Comments.fdf file and the Review.pdf file in the Lesson08 folder. (If you need help comparing the size of files, see "Using the Default Adobe PDF Settings" in Lesson 5.) The Comments.fdf file is approximately 2 KB, whereas the Review.pdf file is approximately 1.1 MB. (File size may vary depending on the platform you are working on.)

5 With the Poster1.pdf document active, choose Document > Import Comments.

6 Select Comments.fdf, located in the Lesson08 folder, and click Select. Click Yes to close the message box.

7 If necessary, click the Comments tab to reopen the Comments window.

8 Scroll to the top of the Comments window.

The Comments window now lists comments from Eamon, as well as those from other reviewers.

9 Click the plus sign next to the name Eamon to expand the Comments window, and then click the note icon in the Comments window to refocus the view of the poster in the document pane and highlight Eamon's note.

Click on a note in the Comments window to go to the note in the document pane.

The imported comment appears in the correct location on the page.

10 Choose File > Save to save the Poster1.pdf file.

You can also import comments directly from one PDF document to another. In the PDF document that you want to consolidate comments in, choose Document > Import Comments. Choose Acrobat PDF files for Files of Type (Windows) or Show (Mac OS), and select the file from which you want to import comments. Click Select to import the comments directly without creating an FDF file.

Exporting Adobe PDF comments to a Word document (Windows only)

In some instances, reviewers make comments in an Adobe PDF document that was created from a Microsoft Word 2002 document in Windows XP. If you need to make changes to the Word document based on these comments, it may be easier for you to import the comments directly into the Word document, rather than switching back and forth between the Word document and Acrobat. You can either export the comments from the PDF document in Acrobat, or you can import the comments from the PDF document into Word. See "Adding comments to a Word document," "Tips for exporting comments to a Word document," and "Selecting which comments to import" in the Complete Acrobat 6.0 Help.

Replying to comments

Before you add comments of your own, you'll use the Reply command to respond to the existing comments. First you'll reply to Eamon's note that you just imported.

1 Double-click on the orange note in the document pane to open it.

Eamon would like to have color applied to the text to soften it, but the poster is running over budget as is, so you'll decline to implement Eamon's suggestion.

2 Click the Set Status button ( ), on the Comments window toolbar, and choose Rejected from the menu.

The status of the comment is recorded in the Comments window.

Now you'll explain your decision to Eamon.

3 Click the Reply button ( ) in the Comments window toolbar.

You'll enter your reply in the note box that opens automatically in the Comments window.

4 Type in your reply. We typed in, "**I agree that a color would be great, but unfortunately adding a color to the text would take us over budget. Let's keep this in mind for the next run.**"

5 Click the Comments tab to close the Comments window.

Your reply to Eamon's comment is opened automatically with a note at the bottom indicating one reply.

6 Click on the "1 reply" label.

A toolbar is displayed below the note, indicating that comment 2 of 2 is displayed. You can display Eamon's comment by clicking the Previous Comment button (◉).

7 Click View All in this toolbar to open the Comments window and display both the initial note and your response.

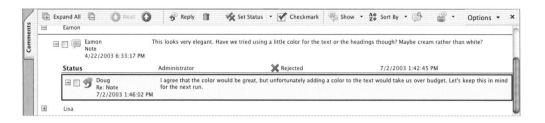

💡 *You can set the status of a comment without creating a reply.*

8 When you're finished, close your note. Closing the note also closes the associated toolbar.

Now you'll deal with the comment about the capitalization of the names of wines.

9 In the Comments window, scroll down to view the three Pencil comments applied by Lisa, and click the pencil icon to select any one of the comments.

10 Click the Reply button on the Comments window toolbar.

11 Click in the text box to create an insertion point, and enter your response. We entered, **"We need to use initial capitals for all wine names. Please be sure that the source text file for this poster is also corrected. I've attached a copy of the source file for you."** (You'll learn how to attach the source file later in this lesson.)

You can also add text formatting to your notes. In this case, you want to emphasize that the source text file needs to be updated. You can only add text formatting to a comment in an associated note text box; you cannot add text formatting in the Comments window.

12 In the document pane, double-click the pencil comment that you replied to. If necessary, click the Next Comment button (⊙) in the toolbar associated with the note to access your reply.

13 Click in the note text box between the first and second sentences, and then drag to select the entire second sentence.

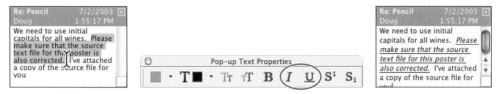

You use the Pop-up Text Properties toolbar to apply formatting to text in notes.

14 In the Pop-up Text Properties toolbar, choose the desired text formatting. We choose Italic (*I*) and Underline (U). Click outside the text selection to see the effect of the fomatting.

Note: If you don't see the Pop-up Text Properties toolbar, choose View > Toolbars> Properties Bar.

You can continue exploring the options available through the Comments window to expand and collapse comments, browse through comments, delete comments, sort comments, print comments, and search comments. When you are finished, be sure to close all the comments boxes and save your work.

15 Click the Comments tab to close the Comments window, and close any open notes.

16 Choose File > Save to save your work.

Adding comments

As you saw in the earlier part of this lesson, you can easily add notes (the equivalent of sticky notes) to a document and respond to these notes. You can also mark up a document with the drawing tools, the Pencil tool, and the highlighting tools, and you can add text edit comments to indicate where text should be added, deleted, or replaced. You can add stamps, such as confidential notices, and you can even attach files and sound clips.

Marking up a document with text markup tools

You use the text markup tools in Acrobat Professional to emphasize specific text in a document, such as a heading or an entire paragraph. You can choose from the Highlighter tool, the Cross-Out Text tool, and the Underline Text tool. You can add a note associated with a text markup to comment on the text being emphasized. Text markups are saved as comments and appear in the Comments window.

You'll highlight text in the poster, and then add a note associated with the highlighted text.

1 Click the Fit Width button (⊟) on the Acrobat toolbar, and scroll down in the document pane until you can see the first paragraph of the poster.

2 Select the Highlighter tool (⊗) in the Commenting toolbar, and drag the I-beam to highlight the last sentence in the first paragraph. The sentence begins with, "The 2000 Noble Riesling ... ."

💡 *You can change the appearance properties of any of the tools, including the color of the highlight, in the Properties toolbar or in the Appearance tab of the Properties dialog box, as you did for the Note tool in "Setting the appearance of notes" on page 233.*

3 Select the Hand tool (✋), and double-click on the highlighted text to open a note.

4 Type in your message. We typed, "**This sentence needs editorial help. At a minimum, replace the first "and" with a comma.**"

5 Click the note's Close button to close the note.

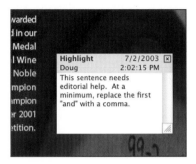

6 Choose File > Save to save your work.

Editing text

In this section, you'll use the text editing tools to indicate the required correction to a subheading on the poster, as suggested by one of the reviewers.

1 Click the Text Edits button (⊤̺) in the Commenting toolbar, and click just before the word GENERAL to create an insertion point in the second heading "WineMaker and General Manager." Drag to select the word "GENERAL." You may need to scroll down the page to see the heading.

2 Click the arrow next to the Text Edits button on the Commenting toolbar, and choose the Replace Selected Text tool.

The word is automatically struck out and a text box opens in which you type the replacement text.

3 In the Inserted Text box, type "VINEYARD".

4 Click the note's Close button to close the note.

Now that you've made the correction to the heading, Lisa's note is no longer relevant so you'll delete it.

Deleting a comment

You can easily delete unwanted comments from a document.

1 Using the Hand tool, move the pointer over the blue note. The contents of the note are displayed, so you're sure to select the correct note to delete.

2 Right-click (Windows) or Control-click (Mac OS), and choose Delete from the context menu.

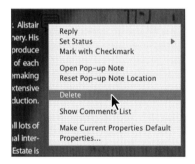

3 Choose File > Save to save the Poster1.pdf file.

You've responded to several of the comments, and you can continue experimenting with this part of the lesson if you wish. You can create a thread of replies for any comment.

Now though, you'll move on to add a few more of your own comments to the poster before you send it off to the designer.

Adding a file attachment

You use the Attach File tool in Acrobat Professional to embed a file at a specified location in a document so that the reader can open it for viewing. You can attach any type of file as a file attachment. To open an attached file, however, the reader must have an application that can recognize the attachment.

Several reviewers observed that the sentence construction and capitalization of the text of the poster needed attention. Unfortunately, the text for this poster was taken verbatim from another document. To ensure that the corrections are made in the source document, Expansion.doc, you'll attach that document to the poster.

1 Select the Attach File tool ( ) in the Advanced Commenting toolbar.

2 Click in the blank space to the left of the poster heading.

3 In the dialog box, select Expansion.doc, located in the Lesson08 folder, and click Select. Be sure the Files of Type (Windows) or Show (Mac OS) option is set to All Files.

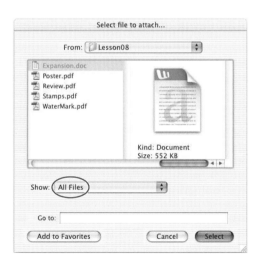

4 On the Appearance tab of the File Attachment Properties dialog box, select the Attachment icon to represent this type of file attachment. We used the Paperclip icon.

5 Click the Color button to select a color for the icon. We chose teal.

6 Click the General tab, and for Description, replace the file name with the following: **Source file to be corrected**. Then click Close.

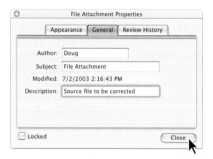

A paperclip appears on the page.

7 Position your pointer over the paperclip.

The description of the file appears below the paperclip.

If you have the appropriate application installed on your system, you can open the file that you have just attached.

8 Double-click the paperclip to open the file. Click OK or Open to confirm that you want to open the file. When you have finished viewing the file, exit or quit the associated application.

9 Choose File > Save to save your work.

Marking up a document with drawing tools

Acrobat Professional's drawing tools let you emphasize a specific area of a document, such as a graphic or table. The Pencil tool creates a free-form line; the Pencil Eraser tool lets you erase any part of a drawing you have created. The Rectangle tool creates a rectangular boundary, the Oval tool creates an elliptical boundary, and the Line tool creates a straight line between two specified points. The Polygon tool creates a closed shape with multiple segments, and the Polygon Line tool creates an open shape with multiple segments. You can add a note associated with a drawing markup to comment on the area of the page being emphasized. Drawing markups are saved as comments and appear in the Comments window.

You'll add a rectangle to the poster indicating where you would like to see the copyright notice attached, and then add a note associated with the rectangle.

1 Click the Fit Page button (▱) so that you can view the entire poster.

2 Click the Rectangle tool (▤) on the Advanced Commenting toolbar.

3 Drag to create a rectangle at the bottom of the poster, directly under the text column and the same width as the text column. This is where you want the designer to place the copyright notice.

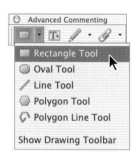
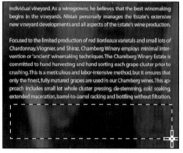

Drag to select Rectangle tool.

Drag to create a rectangle to contain the copyright notice.

4 Double-click the edge of the rectangle to open a note.

5 Type the note text as desired. (We typed the following: "**Please place a copyright notice here.**") Then close the note.

6 Choose File > Save to save your work.

Summarizing comments

At times you may want to display just the text of the notes so that you don't have to open each one individually to read it. You'll summarize the comments on the poster, compiling the text of all the notes in a new PDF document.

1 Choose Document > Summarize Comments.

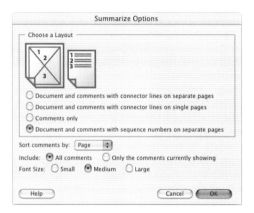

The Summarize Options dialog box lets you choose how the summary will be displayed, whether to sort the summary of comments by page, author, date, or type, as well as whether to include all comments or only the comments currently showing. You can preview the display option by clicking the buttons in the Choose a Layout panel.

2 Click the Document and Comments with Connector Lines on Single Pages option.

You'll use the default values for the other options.

3 Click OK in the Summarize Options dialog box.

A new PDF file named Summary of Comments on Poster1.pdf is created. This document displays the poster on the left side and the contents of the comments on the right, including the note label, and the date and time the comment was added to the file. Because the content of the comments exceeds one page, the poster page is displayed again on a second page with the remaining comments.

4 Choose File > Save As, rename the file **Summary.pdf**, and save it in the Lesson08 folder.

5 Choose File > Close and close the summary file.

Spell checking comments

When you looked at the summary of the comments, you may have noticed that one contains a typographical error—author jo typed "hiphenation" instead of "hyphenation."

You'll use the spell checking feature to quickly spell check all the comments added to the poster.

1 In the Poster1.pdf file, choose Edit > Check Spelling > In Comments and Form Fields.

2 Click Start.

Any unrecognized text string is displayed in the Word Not Found text box. "hyphenation" is the suggested correction for "hiphenation".

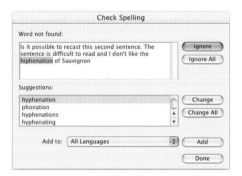

3 Click Change to accept the correction.

4 Click Done to close the spell checking operation.

5 Choose File > Save, and save the corrected file in the Lesson08 folder.

Printing comments

When you print a PDF file that contains comments, you can print the file so that the comment icons print or you can hide all the comment icons.

1 Do one of the following:

• To print the comment icons, choose File > Print, and choose Documents and Comments from the Print What menu in the Print dialog box. You'll see a preview of the print copy in the Print dialog box. Click Cancel to exit the Print dialog box without printing the file.

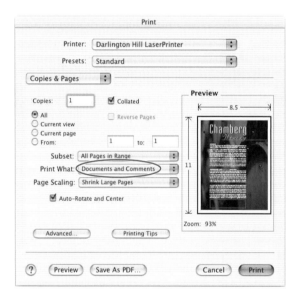

• To print a summary of the comments, choose File > Print with Comments. In the Summarize Options dialog box, choose Comments Only and click Close or OK. In the Print dialog box, click Cancel to exit the Print dialog box without printing the comment summary.

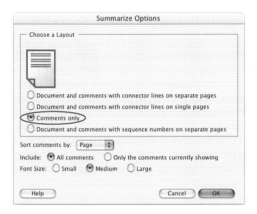

You can also summarize the comments and print both the document and the summary. The options for printing comments are the same as the layout options in the Comment Options dialog box—that is, printing comments on separate pages (with or without connector lines), printing comments on the same page with connector lines, and printing only comments. See "Summarizing comments" on page 248.

2 Choose File > Close to close the file when you have finished looking at the print options.

3 Close the Commenting, Advanced Commenting, and Properties toolbars.

Exploring on your own: Custom stamps

The commenting toolbar allows you to add stamps to your PDF document, as well as notes and text markups. Acrobat Professional provides a number of traditional stamps, but you can also create custom stamps.

Each illustration or graphic for a stamp must be on a separate page in a PDF file. Each stamp can be in a separate PDF file, or several stamps may be contained in one PDF file. We've provided a PDF file with two images that you can use for practice, or you can use your own artwork or photo images saved as PDF files. You can create custom stamps from any files in common graphic formats such as those created using Adobe Illustrator and Adobe Photoshop.

You can create stamps from supported image type files (JPEG, TIFF, BMP, PNG, etc.). The image files are converted to Adobe PDF automatically as you create the custom stamp. Be aware, though, that the image files must be sized correctly. You cannot resize the image once you have created a stamp. You can, however, fit the stamp within a rectangle that you drag with the stamp tool.

Creating a custom stamp

1 Open Acrobat Professional.

2 If the Commenting toolbar isn't open, choose View > Toolbars > Commenting.

3 Click the arrow next to the Stamp tool (), and choose Create Custom Stamp from the menu.

4 In the Create Stamp dialog box, click the Select button and then click the Browse button to locate the image file that you're going to use to create the custom stamp. If you're creating a stamp directly from an image file (rather than a PDF file), be sure that you choose the appropriate file type from the Files of Type (Windows) or Show (Mac OS) menu. We selected the Stamps.pdf file in the Lesson08 folder.

5 Click Select, and preview the sample image. If the target file contains more than one image, use the scroll bar to select the image that you want to use as the stamp. Our target file contains three images. We chose to use the image on page 1.

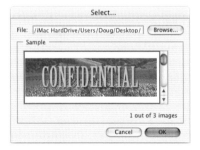

6 Click OK to return to the Create Stamp dialog box.

Now you'll create a category for the stamp and give the stamp a name. The category name appears in the drop down menu associated with the Stamp tool on the commenting toolbar. The stamp name appears in the category name's submenu.

7 Enter a name for the category of your stamp. We used **Chamberg**.

8 Enter a name for the stamp. We used **Confidential**.

9 Click OK.

That's all there is to creating custom stamps.

Now you'll add your custom stamp to a document.

Applying a custom stamp

1 Open the Review.pdf file in the Lesson08 folder.

2 Click the arrow next to the Stamp tool (🏷), and choose Chamberg > Confidential from the menu, and click the stamp image.

3 Use the Stamp tool to drag a rectangle on the document where you want the stamp to appear.

You can move the stamp by dragging it across the page of the document. You can resize the stamp by moving the pointer over a corner of the stamp until the pointer changes to a double-headed arrow, and then dragging the stamp out to the required size.

When you are finished, close Review.pfd without saving your work.

Exploring on your own: Email-based reviews

An email-based review is easy to set up and yet gives you powerful tools for managing the review process. You can experiment with setting up an email-based review if you have an email address, a connection to the Internet, and a colleague to work with.

Setting up an email-based review

In this exercise, you'll email a PDF document to a friend for review and then receive the friend's comments.

Note: You cannot email a PDF document to yourself as part of an email-based review unless you have at least two separate computer systems. The process will not work. You need to collaborate with a colleague to complete this part of the lesson.

1 In Acrobat Professional, choose File > Open, and open the Watermark.pdf file.

This is a new graphic that the winery is considering for use as a watermark or background image that will appear on all correspondence, invoices, etc. You're going to send out the file for review to a friend or a colleague.

2 Choose File > Send by Email for Review.

3 Enter your own email address in the message box, and click OK. This is the email address that will be used when reviewers return comments to you.

Note: You are only required to enter your email address the first time you invoke the Send by Email for Review command.

4 Enter your colleague's email address in the To: box. You can enter as many addresses as your email application supports.

If necessary, scroll down the email message to read the entire message that is sent to reviewers along with the PDF file that is being reviewed. You can add a personal comment at the beginning or end of the message if you like, but we recommend that you don't change the instructions in the message. You might want to add an explanation of the document, the review timeline, and the criteria to be used in the review, for example.

5 Click Send (the location and name of the command that sends your email will vary with your email application), and follow any on-screen prompts to complete the email process.

6 Close the Watermark.pdf file, and exit or quit Acrobat Professional.

Participating in an email-based review

As a participant in an email-based review, your colleague will check their email.

1 Open the email application, and check the mail. Your colleague should have received a message with an .fdf attachment.

2 Read the email message, and double-click the attachment to open it.

When the file opens, a Document Status dialog box explains the process.

A document that is part of an email-based review will have a document status icon at the left of the status bar. Clicking this icon will open the informational Document Status dialog box.

3 After reading the message, click Close to close the dialog box.

Acrobat Professional opens with the How To window open to give novice users help in participating in an email review. The Commenting toolbar also opens automatically.

4 Have your colleague add a note or two to the file, and then save the file to the desktop.

5 Click the Send Comments button on the Commenting toolbar.

Acrobat automatically opens the default email application and attaches the document to a pre-addressed and pre-written email message. (Your colleague will email the file back to you. Your email address should be the default address.)

6 Click the Send button in the email application and follow any on-screen prompts.

7 Close and save the Watermark.pdf file.

Receiving review comments

Now you'll check your email again to see what your colleague has sent to you.

1 Check your email. You should have received the reply with a file attached.

2 Double-click the .fdf attachment. You're advised that the comments have been added automatically to your master file.

Acrobat automatically opens the PDF file on your system and adds the review comments to it.

3 Double-click the original copy of the PDF file that you sent for review (Watermark.pdf) to open it. The reviewers comments are attached automatically.

Again, the How To window opens to display the appropriate information. Each time you open an email reply to your request for review, comments will be added to your master file.

Note: If you receive more than one reviewed file, you will be asked if you want to open this copy or a tracked PDF. Click the Open Tracked PDF to consolidate review comments into one document.

Managing email-based reviews

1 In Acrobat Professional, click the arrow next to the Review & Comment button on the Acrobat toolbar, and choose Track Reviews.

The Review & Comment pane opens on the right of your screen.

2 In the Review & Comment pane, make sure that All is selected from the Review Tracker Show menu. All is selected when it has a check mark next to it.

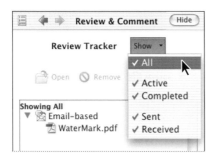

All your email-based review documents are listed.

3 Select the Watermark.pdf file in the listing. Details of the email-based review are displayed in the lower part of the pane.

If you had sent the PDF file to more reviewers, all would be listed in this pane, along with when review comments were received.

You can open the master file for an email-based review by selecting the file in this panel and clicking the Open button (   ). Similarly you can remove a file from the email-based review process, by selecting the file name and clicking the Remove button (   ).

The Manage menu contains several commands that make contacting reviewers easy.

When you're finished exploring the commands available, choose File > Close, and save and close the PDF file.

It is difficult to reproduce the rich experience of using the email review feature without a group of participants. We encourage you to experiment with this feature when you have a document to review with your colleagues.

Review questions

1 How can you send a PDF file out for review?

2 How can you consolidate comments made in several identical copies of a PDF file?

3 How can you change the author name on a note?

4 What are the advantages of using a structured email review process?

Review answers

1 There are several ways to send a PDF file for review. With the PDF file that you want to have reviewed open, do one of the following:

• Click the Email button on the Acrobat toolbar.

• To set up a more structured review, Choose File > Send by Email for Review.

• On Windows, if all your reviewers have access to a common server, choose File > Upload for Browser-Based Review.

2 You can consolidate comments into one PDF file by exporting the comments from each copy of the PDF file to an FDF file and then importing all the FDF files into one PDF file. Or you can import the comments directly from the PDF files using the Document > Import Comments command. Comments must be imported from identical copies of the PDF files or they will import incorrectly.

3 To change the author name on a note (or any note associated with a comment) you must first change the Acrobat Commenting preferences so that the system log-in name isn't used automatically for authoring comments. Then you can change the note's properties in the General tab of the Note Properties dialog box. Finally, you make the current note's properties the default values if you want to continue using the new author name.

4 When you start a review process using the Send by Email for Review process, the reviewer receives a copy of the PDF file along with instructions on how to complete the review and ready access to the How To window displaying related topics. A Send Comments button is added to the Commenting toolbar to facilitate return of the review comments. As the initiator of the review process, you can automatically consolidate all review comments as you open the documents returned by the reviewers. You also have access to a powerful set of review management tools.

Lesson 9

9 Putting Documents Online

This lesson starts you on the process of putting documents that have been designed for the print environment online. You'll start with a PDF file of a book, set an opening view for the online version, and work with hyperlink features, such as bookmarks and articles, to enhance your electronic publication.

In this lesson, you'll review and learn how to do the following:

- Set an opening view for an online document.

- Create custom bookmarks that link to specific views in the document.

- Create, follow, and edit an article thread.

- Replace a page of a PDF file with a page from a different PDF file.

- Reduce the file size of the finished Adobe PDF file.

This lesson will take about 45 minutes to complete.

If needed, remove the previous lesson folder from your hard drive, and copy the Lesson09 folder onto it.

Note: Windows users may need to unlock the lesson files before using them. For information, see "Copying the Classroom in a Book files" on page 3.

Getting started

In this lesson, you'll work with a reference manual for Adobe Illustrator. You'll create an electronic print-on-demand version of the manual without altering the content or design of the original book.

Viewing the work file

You'll start by opening a PDF version of the Adobe Illustrator book. This Adobe PDF file was created from the original Adobe FrameMaker file.

1 Start Acrobat Professional.

2 Choose File > Open. Select Illus_Excerpt.pdf in the Lesson09 folder, and click Open. Then choose File > Save As, rename the file **Illus_Excerpt1.pdf**, and save it in the Lesson09 folder.

To maximize the screen area used for display, the Adobe Illustrator book has been set to open with the navigation pane closed.

3 Click the Bookmark tab to show the bookmarks.

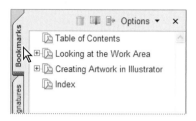

The PDF file contains two chapters, a table of contents, and an index, just as in the original FrameMaker file. The table of contents entries, cross-references, index entries, and text flows in the FrameMaker file have been converted to bookmarks, links, and articles in the PDF file.

You can automatically generate PDF links from files that have been properly formatted in an application that supports this capability, such as Adobe InDesign, Adobe PageMaker, Adobe FrameMaker, and Microsoft Word.

Setting an opening view

You can set the opening view of a PDF document for your user, including the opening page number and magnification level, and whether bookmarks, page thumbnails, the toolbar, and the menu bar are displayed. You can change any of these settings to control how the document displays when it is opened.

In this section, you'll set the opening view to display the bookmarks automatically so the user is sure to find them, and you'll set the view to Fit Page.

1 Choose File > Document Properties, and select Initial View in the left pane.

2 Under Document Options, choose Bookmarks Panel and Page from the Show menu to open the navigation pane with the bookmarks in front. This option also opens the document pane.

3 From the Page Layout menu, choose Single Page to display one page of the document at a time.

4 From the Magnification pop-up menu, make sure that Fit Page is selected to display the entire page in the document pane.

5 Make sure that the Open to Page Number option is selected, and that the page number is set to I.

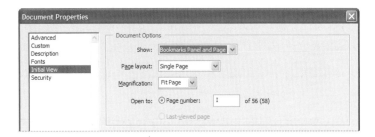

6 Click OK to accept the settings.

7 Choose File > Close, and click Yes (Windows) or Save (Mac OS) in the alert box to save the changes before closing the file.

Changes do not take effect until you save and close the file.

8 Choose File > Open, and open the Illus_Excerpt1.pdf file.

The file now opens with the bookmarks displayed and the entire first page displayed in the document window.

Looking at bookmarks

A bookmark is a link represented by text in the Bookmarks panel. Bookmarks that are created automatically by authoring programs such as Adobe InDesign, Adobe FrameMaker, Adobe PageMaker, or Microsoft Word are generally linked to headings in the text or to figure captions.

You can also use bookmarks to create a brief custom outline of a document or to open other documents.

Additionally, you can use electronic bookmarks as you would paper bookmarks—to mark a place in a document that you want to recall or return to later. Later in this lesson, you'll create custom bookmarks that are linked to an area on a page in the document.

1 If needed, drag the right border of the Bookmarks panel (a double-headed arrow appears) to resize the Bookmarks panel so that you can see more of the bookmark text.

2 If necessary, select the Hand tool ( ), and click the Table of Contents bookmark to view the table of contents.

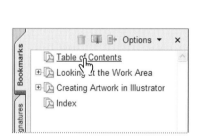

Notice that the icon for the Table of Contents bookmark is highlighted, indicating that the bookmark is linked to the current page of the document.

3 Move the pointer over the contents list in the document pane and notice that the pointing finger appears over each linked entry.

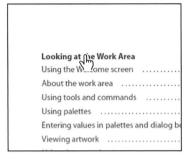

Acrobat Professional automatically linked the table of contents, which was generated using Adobe FrameMaker, to the headings in the document.

4 Click the Index entry at the bottom of the table of contents to view the index listings. In the index, each page number listing links to the appropriate reference in the text. Depending on your monitor, you may need to select the Zoom-In tool (🔍) and click in the document pane to increase the magnification. Reselect the Hand tool when the magnification is sufficient.

5 Position your pointer over the number 5 next to the "Convert Anchor Point tool" entry so that the pointing finger appears. Click to jump to the section about the Illustrator tools.

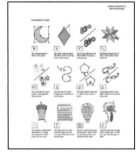

Adding custom bookmarks

Although the basic bookmarks and links for the Adobe Illustrator book have already been generated, you can add your own custom bookmarks and links using the tools in Acrobat Professional. In this part of the lesson, you'll use different methods to add some new bookmarks that link to the overview of the tools and to the Graph family of tools in the book.

Creating new bookmarks

You'll create three new bookmarks—one placeholder labeled *Tools* and two subsidiary bookmarks linked to an overview of the tools and to the Graph family of tools in the Adobe Illustrator book. The placeholder bookmark will not be linked to the document; it will serve only as a hierarchical placeholder.

First you'll create the placeholder bookmark.

1 From the Magnification pop-up menu, choose 100%. A bookmark always displays a page at the magnification set when the bookmark was created.

2 Click in any blank area of the Bookmarks panel to make sure that no bookmark is selected.

3 Click the Options button at the top of the Bookmarks panel to display the Options menu, and choose New Bookmark. A new bookmark appears at the bottom of the Bookmarks panel.

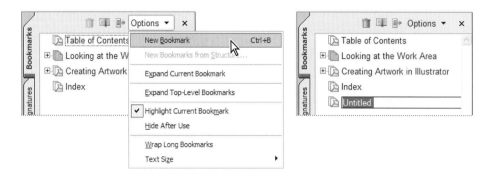

4 If the bookmark text isn't selected, click in the bookmark label area to select the text.

5 Type **Tools** to name the bookmark. Click outside the bookmark to deselect it.

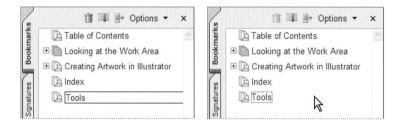

Now you'll create the remaining two bookmarks. You'll create the first bookmark using the keyboard shortcut for the New Bookmarks command. (Many Acrobat Professional commands can be executed using keyboard shortcuts.) You'll create and name the second bookmark by selecting text in the book itself.

6 To create a new bookmark using a keyboard shortcut, press Ctrl+B (Windows) or Command+B (Mac OS), and name the bookmark **Graph tools**. Click outside the bookmark to deselect it.

7 Click the Next Page button (▶) in the status bar.

Click each of the new bookmarks in turn. Notice that the Tools bookmark links to whatever page was open when you set the link. The Graph tools bookmark also links to that same page unless you changed the page view between creating links. You'll change the destination of these links in the next section.

Now you'll create the third bookmark using a different method—one that automatically sets the correct link.

8 Select the Select Text tool ([T]) in the toolbar.

9 Move the I-beam into the document page, and drag to highlight the text "Overview of tools" at the top of the page.

Be sure to leave the magnification at 100%. Whatever magnification is used will be inherited by the bookmark.

10 Click the Create New Bookmark icon (📑) at the top of the Bookmarks panel. A new Overview of tools bookmark appears at the bottom of the bookmarks list—the highlighted text from the document pane has been used as the bookmark name. By default, the new bookmark links to the current page view displayed on your screen.

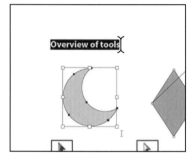
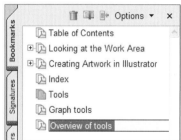

Text selected in the document pane . . .   *. . . is used as the bookmark name.*

If no bookmark is selected when you create a new bookmark, the new bookmark always appears at the bottom of the list.

11 Click in the blank space beneath the bookmark list to deselect the bookmark text.

12 Test the new bookmark by clicking the First Page button (◀|) to go to the beginning of the book. Select the Hand tool (🖑), and click the Overview of tools bookmark to jump to the corresponding section.

13 Choose File > Save to save your work.

Moving bookmarks

After creating a bookmark, you can easily move it to its proper place in the Bookmarks panel by dragging.

Before you set links for the two bookmarks you created earlier, you'll nest the Graph tools and Overview of tools bookmarks under the Tools bookmark.

1 Click in the blank space beneath the bookmark list to deselect any bookmark.

2 Hold down Shift and click the Graph tools and Overview of tools bookmarks to select them both, and then release Shift.

3 Position the pointer on one of the selected bookmarks, hold down the mouse button and drag the bookmarks up. When the red sideways arrow appears directly under the Tools bookmark icon (not the text), release the mouse.

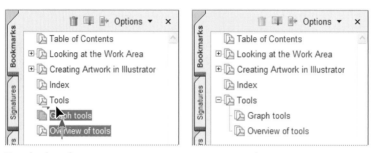

Drag bookmarks up . . .   . . . to nest them.

4 Click in the blank area of the Bookmarks panel to deselect the bookmarks.

5 Choose File > Save to save your work.

Resetting bookmark destinations

Whenever you create a bookmark, the bookmark destination is set automatically to the current document view that your screen displays. Sometimes it is easier to create a series of bookmarks and set the destinations later (as with the first two bookmarks you created); sometimes it is easier to set the destination as you create the bookmark (as with the third bookmark you created).

Now you'll assign a correct destination and action to the Tools and Graph tools bookmarks. The graph tools are discussed on page 9 of the book.

1 Click the Graph tools bookmark to select it.

2 If needed, go to page 9 in the document pane by dragging the scroll bar or by choosing View > Go To > Page, entering **9**, and clicking OK.

3 Select the Zoom-In tool (⌖), and marquee-drag around the two rows of graph tools. You may need to scroll down the page to see the two rows of graph tools.

4 Choose Set Bookmark Destination from the Options menu. At the prompt, click Yes.

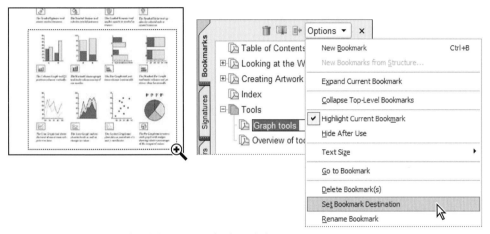

Use Zoom-In tool to magnify sidebar.   *Set bookmark destination.*

Next you'll turn the Tools bookmark into a placeholder heading for its nested bookmarks.

5 Click the minus sign or triangle to the left of the Tools bookmark to hide its nested bookmarks.

6 Click the Tools bookmark or its icon to select the bookmark.

7 Click the Options button at the top of the Bookmarks panel, and choose Properties from the Options menu.

8 Click the Actions tab, select the action Go To a Page in This Document in the Actions window, and click Delete. This effectively sets the action as "none."

9 Click Close.

10 In the Bookmarks panel, click in the blank area to deselect all bookmarks. Click the plus sign or triangle next to the Tools bookmark to display its nested bookmarks.

11 Use the Hand tool to test your new bookmarks. Click the Graph Tools bookmark, and then click the Tools bookmark. Notice that nothing happens when you click the Tools bookmark. This bookmark now functions not as a link but as a hierarchical placeholder.

12 Choose File > Save to save your work.

Looking at articles

Although the Adobe Illustrator book has been converted to an online format, it still uses a layout associated with printed documents. The size restrictions of the screen can make the reading of some documents quite difficult. For example, documents created in a column format can be particularly difficult to follow using the traditional page-up or page-down tools.

Acrobat Professional's article feature lets you guide users through material organized in columns or across a series of nonconsecutive pages. You use the Article tool to create a series of linked rectangles that connect the separate sections of the material and follow the flow of text. You can also generate article threads automatically from a page layout file when you convert the file to Adobe PDF.

In this part of the lesson, you'll examine an article that was created automatically. Later in this lesson, you'll learn how to create a customized article thread.

1 If necessary, click the plus sign or triangle next to the Chapter 1, Looking at the Work Area bookmark to expand the bookmark.

2 Click the Using the Welcome Screen bookmark to jump to its corresponding section of information. Then move your pointer over the column of text and notice the downward pointing arrow inside the hand pointer that indicates an article thread.

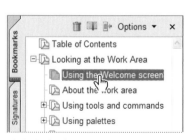

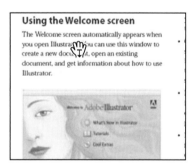

Click the bookmark to go to the text.   A downward arrow indicates an article thread.

3 Click to enter the article. Click again to follow the article. Press Enter or Return several times to continue to follow the article thread.

When you read an article, Acrobat Professional zooms in or out so the current part of the article fills the screen.

Because this article thread was created automatically, it treats the image area on each page as one article box. Now you'll redefine the article to more conveniently follow the column layout.

Deleting an article

First you'll delete the existing article.

1 If the Articles panel is not visible, choose View > Navigation Tabs > Articles to display the panel. Drag the Articles tab to the navigation pane to dock the panel. Click the Close button on the Destinations panel to close the Destinations panel and give yourself a clear view of the document pane.

2 Double-click the "A" text label in the Articles panel to go to the beginning of the article.

3 Choose Tools > Advanced Editing > Show Advanced Editing Toolbar. Select the Article tool () from the toolbar.

The first article box, labeled 1-1, is displayed. (You may have to scroll up or click the Fit Page button (▢) to see the top of the article box.)

4 Select the Hand tool (✋).

5 Select the A text article in the Articles panel, and drag it to the trash can at the top of the panel.

6 Click OK in the alert box to delete the article.

Defining an article

You have deleted the article box that was defined automatically. Now you'll replace it with your own article thread to connect the text columns.

1 If necessary, click the Fit Page button ( ) to view the entire page.

2 Select the Article tool ( ), and drag a marquee around the left column of text. (When you first use the Article tool, it appears as a cross-hair pointer in the document window.) An article box appears around the enclosed text, and the pointer changes to the article pointer ( ).

The 1-1 label at the top of the article box indicates that this is the first box of the first article in the file. Now you'll add another article box to continue the thread.

3 Go to the top of the right text column, and drag a marquee around the column of text. An article box, labeled 1-2, appears around the enclosed text.

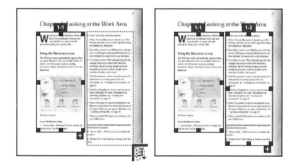

4 Go to the next page by clicking the Next Page button ( ) or by choosing View > Go To > Next Page.

On page 2, you see two columns of text at the top of the page, and one illustration at the bottom of the page that straddles the two columns.

5 Drag a marquee around the column of text on the left, then drag a marquee around the column of text on the right. Finally, draw a marquee around the illustration.

6 Press Enter or Return to end the article thread, or click End Article at the bottom of the document window.

The Article Properties dialog box appears.

Note: You can also display the Article Properties dialog box by selecting an article in the Articles panel and choosing Properties from the Options menu.

7 Do the following:

• For Title, enter **Work Area**, and press Tab. (This is the text that appears in the Articles panel.)

• For Subject, enter **Adobe Illustrator Book**.

• Leave the Author and Keywords fields blank, and click OK.

8 Choose File > Save to save your work.

Reading an article

In this section, you'll look at the various ways you can move through an article.

1 Select the Hand tool ( ).

2 Double-click Work Area article icon in the Articles panel.

The contents of the first article box you created appear on-screen.

You control the magnification of article boxes by adjusting the Max "Fit Visible" Zoom Magnification preference, which you set in the Page Display Preferences dialog box.

3 Move through the article using any of these techniques:

- To advance through the article, press Enter or Return.

- To move backward through the article, hold down Shift and press Enter or Return.

- To move to the beginning of the article, hold down Ctrl (Windows) or Option (Mac OS) and click inside the article.

4 To go to the end of an article, press Shift-Ctrl (Windows) or Shift-Option (Mac OS) and click in the document pane.

5 Choose File > Save to save your work.

Replacing a page

Sometimes you may want to replace an entire page in a PDF file with another PDF page. For example, if you want to change the design or layout of a PDF page, you can revise the source page in your original design application, convert the modified page to PDF, and use it to replace the old PDF page. When you replace a page, only the text and graphics on the original page are replaced. The replacement does not affect any interactive elements associated with the original page, such as bookmarks or links.

The plain title page that currently opens the PDF document is the first page of the printed version of the book. To make your PDF book look more like an actual book, you'll replace this title page with the full-color illustration that was used to create the front cover of the printed guide.

1 Click the Articles tab to close the navigation pane.

2 Click the First Page button (◀) to display the current title page, and, if necessary, click the Fit Page button (▯).

3 Choose Document > Pages > Replace.

4 Select Cover.pdf in the Lesson09 folder, and click Select.

5 In the Replace Pages dialog box, make sure that you are replacing page I with 1, and click OK and then Yes. The new cover illustration appears as page I of the document.

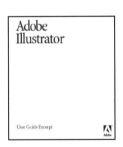

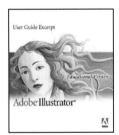

6 Choose File > Save to save the Illus_Excerpt1.pdf file. Leave the file open.

7 Now that your file is finished, you'll make the file smaller to facilitate sharing online.

Reducing the file size

First you'll check the file size.

1 Minimize the Acrobat window, and in Windows, use Windows Explorer to open the Lesson09 folder, and note the size of the Illus_Excerpt1.pdf. In Mac OS, in the Finder, open the Lesson09 folder, and use the List View to view the size of the Illus_Excerpt1.pdf file.

The file size is approximately 1.8MB. File size may vary slightly with your platform.

2 Maximize the Acrobat window, and in Acrobat Professional, choose File > Reduce File Size.

3 Choose the version of Acrobat that you want your file to be compatible with. We choose Acrobat 5.0 and later. Click OK.

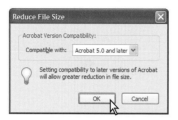

When you choose the compatibility level, be aware that the newer the version of Acrobat that you choose, the smaller the file. If you choose compatibility with Acrobat 6.0, you should be sure that your intended audience does indeed have version 6.0 installed.

4 Save your modified file using a different name. We saved the file in the same directory using the name **SmallerIllus_Excerpt1.pdf**. Click Save to complete the process.

It is a good idea to save the file using a different name so that you don't overwrite the unmodified file.

Acrobat automatically optimizes your PDF file, a process that may take a minute. Any anomalies are displayed in the Conversion Warnings window. Click OK to close the window.

5 Using the same method as you used in Step 1, check the size of the SmallerIllus_Excerpt1.pdf file.

The file size is approximately 1.6MB. Again, file size may vary slightly with your platform.

Choose File > Close and close your file and exit or quit Acrobat.

For more information on how to design your own online book, see Lesson 10, "Optimizing Online Document Design."

Review questions

1 Where do you set the opening view parameters that control how your PDF file opens?

2 How do you create a new bookmark?

3 When you're reading an article on-screen, where can you adjust the view magnification?

Review answers

1 You set the opening view parameters in the Initial View tab of the Document Properties dialog box. To open the Document Properties dialog box, choose File > Document Properties, and then select Initial View in the left pane.

2 First decide on the nature of the bookmark to be added. If no bookmark is selected in the Bookmarks panel, any new bookmark is added at the bottom of the Bookmarks panel. If a bookmark is selected, the new bookmark is added as a child of the selected bookmark. Then do one of the following:

• Click the Create New Bookmark button at the top of the Bookmarks panel.

• Choose the New Bookmark command from the Options menu of the Bookmarks panel.

• Press Ctrl+B (Windows) or Command+B (Mac OS).

3 You can adjust the view magnification of articles in the Page Display preferences. Choose Edit > Preferences (Windows) or Acrobat > Preferences (Mac OS), and select Page Display in the left pane. Set the Max Fit Visible Zoom option to the desired value, and click OK to apply the change.

Lesson 10

10 | Optimizing Online Document Design

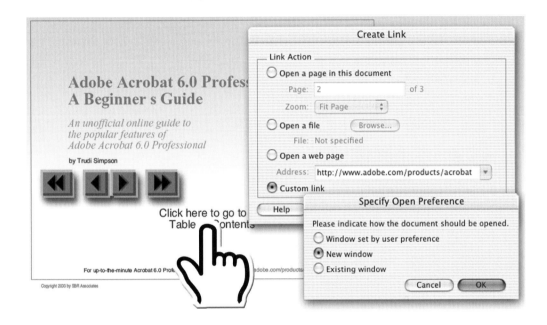

You can greatly improve the usability of online documents by using a page size customized for on-screen viewing and by adding links to help your users navigate through the documents.

In this lesson, you'll learn how to do the following:

- Review factors that affect the design of online documents.

- Add links to help the user navigate through the document.

- Add a link to a Web site.

- Change the formatting and color of text in a document.

- Use JavaScript to set a button destination.

This lesson will take about 45 minutes to complete.

If needed, remove the previous lesson folder from your hard drive, and copy the Lesson10 folder onto it.

Note: Windows users may need to unlock the lesson files before using them. For information, see "Copying the Classroom in a Book files" on page 3.

Getting started

Ideally, online documents should be designed to fit the screen or area of the screen on which they are to be displayed, information should be chunked into screen-sized pages, and pages should have consistent and well-placed navigation aids to help the user work through the documents. In this lesson, you'll work on an online version of a prototype Acrobat Professional user guide, using the tools and techniques you've learned in earlier lessons to convert a simple document into a prototype online presentation.

For information on improving accessibility and flexibility of online documents for motion- and vision-impaired users and for users of hand-held viewing devices, see Lesson 16, "Making Documents Accessible and Flexible."

Looking at design elements in online documents

When you are deciding on your document layout, you should consider how the document will be used. Will it be used in conjunction with other software or on-screen displays, as online help systems often are? Or will it be a standalone document viewed and read more like a traditional book? Will your document be viewed primarily on traditional computer monitors, on handheld devices, or on the newer eBook reading devices? Are your users sophisticated computer users or are they likely to be new to computer systems? These factors and more affect your design decisions.

Creating an online document

In this lesson, you'll work on designing a prototype of an online guide for Acrobat Professional, *Acrobat Professional 6.0—A Beginner's Guide*. The files for this portion of the lesson were created in Adobe FrameMaker and then converted to Adobe PDF. Because this is a prototype document designed simply to illustrate a concept, little effort was put into using the features of FrameMaker to generate automatically linked text. Instead, you'll create just enough links using Acrobat Professional to demonstrate to reviewers how the document is designed to work.

Choosing a page size

Computer monitors generally do not display an 8-1/2 x 11 inch page size in portrait mode well. If you base your document on an 8-1/2 x 11 inch page in portrait mode, your users will probably be inconvenienced by having to use the vertical scroll bar to view material on the lower half of the page. Reducing the page to fit on the monitor screen usually makes the contents hard or even impossible to read. For these reasons, you should consider using a landscape page orientation or you should custom design a page size if your document is to be viewed primarily on-screen.

For this project, you'll use an 8-1/2 x 11 inch page size with a landscape orientation. You can set the opening view for your document to use the Acrobat Professional Fit Page option to ensure that your users always view an entire page rather than a partial page. For information on setting the opening view, see Lesson 9, "Putting Documents Online."

Adding links

We created a title page for *Acrobat Professional 6.0—A Beginner's Guide* for you. This page functions as the welcome page. You'll add two links to this page—a link to the Adobe Web site and a link from this page to the Contents page of the user guide.

You use the Link tool to create new links in a document. To specify an activation area for the link, you drag over the desired area with the Link tool. Then you set the destination view for the link.

1 Open Acrobat Professional.

2 Choose File > Open. Select BGTitle.pdf in the Lesson10 folder, and click Open.

3 Choose Tools > Advanced Editing, and select the Link tool (🖐).

The Link tool appears as a cross-hair pointer when you move it into the document. When you select the Link tool, any existing links in the document appear temporarily as black rectangles.

4 Place the cross hair above and to the left of the Click here to go to the Table of Contents text, and drag to create a marquee that encloses the entire text block.

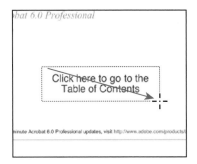

The Create Link dialog box appears. This dialog box lets you specify the type of link to set.

5 Select the Open a Page in this Document option, and enter 2 for the Page number. Leave Zoom at Fit Page, and click OK.

This sets the link action. Now you'll set the appearance of the link in the same Link Properties dialog box. You can also set the link appearance in the Link Properties toolbar, but you can only set the visibility of the link in the Link Properties dialog box.

To open the Properties toolbar, choose View > Toolbars > Properties Bar. The Properties toolbar is dynamic in that the item you have selected determines the tools that appear on the Properties toolbar. For more information on using the Properties toolbar, see "Setting a link to a Web site" on page 293.

6 With the Link tool still selected, double-click in the newly created link box (red) to reopen the Link Properties dialog box.

7 Click the Appearance tab, and choose Invisible Rectangle from the Link Type menu. For Highlight Style, choose None from the menu.

Because we are using an invisible rectangle for the link type, none of the other options—line style, line thickness, and color—is available.

The following illustration shows the different highlight appearances available in Acrobat Professional.

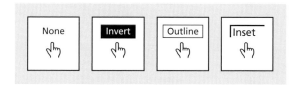

8 Click Close to close the dialog box and set the link. (Your link box remains red and visible until you select the Hand tool.)

Before you test the link, you'll review the other types of actions that you can add to a link. You can add just one action to a link, as you did in the prior steps, or you can add several actions to execute sequentially.

Take a moment to review the types of actions that you can add to links.

9 Double-click in the newly created link box to reopen the Link Properties dialog box.

10 In the Actions tab of the Link Properties dialog box, click the arrow to open the Select Action menu. These are additional actions that you can add to a link. You may need to scroll down to view the entire list. When you are finished reviewing the actions, click outside the menu listing to close the menu without changing the Go To a Page in This Document selection, and click Close to close the dialog box.

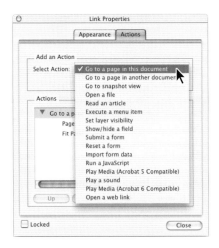

For information on the different types of actions that you can assign to your link, see "About action types" in the Complete Acrobat 6.0 Help.

Now you'll test the link that you set from the Title page to the Contents page, page 2.

11 Select the Hand tool (), and move the pointer over the Click ere to go to the Table of Contents text. The pointing finger indicates the activation area that you have just created.

12 Click the activation area to test your link. You should jump to the Contents page with the same magnification setting.

13 Click the Previous Page button (◀) on the Acrobat status bar to return to the Title page.

14 Choose File > Save to save the file.

Later in this lesson, you'll edit an existing link in the Contents. Now though you'll add a link from the title page to the Adobe Web site.

Designing a link to a Web site

On the title page of your document, you'll add a link to the Adobe Web site that will take users to the Acrobat home page.

At the bottom of the title page, you'll see text that directs users to check the Adobe Web site for any updates to Acrobat 6.0 Professional.

First you'll change the color and style of the text to make the link more obvious, and then you'll create a link.

Adding color to hyperlinks

Traditionally linked text is colored. If you haven't set the color of any text that is designed to be linked in your authoring program, you can add the color in Acrobat Professional. Because this prototype document uses red as a design color, you'll use the Touchup Text tool to change the color of linked text to blue so users won't get confused.

1 Choose Tools > Advanced Editing > Show Advanced Editing Toolbar to open the Advanced Editing toolbar.

2 Select the Touchup Text tool (📝).

3 Drag through the URL (http://www.adobe.com/products/acrobat/) to select it. A bounding box appears. You can edit text anywhere within the bounding box.

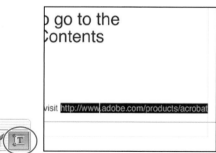

4 Right-click (Windows) or Control-click (Mac OS) the selected text, and choose Properties from the context menu.

5 In the TouchUp Properties dialog box, click the Fill button to open the color palette. Choose a color for the text. We chose blue. Click outside the text selection in the document window to view the colored text.

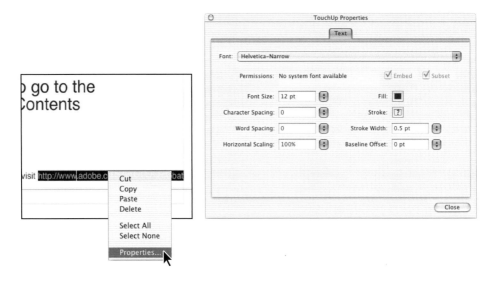

6 When you are satisfied with your color selection, click Close to exit the TouchUp Properties dialog box.

7 Select the Hand tool.

8 Choose File > Save, and save BGTitle.pdf in the Lesson10 folder.

Setting a link to a Web site

Now that you've set the appearance of your link text, you're almost ready to set the link to the Adobe Web site. Before you do though, you'll check that your preferences are set to open web links in a Web browser rather than in Acrobat.

1 Choose Edit > Preferences (Windows) or Acrobat > Preferences (Mac OS), and select Web Capture in the left pane.

2 From the Open Web Links menu, choose In Web Browser.

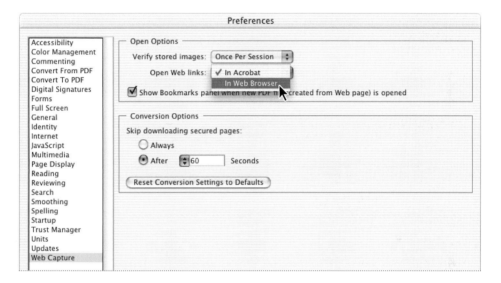

3 Click OK to apply the change.

Now you'll copy the target URL from the title page, ready to paste it into the Address Text box in the Create Link from Selection dialog box.

4 Click the Select Text button (▥) in the Acrobat toolbar, and in the document pane, drag to highlight the URL in the text.

5 Press Ctrl-C (Windows) or Command-C (Mac OS) to copy the URL.

6 With the Select Text tool still selected and the URL text highlighted, right-click (Windows) or Control-click (Mac OS) the URL, and select Create Link in the context menu.

7 In the Create Link from Selection dialog box, click Open a Web Page.

8 In the Address text box, press Ctrl-V (Windows) or Command-V (Mac OS) to copy the URL.

9 Click OK to set the link.

Now you'll set the appearance of the link.

10 Select the Link tool (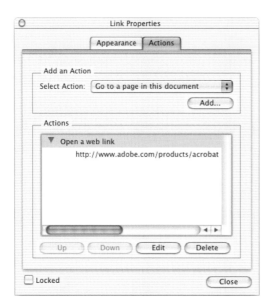) in the Advanced Editing menu, and double-click in the link area to open the Link Properties dialog box.

11 Click the Appearance tab, and choose Invisible Rectangle for Link Type.

12 For Highlight Style, choose None.

13 Click the Action tab, and verify that your URL is set correctly in the Actions window. (Be sure to check the link in the Actions window and not in the Select Action menu.)

14 Click Close.

If you have a Web browser and a connection to the World Wide Web, you can go on to the next step and try out your newly created link.

15 Select the Hand tool ( ), and click on the link. Notice that the Hand tool contains a plus sign (or the letter w), indicating that this is a web link.

16 If necessary, choose OK to clear the message box.

Launch your Web browser if prompted to do so.

The link opens the Acrobat home page on the Adobe Systems Web site.

17 Close the browser window when you have finished viewing the Web site, and return to Acrobat Professional.

18 Choose File > Save, and save BGTitle.pdf in the Lesson10 folder.

If you receive a document that contains URLs that are not linked to their respective Web sites, you can quickly make the links active using the Advanced > Links > Create from URLs in Document command.

Underlining links

Now you'll underline the linked text.

You set the Underline Text tool properties in the Properties toolbar.

1 Choose View > Toolbars > Properties Bar to open the Properties toolbar.

2 Choose Tools > Commenting > Show Commenting Toolbar to open the Commenting toolbar.

3 If necessary, drag the Commenting toolbar to the side so that it doesn't overlap the Properties toolbar.

4 Click the arrow next to the Highlighter tool (🖍) on the Commenting toolbar, and choose Underline Text tool from the menu.

The Properties toolbar becomes the Underline Text Tool Properties toolbar.

5 On the Underline Text Tool Properties toolbar, click the arrow next to the color field and select the same color that you chose for the web link. We chose blue.

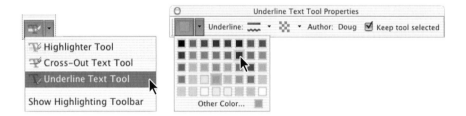

Until you change the settings, all subsequent underlining will be done in blue.

6 In the document pane, drag to select the URL text that you want to underline.

When you release the mouse button, your text is underlined in the color that you selected in the Properties toolbar.

7 Select the Hand tool.

8 Click the Close button on the Properties toolbar.

9 Choose File > Save, and save BGTitle.pdf in the Lesson10 folder.

Editing a link type and destination

In this section, you'll edit an existing link on the contents page of your document to correct the link destination. You can edit a link at any time—changing its activation area, appearance, or link action.

First you'll change the Acrobat preferences so that links to other documents open in a new Acrobat window. Otherwise, you'd have to close the currently open document whenever you opened a link to another document.

1 Choose Edit > Preferences (Windows) or Acrobat > Preferences (Mac OS), and select General in the left pane.

2 Click the check box for the Open Cross-Document Links in Same Window option. This option is off when the check box is empty. For this lesson, you want the option to be off (unchecked).

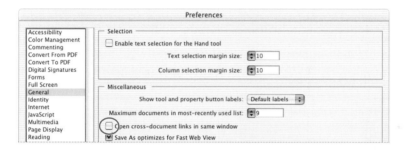

3 Click OK to apply the change.

Now you'll look at the link that needs to be edited.

4 Using the Hand tool, click the Click here to go to the Table of Contents text to go to the main table of contents.

5 Click the Signing PDF Files text to follow its link. (On Mac OS, you may need to save and close the BGTitle.pdf file.)

Notice that the link does not take you to the correct section.

6 Click the Previous View button () to return to the Contents.

The Previous View button takes you to the previous view, even if it is in a different file.

7 Select the Link tool ( ) in the Advanced Editing toolbar, and double-click inside the rectangle surrounding the Signing PDF Files text to open the Link Properties dialog box.

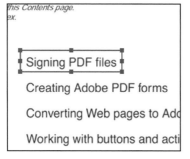

You'll edit the destination of the selected link.

8 Click the Action tab, and select the Open a File action in the Actions window.

9 Click the Edit button to reset the destination for the link.

10 In the Select File to Open dialog box, select the Signing.pdf file in the Lesson10 folder, and click Select.

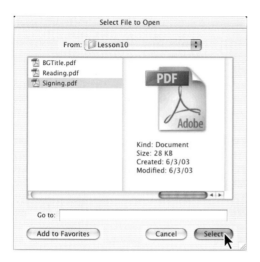

Notice that if the file name is truncated in the middle. You can always see the beginning of the path and the file name.

11 In the Specify Open Preference dialog box, choose New Window to ensure that the new document opens in a new window, and click OK and then click Close.

12 Select the Hand tool, and click the Signing PDF Files link to test your revised link.

You should now jump to the correct section.

13 Click the Previous View button to return to the Contents.

14 Choose File > Save to save your work.

Now that you've edited the type and destination of a link, you'll change the activation area of a link.

Editing a link activation area

You'll navigate to the section on Reading PDF Files and adjust the activation area of a link on this page.

1 Click the Reading PDF Files link to go to the table of contents for this section. (On Mac OS, you may need to save and close the BGTitle.pdf file.)

Notice the topics that are listed under the heading Paging Through a Document.

2 Click the Paging Through a Document Link.

All the topics listed under the heading Paging Through a Document are covered on the same page. Rather than create a link for each topic, you'll expand one existing link on the contents page to cover all the topics.

3 Click the Previous View button (⊙) to return to the contents page for Reading PDF Files.

4 Select the Link tool (🔧), in the Advanced Editing toolbar, and move the pointer inside the rectangle surrounding the Next Page text.

Handles appear on the edges of the rectangle, indicating that the link is selected.

5 Move the pointer over the bottom right handle so that the double-headed arrow appears. Then drag to stretch the rectangle around the entire text block below the Paging Through a Document heading.

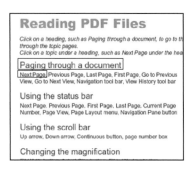
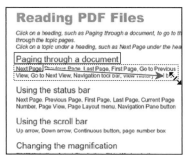

6 Select the Hand tool, and move the pointer over the topics. Notice that the activation area includes the entire block of topics.

7 Click the activation area to test your link.

8 Click the Previous View button to return to the contents page for this section.

9 Choose File > Save to save your work.

Linking to a destination

When you set up an online document, you often find that you want to take users to a page other than the first, last, previous, or next page, which are the standard actions available for an Execute Menu Action link. An easy way to do this is to set a page destination using JavaScript.

Note: You can also create a destination on a page in a PDF file and set a link to that destination.

Before you set a link using JavaScript, you'll look at how the author and designer of this user guide created the links for the next page, previous page, first page, last page buttons that were added to the foot of the page.

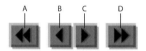

A. First page B. Previous page
C. Next page D. Last page

1 Click the Link tool ( ), and move your pointer over the blue next page button at the bottom of the document page. When the link displays as a red rectangle with handles, right-click (Windows) or Control-click (Mac OS), and choose Properties from the context menu.

In the Link Properties dialog box, notice that the selected action in the Actions window is Execute a Menu Item. (Be sure to check the Actions window and not the Select Action menu.)

2 Click the Edit button to see how the menu item is selected.

3 Click Cancel to exit the dialog box without making any changes, and click Close.

Using JavaScript to set a button destination

Now you'll add a link to page 2 in the Reading PDF Files section that links to the first page in the section (the section contents). The image for the link was created in the authoring program, Adobe Framemaker. Although you could create this link using the Execute a Menu Item action and setting the action to go to the first page, for practice you'll add a link to the image and set the link action using JavaScript.

1 Select the Hand tool (✍️) and click the Next Page button (▶) on the Acrobat Professional status bar to go to page 2 of the Reading.pdf file.

2 Select the Link tool (🔗), and drag a rectangle around the Contents button image at the bottom right of the document page.

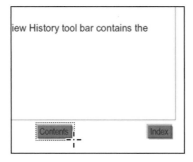

3 In the Create Link dialog box, choose Custom Link and click OK.

4 Choose Run a JavaScript from the Select Action menu, and click Add.

5 In the JavaScript Editor dialog box, type in the following code exactly as it appears here:

this.pageNum = 0;

Note: It doesn't matter whether you include spaces around the equal sign.

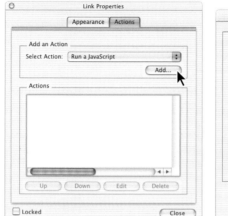

JavaScript considers the first page in a document to have the page number 0. Hence the first page in your document is page 0 in the JavaScript code.

6 Click OK to close the JavaScript Edit dialog box.

Now you'll set the appearance of the link. Because you have an image for the link, you'll want your link area to be invisible.

7 Click the Appearance tab.

8 Choose Invisible Rectangle for Link Type, and choose None for Highlight Style.

9 Click Close to finish setting the link.

10 Test your link by selecting the Hand tool and clicking the Contents link. You'll go to page 1 of the Reading.pdf file.

11 Choose File > Save, and save your changes to the Reading.pdf file.

12 Click the Close buttons to close the Commenting and Advanced Editing toolbars.

13 Choose Window > Close All to close all open files.

You have created a button that will take your users to the first page (the contents page for the Reading PDF Files section) of the document whenever they click on it. You can use the same approach to create a link to the index, or you can use the Go To a Page in Another Document action if the index is in a separate file.

The Link Properties dialog box gives you many ways to create links and allows you to customize their appearance and actions. You can associate several actions with one link. For example, you can set the first action to play a sound, such as a chime, and then set the second action to move to a new page.

Now that the navigation in your file is finished, you need to think about some house-keeping issues that will make your files easier to access and use.

Adding document properties information to PDF files

The Description panel of the Document Properties dialog box provides users with basic information about a file as well as another way to search for a file in a collection of indexed documents. (Documents can be indexed only in Acrobat 6.0 Professional, but the index can be searched by Acrobat 6.0 Professional users.) The Title, Subject, Author, and Keyword fields in the Document Properties dialog box can be completed and edited in Acrobat Professional.

First take a look at the information loaded in the fields for the document.

1   Choose File > Open, and open the BGTitle.pdf file in the Lesson10 folder.

2   Choose File > Document Properties > Description.

By default, the filename BGTitle.fm appears in the Title field. The author's name is Emily Grace. Note that the Subject and Keyword fields are empty. The other entries represent file information generated by the application used to create the PDF file.

Because many Web search engines use the document properties information fields to search for information and display results in a Search Results list, you should fill in document properties information fields for each document you distribute. Because the filename often is not an adequate description of the document, consider replacing it with the document title.

In this section, you'll enter document properties information in only the BGTitle.pdf file. In a normal workflow, you would enter document properties information for all files in a document collection.

3 In the Document Properties dialog box, fill in the following text boxes:

• Title. (We entered **Acrobat 6.0: A Beginner's Guide.**)

• Subject. (We entered **Acrobat 6.0 Professional.**)

• Keywords. (We entered **Acrobat, text book, user guide, help.** Be sure to enter a comma and space between each keyword.)

4 Click OK.

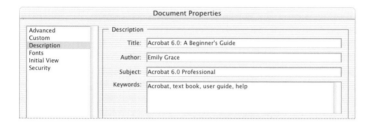

5 Save the file.

Optimizing for page-at-a-time downloading

If you're distributing your documents on the Web or via a company intranet, you should use the Fast Web View option to remove unused objects, consolidate duplicate page backgrounds, and reorder objects in the PDF file format for *page-at-a-time downloading*. With page-at-a-time downloading (also called byte-serving), the Web server sends only the requested page of information to the user, not the entire PDF document. This is especially important with large documents, which can take a long time to download from the server.

First you'll check whether your file is already optimized for Fast Web View.

1 Choose File > Document Properties, and select Description in the left pane.

2 At the bottom right of the dialog box, you'll see that the document is not optimized for Fast Web View. Click Cancel to exit the dialog box.

To restructure the document for Fast Web View, you'll check your preferences to make sure that the Save As Optimizes for Fast Web View option is on and then re-save the file.

3 Choose Edit > Preferences (Windows) or Acrobat > Preferences (Mac OS), and select General in the left pane.

4 Under Miscellaneous, make sure that the Save As Optimizes For Fast Web View option is checked. (This option is checked by default.) Click OK.

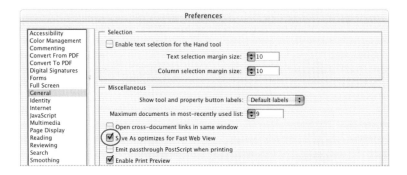

5 Choose File > Save As and save the file using the same file name and location to overwrite the non-optimized file. If you recheck the Document Properties, you'll see that your file is now optimized for fast web view.

6 Choose File > Close to close the file.

7 Exit or quit Acrobat.

Now when users view your file on the Web, only the requested page of information will be downloaded, rather than the entire PDF file. This shortens perceived download times with large documents.

Adding Adobe Reader installers

Adobe Reader is available free of charge for distribution with your documents to make it easier for users to view your PDF documents. It's important either to include a copy of the Reader installers on your CD or to point Web users to the Reader installers on the Adobe Web site at www.adobe.com.

If you're including the Reader installers on a CD-ROM, include a ReadMe text file at the top level of the CD that describes how to install Reader and provides any last-minute information. If you're posting the Reader installers on a Web site, include the Reader installation instructions with the link to the downloadable software.

If you're distributing documents on the Web, you'll probably want to point users to the Adobe Web site for the downloadable Reader software.

You may make and distribute unlimited copies of Reader, including copies for commercial distribution. For complete information on distributing and giving your users access to Adobe Reader, visit the Adobe Web site at http://www.adobe.com/products/acrobat/.

A special "Includes Adobe Acrobat" logo is available from Adobe for use when distributing Reader. See the Adobe Web site for details.

Review questions

1 How do you change the color of the underline for the Underline Text tool?

2 Why should you optimize your PDF files for page-at-a-time downloading?

3 Can you edit an existing link in a PDF document?

4 Why is it important to add document information to a PDF file?

Review answers

1 You change the color of the underline in the Underline Text Tool Properties toolbar. Open the Properties toolbar by choosing View > Toolbars > Properties Bar. Select the Underline Text tool in the Commenting toolbar, and change the underline color in the Properties toolbar.

2 If your file is large, it may download slowly, especially if users have a slow Internet connection. Optimizing a file for page-at-a-time downloading makes the download process seem faster.

3 Yes. Select the Link tool in the Advanced Editing toolbar. All links defined in the document are outlined in black. Double-click on any link to edit its properties in the Link Properties dialog box.

4 Document information is often used by Web search engines and can also be used when an index is created using the Catalog feature of Acrobat Professional. Adding a descriptive title, keywords, and author information, makes it more likely that your document will be found in a search.

Lesson 11

11 | Adding Signatures and Security

You can digitally sign or certify Adobe PDF files to attest to the validity of the contents of the file. You can also protect your Adobe PDF files by applying security that limits how users can manipulate the contents of your files and even who can open your files.

In this lesson, you'll learn how to do the following:

• Digitally sign documents.

• Create a digital ID.

• Verify a digital signature.

• Certify a document.

• Apply password protection to a file to limit who can open it, and apply permissions passwords to limit printing and changing of the file.

• Create a picture signature.

This lesson will take about 45 minutes to complete.

If needed, remove the previous lesson folder from your hard drive, and copy the Lesson11 folder onto it.

Note: Windows users may need to unlock the lesson files before using them. For information, see "Copying the Classroom in a Book files" on page 3.

Getting started

You can set the appearance of your digital signature, select your preferred digital signature signing method, and determine how digital signatures are verified in the Digital Signatures preferences.

First you'll take a look at the default preferences for digital signatures.

1 Start Acrobat Professional.

2 Choose Edit > Preferences (Windows) or Acrobat > Preferences (Mac OS), and select Digital Signatures in the left pane.

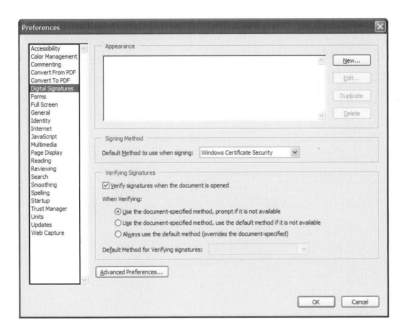

Unless you have already defined an appearance for your digital signature, the Appearance window is blank.

3 Click New to open the Configure Signature Appearance dialog box where you personalize your digital signature. The Preview pane shows the default digital signature appearance. You'll add a graphic to your signature later in the lesson. For now, click Cancel to return to the Preferences dialog box.

4 Make sure that Default Certificate Security is selected for the default method to use when signing. *You must have this option selected to complete this lesson and Lesson 12.*

5 Make sure that signatures are verified using the document-specified method when a document is opened.

6 Choose Cancel to close the Preferences dialog box without making any changes, or choose OK if you changed any of the defaults.

Opening the work file

In this lesson, you'll return an advertisement for Clarity skin lotion to the advertising agency for finalization. Now that you've reviewed the document and made required changes, you'll sign the revised advertisement electronically. Signing a document electronically offers several advantages, not least of which is that you can email the signed document rather than having to fax it. Although digitally signing a document doesn't prevent people from changing the document, it does allow you to track any changes made after the signature is added and revert to the signed version if necessary. (You can also prevent users from changing your document by applying appropriate security to the document, as you'll see later in this lesson).

Choose File > Open. Select Lotion.pdf in the Lesson11 folder, and click Open. Then choose File > Save As, rename the file **Lotion1.pdf**, and save it in the Lesson11folder.

About digital IDs

A digital ID contains your signature information. Digital IDs are also referred to as credentials or profiles. You can get a digital ID from a third-party provider, or you can create a self-signed digital ID and share your signature information with others in a certificate. A certificate is a confirmation of your identity and contains information used to protect data.

You can use two types of digital IDs: those that you create yourself (self-signed), and those that are issued to you by a third-party provider. Generally, digital IDs issued by a third party are required for use in any official capacity. The provider of digital ID certificates is sometimes called a signature handler. You may want to create more than one digital ID if you sign documents in different roles, or with different certification methods.

—From the Complete Acrobat 6 Online Help.

Creating a digital ID

You can create a digital ID at the same time that you sign a document, but in this lesson you'll create your Acrobat self-signed digital ID before you sign the document.

You can create more than one digital ID to reflect different roles in your life. For this section of the lesson, you'll create a digital ID for T. Simpson, Director of Advertising. Later in the lesson, you'll experiment with creating a picture signature.

1 Choose Advanced > Manage Digital IDs > My Digital ID Files > Select My Digital ID File.

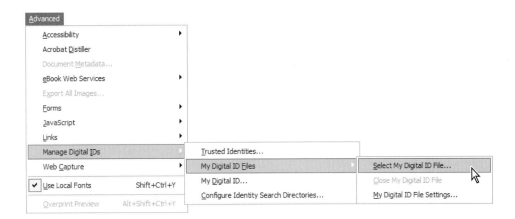

2 In the Select My Digital ID File dialog box, click the New Digital ID File button.

In this lesson, you'll create a self-signed digital ID which you can share directly with your colleagues. While this method is adequate for most unofficial exchanges, a more secure approach is to obtain a digital ID from a third-party provider (sometimes called a signature handler or certificate authority).

3 Click Continue to close the alert box.

4 Enter the name you want to appear in the Signatures panel and in any signature field that you complete, and enter a corporate name and an email address. We entered **T. Simpson, Director** for the name, **Clarity** for the Organization Name, and **clarity@xyz.net** for the email address. Make sure that you select a Country/Region. We selected **US - United States**.

5 Choose a Key Algorithm to set the level of security. We chose **1024-bit RSA**. Although 2048-bit RSA offers more security protection, it is not as universally compatible as 1024-bit RSA.

Now you'll specify what the encryption applies to. You can use the digital ID to control digital signatures, data encryption, or both. When you encrypt a PDF document, you specify a list of recipients from your Trusted Identities, and you define the recipients' level of access to the file—for example, whether the recipients can edit, copy, or print the files.

For this lesson, you'll chose digital signatures.

6 From the Use Digital ID For menu, choose Digital Signatures.

7 Now you must set a password. We used **Lotion123** as the password. Reenter your password to confirm it. Remember that the password is case-sensitive. Be sure to make a note of your password in a safe place. You cannot use or access your digital ID without this password.

*Note: Your password may not contain double quotations marks or the characters ! @ # $ % ^ & * , | \ ; < > _ .*

8 Click Create, and save the digital ID file in the Security folder. Make sure that the file type is Acrobat Self-Sign Digital ID file.

On Windows, the file is saved as a .pfx file; on Mac OS, the file is saved as a .p12 file.

Now you'll sign the advertisement and return it to the agency.

Signing the advertisement

1 Click the Sign button (✐) on the toolbar, and choose Sign This Document from the menu.

Acrobat first reminds you that you are the first to sign this document and asks if you want to certify the document or sign it. When you certify a document, you attest to its contents and specify the type of changes that a user can make to the document without invalidating the signature. When you sign a document, any subsequent changes to the document affect the validity of the signature. Because you want the advertising agency to know that the changes to this advertisement are approved and you want them to be sure that the document is unchanged since you approved it, you'll create a visible signature field and sign the document.

Later in this lesson you'll certify a document.

2 Click the Continue Signing button to clear the certification warning.

3 Make sure that the Create a New Signature Field to Sign option is selected, and click Next.

4 Click OK to close the alert box, and drag to create a signature field. We dragged a signature field in the area below the headline.

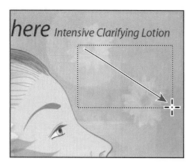

5 In the Apply Digital Signature dialog box, select the digital ID that you just created. We selected **T. Simpson, Director.** Click OK.

Note: If you get an error message saying that you don't have a suitable digital ID, click the Add button and recreate your signature.

6 Type your password in the Confirm Password text box. We typed in **Lotion123.**

7 Choose a reason for signing the document. We chose **I Am Approving This Document.**

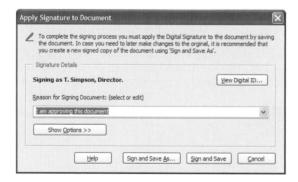

Before you complete the signature process, you'll adjust the appearance of your signature.

Adding an image to a digital signature

1 Click the Show Options button to display the signature appearance options.

2 Click the New button to open the Configure Signature Appearance dialog box where you can modify your signature appearance.

The Preview pane shows the default digital signature appearance.

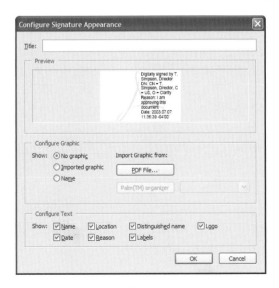

First you'll name your signature and then add your corporate logo to the signature block.

3 In the Title text box, enter a name for your signature. We entered **Logo** because we're going to add our corporate logo to the signature line. You should use a name that is easy to associate with the contents of the signature.

Note: You can add any image or graphic that is contained on one page of a PDF file.

4 In the Configure Graphic section of the dialog box, select the Imported Graphic option, and click the PDF File button to locate the PDF file of the logo.

5 In the Select Picture dialog box, click the Browse button and locate the Clarity_Logo.pdf file in the Lesson11 folder. Click Select, and then click OK to return to the Configure Signature Appearance dialog box.

♀ *You can also create a new signature appearance in the Digital Signatures preferences.*

Now you'll specify the information to be included in the text block of your signature. You'll include your name, the reason for signing the document, and the date.

6 In the Configure Text area of the Configure Signature Appearance dialog box, leave Name, Date, and Reason selected. Deselect all the other options.

7 When you're happy with the preview of your signature block, click OK.

8 Click Sign and Save in the Apply Signature to Document dialog box to apply the signature. (On Mac OS, you may need to enter your password again before you can sign and save the document.) Click OK to close the alert box.

When you digitally sign a document, you embed a unique fingerprint with encrypted numbers. The recipient of the signed document needs your signer's certificate to validate the digital signature.

Modifying a signed document

Just for fun, you'll add a comment to the signed document to see how the digital signature information changes. But first you'll look at the signatures panel to see what a valid signature looks like.

1 Click the Signatures tab, and if necessary, drag the right margin of the Signatures panel so that you can see all the signature information. Notice that the Signature panel contains much more information that the digital signature. If you recall, you streamlined the information included in your digital signature in the previous section.

Now you'll add a note to the advertisement and see how the addition changes the digital signature.

2 Choose Tools > Commenting, and click the Note tool ( ).

3 Click anywhere on the document page to add a note. We added a note saying, **"Good work."**

As soon as you add the note, the status of the signature changes from valid to unknown.

4 Right-click (Windows) or Control-click (Mac OS) on the signature box in the document pane, and choose Validate Signature. The alert box explains that although the signature is valid, a change has been made. Click Close to close the warning box.

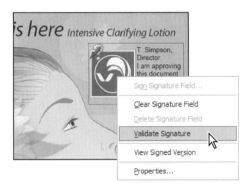

5 Choose File > Save.

Even after you have saved the document, you can easily revert to the copy that was signed.

6 Right-click (Windows) or Control-click (Mac OS) on the signature box in the document pane, and choose View Signed Version.

The View Signed Version option allows you to recover your unchanged file.

7 Choose Window > Close All, and close all open files.

Using the Signatures Tab

The Signatures tab lists all the signature fields in the current document. Each signature in the panel has an icon identifying its current verification status. A blue ribbon icon indicates that the certification is valid. The digital signature icon along with the name of the field in the Signatures panel indicates the presence of the empty signature field. A check mark icon indicates that the signature is valid. A question mark icon indicates that the signature has not been verified. A warning sign icon indicates that the document was modified after the signature was added.

You can collapse a signature to see only the name, date, and status, or you can expand it to see more information.

To display the Signatures tab:

* *Choose View > Navigation Tabs > Signatures, or click the Signatures tab on the left side of the document window.*

Tip: You can right-click (Windows) or Control-click (Mac OS) a signature field in the Signatures tab to do most signature-related tasks, including adding, clearing, and validating signatures. In some cases, however, the signature field may become locked after you sign it.

To expand or collapse a signature in the Signatures tab:

* *Click the plus sign (Windows) or triangle (Mac OS) to the left of the signature to expand it. Click the minus sign (Windows) or the rotated triangle (Mac OS) to the left of the signature to collapse it.*

—From the Complete Acrobat 6.0 Online Help.

Certifying a PDF file

In the prior section of this lesson, you signed a PDF document to signify that you had approved the content and requested changes. You can also certify the contents of a PDF document. Certifying a document rather than signing it is useful if you want the user to be able to make approved changes to a document. As you saw in the previous section, if you sign a document, and anyone (even you as the signer) makes changes, the signature is invalidated. However, if you certify a document and the user makes approved changes, the certification is still valid. You can certify forms for example, to guarantee that the content is valid when the user receives the form. You, as the creator of the form, can specify what tasks the user can perform. For example, you can specify that readers can fill in the form fields without invalidating the document. However, if a user tries to add or remove a form field or a page, the certification will be invalidated.

Now you'll certify a form to be sent to clients of a winery, asking them to estimate their purchases. By certifying the form, you are sure that the client fills out the form as you designed it, with no additions or deletions to the form fields.

1 Choose File > Open, and open the Final_Survey.pdf file in the Lesson11 folder.

2 Choose File > Document Properties, and click Security in the left pane.

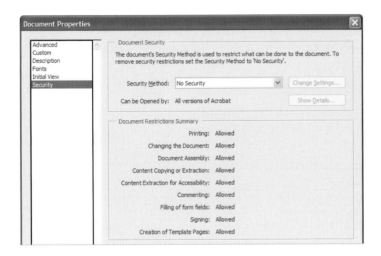

The information in the Document Properties dialog box shows that no security and no restrictions have been applied to the document.

3 Click Cancel to close the Document Properties dialog box without making any changes.

4 Choose File > Save As Certified Document.

5 Click OK to clear the message box. You'll use the Digital ID that you created earlier in the lesson to certify the file.

6 From the Allowed Actions menu, choose Only Allow Commenting and Forms Fill-in Actions on This Document.

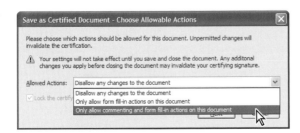

7 Click the box for the option that locks the certifying signature so that no one can modify or delete your certification. (The option is selected when a check mark is visible in the box.) Then click Next.

8 Click Next again to clear the warning box.

In the Select Visibility dialog box, if you choose the Show Certification on Document option, your signature will appear on the document alongside a blue ribbon certification. For this lesson, you'll choose not to show the certification on the form.

9 Select the Do Not Show Certification on Document option, and click Next.

10 Choose your Digital ID from the Digital ID File menu. We chose **T. Simpson, Director**. Then click OK.

11 Enter your password in the Confirm Password box. We entered **Lotion123**.

12 Choose a reason for signing the document. We choose to certify that we attested to the accuracy and integrity of the document.

13 Click the Sign and Save button and complete the certification process.

14 Click OK to clear the message box.

15 Click the Signatures tab to review what actions the certification allows.

Important: The note about potentially malicious content refers only to the presence of JavaScript actions in the form. This file contains no content that is harmful to your computer or your system.

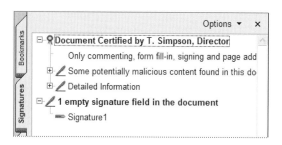

16 When you've finished reviewing the certification information, click the Signatures tab to close the Signatures panel.

 Whenever you open a certified document, you'll see a Certification icon ( ) at the left of the status bar. You can click on this icon at any time to see certification information for the document.

Signing a certified document

Now you'll sign the document that you just certified to verify that filling in a signature field doesn't invalidate the certification.

1 Click the Sign button ( ) on the toolbar, and choose Sign This Document from the menu.

2 In the Sign Document dialog box, make sure that the option to Sign an Existing Signature Field is selected, and click Next.

3 Click OK to clear the alert box.

4 Click anywhere in the empty signature field at the bottom of the survey, and click Next to clear the warning box.

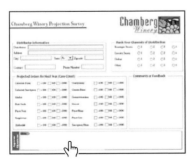

5 Choose your Digital ID (**T. Simpson, Director**), and click OK.

6 Enter your password in the Confirm Password box. We entered **Lotion123**. You can select a reason for signing the document if you wish. Then click Sign and Save to complete the process. Click OK to clear the alert box.

7 Click the Signatures tab to open the Signatures panel.

In the Signatures panel, notice that the certification is still valid even though a signature has been added. Remember that when you signed the document earlier in the lesson and then added a comment, your signature became invalid. Note, however, that if you attempt to fill in any of the form fields, after you have signed the document, your signature is invalidated. The form is still certified, though.

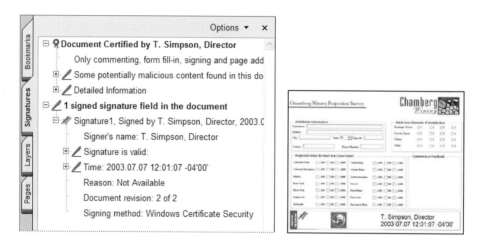

Important: As before, the note about potentially malicious content refers only to the presence of JavaScript actions in the form. This file contains no content that is harmful to your computer or your system.

8 Choose File > Close.

Looking at security settings

As you have seen, you can digitally sign a document or certify a document to attest to the contents of the document at the time of signing or certification. There are times, however, when you simply want to restrict access to a document. You can do this by adding security to your Adobe PDF files.

When you open a document that has restricted access or some type of security applied to it, you'll see an icon in the bottom left of the status bar. Clicking this icon at any time opens a dialog box that tells more about the restrictions applied to the document.

1 Choose File > Open, and open the Secure_Survey.pdf file in the Lesson11 folder.

2 Click the Sign button ( ) on the Acrobat toolbar, and notice that the Sign This Document command is grayed out.

3 Choose Tools > Commenting > Show Commenting Toolbar, and again notice that all the commenting and text markup tools are grayed out. Then click the Close button to close the Commenting toolbar.

4 Click the Secure button ( ) on the Acrobat toolbar, and choose Display Restrictions and Security from the menu.

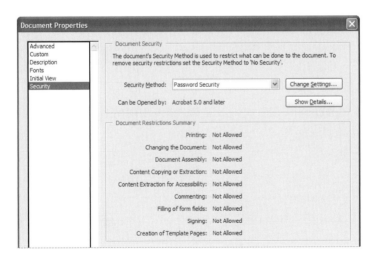

The dialog box lists the actions that are allowed and those that are not allowed. As you read down the list, you'll see that signing and commenting are not allowed, which is why the related tools are grayed out on the Commenting toolbar (steps 2 and 3).

5 When you have finished reviewing the information, click Cancel to close the Document Properties dialog box.

6 Choose File > Close to close the Secure_Survey.pdf file.

Now you'll change the security settings for one of your own files.

Adding security to your PDF files

You can add security to your Adobe PDF files when you first create them or after the fact. You can even add security to files that you receive from some one else, unless the creator of the document limited who can change security settings.

In Acrobat Professional, you have several ways of adding security:

• You can apply password protection to your files to limit what a user can do with your files. For example, you can disallow printing, editing, or adding comments to your files.

• You can apply password protection to limit who can open your files.

• You can apply password protection to limit who can change the security settings on your files.

• You can encrypt your files to limit access to your files to a predefined set of users and to limit the types of actions they can perform on your files.

• You can certify your documents to attest to the contents and to allow users to make certain types of changes. Unlike a digital signature, a certification isn't invalidated if the user makes the approved types of changes.

In this part of the lesson, you'll add password protection to limit who can open your document and who can change the security settings.

Adding passwords

You can add two kinds of passwords to protect your Adobe PDF documents. You can add a Document Open password so that only users who have the password can open the document, and you can add a Permissions password so that only users who have the password can change the permissions for the document.

You'll add password protection to your logo file so that no one can change the contents of the logo file and so that unauthorized users can't open and use the file.

1 Choose File > Open, and open the file SBR_Logo.pdf. Click OK to close the Adobe Picture Tasks dialog box.

2 Choose File > Save As, and name the file **SBR_Logo1.pdf** and save it in the Lesson11 folder.

3 Click the Secure button on the Acrobat toolbar, and choose Display Restrictions and Security. Click Security in the left pane.

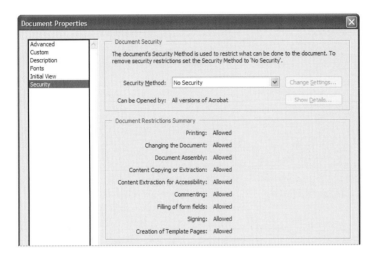

No security at all has been applied to this file. You'll first choose the type of security to add.

4 From the Security Method box, choose Password Security. The Password Security Settings dialog box opens automatically.

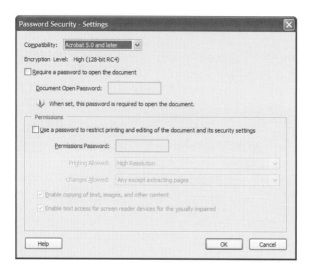

First you'll set the compatibility level.

The default compatibility level is compatibility with Acrobat 5 or later. If you're sure that all your users have Acrobat 5 or later, this compatibility level is the preferred setting. If you think that some of your users may still be running Acrobat 4, then you should select Acrobat 3 and later. Note, however, that this is a lower encryption level.

5 Select your compatibility level from the Compatibility menu. We used **Acrobat 5 and later.**

6 Check the box for the Require a Password to Open the Document option, and then type in your password. We typed in **SBRLogo**.

You'll share this password with anyone that you want to be able to open the document. Remember that passwords are case-sensitive.

Always record your passwords in a secure location. If you forget your password, you can't recover it from the document. You might prefer to store an unprotected copy of the document in a secure location.

Now you'll add a second password that controls who is allowed to change printing and editing and security settings for the file.

7 Under Permission, check the box for the Use a Password to Restrict Printing and Editing of the Document and its Security Settings, and type in your password. We typed in **SBRPres**.

Note: Your open password and permissions password can't be the same.

8 From the Printing Allowed menu, choose whether to allow printing at all, printing at low resolution, or printing at high resolution. We chose Low Resolution.

9 From the Changes Allowed menu, choose the type of changes you will allow users to make. We chose **Commenting, Filling in Form Fields, and Signing** to allow users to comment on the logo.

10 Click OK to apply your changes.

11 In the first dialog box, re-enter the Open Password. We entered **SBRLogo**. Then click OK, and click OK again to clear the alert box.

12 In the second dialog box, re-enter the Permissions Password. We entered **SBRPres**. Then click OK, and click OK again to clear the alert box.

Notice that the actions available to users have changed. For more information on the security applied, click the Show Details button.

13 Click OK to close the Document Properties dialog box.

14 Click File > Save to save your work and apply the security changes.

15 Choose File > Close to close the SBRLogo1.pdf file.

Now you'll check the security that you've added to your file.

Opening a password-protected file

1 Choose File > Open and re-open the SBRLogo1.pdf file in the Lesson11 folder.

You're prompted to enter the required password to open the file.

2 We entered **SBRLogo,** and clicked OK. Then click OK to clear the Adobe Picture Tasks dialog box.

Now you'll test the Permissions Password.

3 Click the Secure button ( ) on the toolbar, and choose Display Restrictions and Security from the menu.

4 In the Document Properties dialog box, try changing the Security Method from Password Security to No Security.

Acrobat prompts you to enter the Permissions password.

5 We entered **SBRPres** and clicked OK and then OK again.

All restrictions have been removed from the file.

6 Click OK to close the Document Properties dialog box.

7 Choose File > Close, and close the file without saving the changes.

Review questions

1 Where do you change the appearance of your digital signature?

2 How many digital signatures can you create?

3 Why would you want to apply password protection to a PDF file?

4 When would you apply permissions protection?

Review answers

1 You change the appearance of your digital signature in the Configure Signature Appearance dialog box. You can access this dialog box from the Digital Signatures Preferences dialog box. You can also change the appearance of your digital signature in the Apply Signature to Document dialog box during the signing process.

2 You can have numerous digital signatures. You can create different digital signatures for the different identities that you use. You can have personal signatures, corporate signatures, family signatures, etc.

3 If you have a confidential document that you don't want others to read, you can apply password protection. Only users with whom you share your password will be able to open the document.

4 Permissions protection limits how a user can manipulate the contents of your Adobe PDF file. For example, you can specify that users cannot print the contents of your file, or copy and paste the contents of your file. Permission protection allows you to share the content of your file without losing control over how it is used.

Lesson 12

12 | **Filling Out Forms**

Acrobat Professional lets you fill out electronic forms, and submit the form data by email or over the World Wide Web. You can also digitally sign forms.

In this lesson, you'll learn how to do the following:

• Examine a password-protected form.

• Fill out an Adobe PDF form and spell check the entries.

• Export information from one form and import it into a blank form.

• Set the Acrobat Professional preferences to automatically complete fields when the necessary information is available.

• Add a digital signature field to a form, and digitally sign the form.

This lesson will take about 45 minutes to complete.

If needed, remove the previous lesson folder from your hard drive, and copy the Lesson12 folder onto it.

This lesson assumes that you have created a digital ID, as described in Lesson 11, "Adding Signatures and Security."

Note: Windows users may need to unlock the lesson files before using them. For information, see "Copying the Classroom in a Book files" on page 3.

Getting started

With Adobe Acrobat Professional, it's easy to complete electronic forms. You can even add a signature field and digitally sign your completed form. You can fill out a form on the Web, you can email a completed form, or you can send just the information you entered in the form fields rather than the entire form, making your email attachment much smaller.

In the first part of the lesson, you'll fill out a survey projecting the amount of wine, by type, that your business anticipates ordering, identifying your distribution channels, and giving your corporate information. In the second part of the lesson, you'll add a signature field and sign a form completed by colleagues, and you'll export the information to an FDF file, which is small and easy to email, and then you'll import the data into a blank form to see how the form and data are reassembled in Acrobat Professional.

If you need to create electronic forms or add form fields to existing Adobe PDF documents (other than for digitally signing a document), you need to upgrade to Acrobat Professional. Acrobat Professional allows you to fill out forms and add digital signature fields only.

Opening a password-protected form

1 Start Acrobat Professional.

2 Choose File > Open. Select Survey.pdf in the Lesson12 folder, and click Open.

When you open the document, you'll notice a lock at the left of the status bar.

3 Click the lock icon to open the Document Status dialog box. When you have read the content of the box, click the Close button.

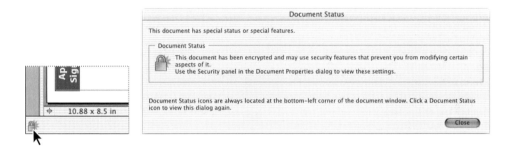

As noted in the Document Status dialog box, you can check the security that has been applied to the file in the Security panel of the Document Properties dialog box. You'll do this now.

4 Choose File > Document Properties, and select Security in the left pane.

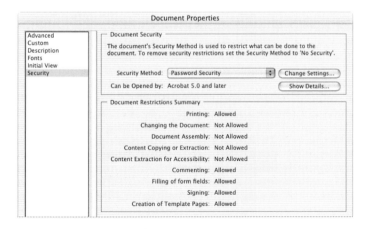

Notice that password security has been applied to this form and that only printing, commenting, filling in form fields, signing, and creation of template pages are allowed.

5 Click OK to close the dialog box when you have finished reviewing the settings.

Filling out a form

1 Choose File > Save As, rename the file **Survey1.pdf**, and save it in the Lesson12 folder.

This electronic form was designed using a page-layout application and then converted to Adobe PDF. Form fields were added using Acrobat Professional so that you can fill out the form from within Acrobat Professional or Adobe Reader.

You use the Hand tool ( ) to enter information in form fields.

2 Click in the Distributor text box, and enter your company name. We entered **SBR Associates**.

3 Press Tab to move to the next field.

You may see an Auto-Complete feature message advising you that Acrobat can remember entries and automatically prompt you with the correct information for subsequent entries.

4 If you are completing this lesson on your own system, click Yes. If you are working on a public system or on someone else's system, click No and move on to step 5 in "Completing form fields automatically" on page 342.

Completing form fields automatically

Acrobat Professional offers an Auto-Complete feature to save you time when filling in forms. If the first few characters you type in a form field match something you've typed in a previous form field, the Auto-Complete feature automatically fills in the remaining characters. The Auto-Complete feature is off by default. You turn it on in the Preferences dialog box.

When you turn on the Auto-Complete feature, you can select to view a list of matching entries. You can also edit the list of matching entries.

1 Choose Edit > Preferences (Windows) or Acrobat > Preferences (Mac OS), and select Forms from the list.

2 Select Off, Basic, or Advanced in the Auto-Complete menu. You can see a description of each option in the window below the menu. We chose **Basic**.

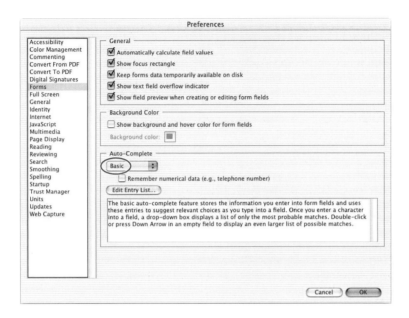

3 Select the Remember Numerical Data option if you want Acrobat to remember your phone number, for example.

4 Click OK to apply the settings.

After you enter your phone number on the form, you'll test this feature.

5 Click in the Address field to create an insertion point, and enter your street address. We entered **10157 Walnut Street**.

6 Press Tab, and enter your city. We entered **San Jose**.

💡 *If you make an incorrect entry in a form field, you can quickly clear the field by pressing the Esc key.*

Pressing Tab after each entry moves you to the next field. (Pressing Shift+Tab moves you to the previous field.) The designer of the form sets the Tab order of fields. If you want to change the tabbing order of the fields, you can do so by selecting the page thumbnail in the Pages panel, and choosing Page Properties from the Options menu. You reset the tabbing order in the Tab Order panel of this dialog box.

7 Choose a state from the State menu. We chose **CA**.

8 Enter your zipcode. We entered **951100**. Notice that the last digit is rejected. The creator of the form limited the entry in this field to 5 digits, the length of a correct zipcode number. We left the entry as 95110.

9 Enter a contact name. We entered **Trudi Simpson**.

10 For the phone number, enter 5551231234 and press Enter or Return.

Press Enter or Return to format the phone number.

Notice that the phone number is automatically formatted. The creator of the form added this feature using Acrobat Professional.

Now you'll test the Auto-Complete feature. First you'll delete the phone number that you just entered and then re-enter it.

11 Create an insertion point at the beginning or end of the phone number entry, and drag to highlight the phone number that you just entered. Then press Delete to erase the entry.

Because you have turned on the Auto-Complete feature, a drop-down menu displays all the entries that you have made for the form.

12 Select the phone number from the drop-down menu, and press Enter or Return to complete the formatting of the entry.

Using check boxes and radio buttons

Now you'll enter your projections for cases of wine ordered.

1 Move your cursor into the Cabernet Franc line and click the "<100" box.

But you remember that Cabernet Franc is an increasingly popular wine, so maybe you need to order 500 cases.

2 Click the "500" box. Notice that your original entry is automatically erased. The ability to select only one of the three choices was built-in by the creator of the form.

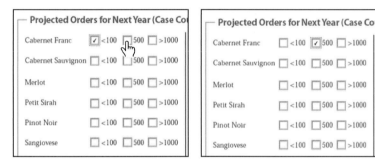

💡 *Pressing Enter or Return toggles the value in a selected check box. If a selected box is checked, pressing Enter or Return clears the check box; if the check box is empty, pressing Enter or Return adds a check mark.*

If you wish, you can fill out the projected case orders for the other wine types. Now though, you'll move on to ranking your distribution channels.

3 Move your cursor into the area in which you'll rank distribution channels.

4 Click the "1" button for Boutique Stores.

5 Then click the "1" button for Grocery Stores.

You can only select one distribution channel as your primary channel.

Notice that the selection for Boutique Stores is deleted automatically. You can only have one first-place selection. Again this is a feature of the form field created in Acrobat Professional.

You can experiment with ranking the various distribution channels. When you're finished you'll add a comment to the survey.

6 Click in the Comments or Feedback box to create an insertion point, and enter a comment. We typed in, "**If we find that we've underestimated the Cab Franc market, what are the chances that we can biy more in June, for example?**"

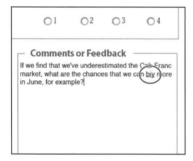

Notice that we deliberately misspelled "buy" so that we can demonstrate the spell check feature for form fields.

7 Choose File > Save to save your work.

Spell checking your entries

You can check the spelling in any form field if the creator of the form has enabled spell checking.

1 Choose Edit > Check Spelling > In Comments and Form Fields.

2 Click Start to begin spell checking.

Unrecognized words appear in the first window.

3 Click Ignore to leave the word as is. Click Change to accept the suggested correction that is highlighted.

If you misspelled the word "biy" as we did, "biy" is displayed in the first window, and "buy" is displayed as an option in the Suggestions window. You may need to scroll down to see it.

4 Select "buy," and click Change to accept the change. The misspelling is corrected in the Comments or Feedback window.

5 Click Done to terminate the spell checking operation.

6 Choose File > Save, and save your work.

For the spell check feature to work correctly, the designer of the form must have turned on the spell checking feature when creating the form.

Now that you've completed the form, you'll sign it before you return it to the winery.

Signing the form

1 Click the arrow next to the Sign button on the Acrobat toolbar, and choose Sign This Document from the menu.

2 Click the Continue Signing button to close the alert box, and click OK to close the message box that directs you to click in the signature field to sign the document.

3 Click in the signature field at the bottom of the document, and click the Continue Signing button again.

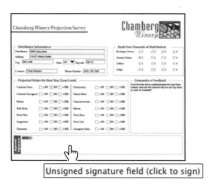

Unsigned signature field (click to sign)

You'll use the digital ID that you created in Lesson 11, "Adding Signatures and Security," to sign the document. If you didn't create a digital ID, you'll need to create one before you can sign the form. To create a digital ID, follow the steps in Lesson 11, in the section "Creating a Digital ID" and "Adding Signatures and Security." Also, be sure that your Digital Signatures preferences are set to use Default Certificate Security for the default method to use when signing.

4 In the dialog box select the digital ID that you created in Lesson 11, and click OK.

5 Enter the password that you used to create your digital ID in the Confirm Password text box. We entered **Lotion123**.

6 Choose the "I am approving this document" option from the Reason for Signing Document menu, and click Sign and Save.

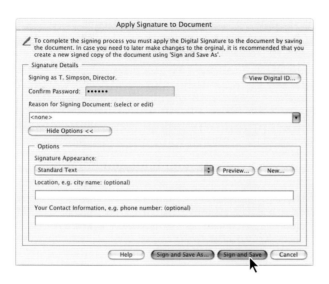

7 Click OK to clear the alert box.

Your form is now completed, signed, and saved.

💡 *You can clear a form before you save it by choosing File > Revert to revert to the last-saved copy of the file. Clearing a form resets all the form fields to empty.*

In a real-life situation, you would probably want to email your completed form to the winery. To do so, you'd just click the email button on the Acrobat toolbar and follow the steps outlined below. If you had not signed the form, you could export the form data and send it as an FDF file, as you will in "Exporting form data" on page 352.

Note: A digital signature field is not included in data imported or exported as an FDF file. For a digital signature to be available, the entire PDF file must be made available.

Emailing the completed form

You can email your completed form without leaving Acrobat Professional.

1 Click the Email button ( ) on the Acrobat Professional toolbar.

Acrobat automatically launches your default email application and attaches the PDF file that is open (your completed form) to an empty email message window. All you need to do is add the email address of the recipient in the To: box, and send the message. You can send the message to your own email address if you have an Internet connection open and an email application on your system. The actual steps for sending the email message will vary with your email application. Send or close your email message and close your email application program when you are finished. (On some systems, the form may not display data that you have entered into the fields. You can check that the data is saved and sent by sending the message to yourself and opening it.)

2 In Acrobat, choose File > Close to close the Survey1.pdf file.

About Digital ID providers

Here are some common providers of digital IDs:

• *The Default Certificate Security lets you create a password-protected digital ID file. To sign documents using a self-signed digital ID, you must distribute your certificate to those who need to validate your digital signatures. Default Certificate Security uses a private/public key (PPK) system to validate the authenticity of signatures. The private key encrypts a fingerprint that is stored with a signature when you sign. The public key uses the certificate to decrypt the fingerprint when you or someone else verifies the signature.*

• *Windows Certificate Security is a Windows security service that allows client and server applications to gain trust in each other's authentication credentials. You can use Windows digital IDs in PDF documents without having to type a password. A certificate store is the system area where Windows certificates are stored.*

• *Third-party signature handlers, such as VeriSign® or Entrust®, often include advanced features such as certification by a third party. See the Adobe Web site for information on using signature handlers with advanced security features.*

–From the Complete Acrobat 6.0 Help.

Adding a signature field

In addition to the survey you've just returned to the Chamberg Winery, they've asked for a summary of last year's purchases. An associate has compiled the data and completed the form. In this part of the lesson, you'll add a signature field to the form and sign it.

Adding a signature field and signing it is very similar to the process that you used to sign the Chamberg Survey in the earlier section, so we'll minimize the steps. If you need more detail, refer back to "Signing the form" on page 347.

1 Choose File > Open and open the file LastYr.pdf in the Lesson12 folder.

2 Choose File > Save As, and save the file as **LastYr1.pdf** in the Lesson12 folder.

3 Click the Sign button on the Acrobat toolbar, and choose Sign This Document from the menu.

If you wanted to create a signature field for someone else to sign, you would choose Create a Blank Signature Field from the menu. (For information on creating a blank signature field, see "Exploring on your own" on page 355.)

4 Click the Continue Signing button in the alert box.

For information on certifying a document rather than signing a document, see Lesson 11, "Adding Signatures and Security."

5 Make sure that the Create a New Signature Field to Sign option is selected, and click Next.

6 Click OK to clear the alert box, and drag to create a signature field. We dragged a signature field at the bottom of the document in the Approval Signatures block.

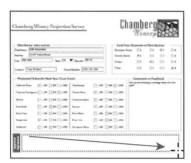

7 Select the Digital ID that you created in Lesson 11, and click OK.

8 Enter your password in the Confirm Password box, we entered **Lotion123**, and choose a reason for signing the document from the menu.

9 Choose a reason for signing the document.

10 Click Sign and Save to complete the process.

11 Click OK to clear the alert box.

You've added a signature field and signed the form. Now you'll export all the forms data.

Exporting form data

Forms files can be large, and sometimes it is easier to send just a file containing the data entered into the form rather than the entire form. You can use the Export Forms Data in Acrobat to export the data in the form as an FDF file, which is generally small and easy to email. The recipient can then import the data from your FDF file into a blank form to recreate your form.

You can also use the Export Forms Data feature to archive form data from a collection of forms without having to archive multiple copies of the completed form. You need only archive one blank copy of the form to import the forms data into.

Note: A digital signature field is not included in data imported or exported as an FDF file. For a digital signature to be available, the entire PDF file must be made available.

1 Choose Advanced > Forms > Export Forms Data.

2 Name the file **LastYr1.fdf,** and click Save to save it in the Lesson12 folder. Make sure that Acrobat FDF Files is selected for Save as Type (Windows) or Format (Mac OS).

FDF stands for Forms Data Format, the file format for exported form data.

3 Choose File > Close to close the LastYr1.pdf file.

This FDF file that you've just created contains all the data entered on the form, and it is the file that you would email as an attachment to the winery.

Comparing FDF and PDF file sizes

Take a moment to compare the file sizes of the completed PDF form file and of the FDF file that contains only the data entered in the form.

1 On Windows, use Windows Explorer to open the Lesson12 folder, and note the sizes of the two files, LastYr1.pdf and LastYr1.fdf. On Mac OS, open the Lesson12 folder in the Finder, select file the LastYr1.pdf, and use the List View to determine the file size. Do the same for the LastYr1.fdf file and note the comparative file sizes.

The FDF file is approximately 4KB; the PDF file is approximately 140KB.(File sizes may vary slightly depending on whether you are using a Windows or Mac OS system.)

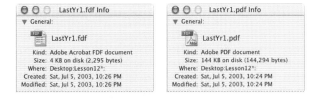

2 Close all open windows.

Importing form data

In real life, you'd send the LastYr1.fdf file as an email attachment to your contact at the Chamberg Winery. For the purposes of this lesson, however, you'll open a blank form and import the LastYr1.fdf file to populate the form fields with the data you just exported.

Note: A digital signature field is not included in data imported or exported as an FDF file. For a digital signature to be available, the entire PDF file must be made available.

1 In Acrobat, choose File > Open. Select BlankYr.pdf in the Lesson12 folder, and click Open.

2 Choose Advanced > Forms > Import Forms Data. Select LastYr1.fdf in the Lesson12 folder, and click Select.

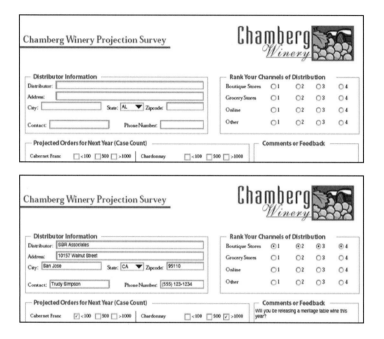

The values you entered in your survey are automatically imported into the corresponding fields in the blank survey. (Note that the signature information is not imported.)

3 Choose File > Close to close the form without saving it.

Exploring on your own

Earlier in this lesson, you signed a form that you completed using a signature field added by the creator of the form, and you added a signed signature field to a second form. You can also add a blank signature field to any PDF document unless the person who created the document has disallowed changes to the document.

💡 *You can check if the creator of a document has applied any restrictions. With the document open, choose File > Document Properties, and choose Security in the left window. Any restrictions are listed in this dialog box.*

You'll open a copy of a document that isn't certified or password-protected, and you'll create a signature field that will allow other users to sign the form digitally.

1 Choose File > Open, select the Lotion.pdf file in the Lesson12 folder, and click Open.

2 Choose File > Save As, and save the file as **Lotion1.pdf** in the Lesson12 folder.

3 Click the Sign button on the toolbar, and choose Create a Blank Signature Field from the drop-down menu.

4 If necessary, click OK to close the alert box.

5 Drag a box that fills the area under the heading and to the right of the face.

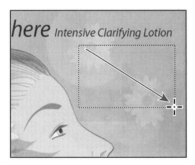

6 Click the General tab in the Digital Signature Properties dialog box. For Name, enter **Signature**, and for Tooltip, enter **Sign Here**. The tooltip is displayed when the user holds the cursor over the empty signature field.

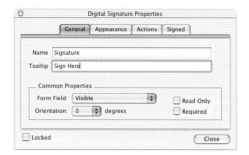

7 Click the Required check box to select it.

You'll leave the Form Field as visible so users know where to sign.

8 Click the Appearance tab. Click the Border Color box, and select a color. We chose blue. You'll need a border color to more easily identify the area to be signed. Leave the line thickness and line style as is.

9 Click the Signed tab. If this were a form, you could select the Mark as Read Only option and select All Fields from the pop-up menu so that no field values could be changed after the document was signed. Since you're adding only a signature box, you'll leave these options unchanged.

10 Click Close to finish adding the signature box. (Note that the signature box is still red. It will remain red until you select the Hand tool.)

You've added a signature box that anyone, including yourself, can sign.

11 To test your tooltip, select the Hand tool, and move the cursor over the signature label. Your tooltip should be visible.

12 When you're finished, choose File > Close, and save and close the Lotion1.pdf file.

Review questions

1 If you type the wrong information into a form field, how can you clear the field and start over?

2 How do you move from one field to the next?

3 Can you sign a form if the person who created the form didn't add a signature field?

4 Why would you want to export data from a form to an FDF file?

Review answers

1 If your cursor is still in the field that you want to clear, press Esc. If you've moved to another field, return to the entry that you want to change, click to create an insertion point and drag to select the entry. Click Delete, or simply type in new information to replace the highlighted material.

2 Press Tab to move to the next field. Press Shift+Tab to move backwards through the fields. The person who created the form determines the tabbing order of the form.

3 Yes. You can create your own signature field using the Sign > Sign this Document or Create a Blank Signature Field command.

4 An FDF file is much smaller than the PDF file for a completed form. As long as the recipient has a blank copy of the form to import the FDF file into, it is much easier to export form data to an FDF file and email the FDF file as an attachment. FDF files are also easier to archive because they are compact. Again, you just need to be sure that you keep one blank copy of the form to import the data into.

Lesson 13

13 | Preparing Presentations

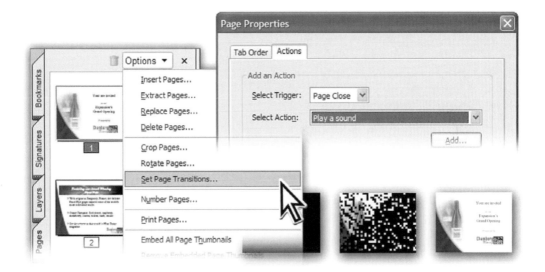

You can set your Adobe PDF file to open in full-screen view with all the Acrobat commands and tools hidden. You can add page transitions that display as you move through the pages of the presentation, and you can even add sounds to enhance your page transitions. Take time to experiment with this lesson and find a presentation format that work best for you.

In this lesson, you'll set up a PDF file in a "slide-show" presentation format. You'll do the following:

• Set your Adobe PDF document to always open in full-screen view.

• Set special effects that control how your presentations look as you move from page to page.

• Add a sound to enhance page transitions.

• Replace a page in a presentation.

This lesson will take about 30 minutes to complete.

If needed, remove the previous lesson folder from your hard drive, and copy the Lesson13 folder onto it.

Note: Windows may users need to unlock the lesson files before using them. For information, see "Copying the Classroom in a Book files" on page 3.

Getting started

Generally when you make a presentation to a group of people, you want the document to take over the entire screen, hiding distractions such as the menu bar, toolbar, and other window controls.

You can set up any PDF file to display in full-screen view, and you can set a variety of transition effects and sound effects to play as you move between pages. You can also convert presentations that you've prepared in other programs, such as PowerPoint, to Adobe PDF, preserving many of the authoring program's special effects. For information on converting PowerPoint presentations to Adobe PDF, see Lesson 3, "Converting Microsoft Office Files."

In this lesson, you'll learn how to set up a full-screen presentation, using an invitation to the Chamberg winery's expansion opening. You'll set up a PDF file to work as a full-screen slide show on your computer, with pages that turn automatically.

The full-screen view is very useful for presentations that don't require input from the user. However, if you use this format for interactive presentations, you should have controls and buttons built into the PDF pages to allow users to exit the presentation or page through the presentation at their own pace.

Opening the work file

The document that you'll work with in this lesson is an invitation by wine master Alistair Eamon to a Pinot Noir tasting to celebrate the expansion of the Chamberg winery. You'll set up the file to run as an unattended display at a convention for wine buyers.

1 Start Acrobat Professional.

2 Choose File > Open, select Invite.pdf in the Lesson13 folder, and click Open.

3 Choose File > Save As and save the file as **Invite1.pdf** in the Lesson13 folder.

4 Click the Fit Page button (⊡) so that you can view the entire page.

5 Use the Next Page button (▶) and the Previous Page button (◀) to page through the invitation. When you're finished, click the First Page button (|◀) to return to the first page of the invitation.

Setting a full-screen view

First you'll set the file to open automatically in full-screen view.

1 Choose File > Document Properties, and select Initial View in the left pane.

2 From the Page Layout menu, choose Single Page. From the Magnification menu, choose Fit Page. Under Window Options, click the empty check box next to the Open in Full Screen Mode option to select the option. (The option is selected when the box contains a check mark.)

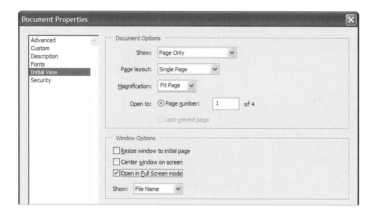

3 Click OK.

4 Choose File > Save to save your work.

The next time the file is opened, the page image with a solid background will automatically fill the entire screen.

In the next section, you'll set page transitions so that the presentation moves automatically from page to page at a predetermined speed. You'll also add a transition effect that displays as the pages change.

Setting page transitions

1 If necessary, click the First Page button ( ) on the status bar to return to page 1 of the document.

2 Click the Pages tab to open the Pages panel.

3 Click the Options button at the top of the Pages panel, and choose Set Page Transitions from the Options menu.

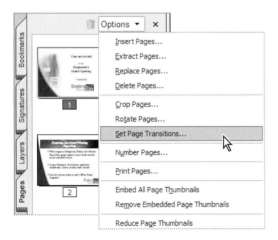

You use the Set Transitions dialog box to set page transitions for all or selected pages in a PDF document. You can set a transition effect and the speed of the effect, as well as set the speed at which the pages are turned.

First you'll choose the pages that the transition will be applied to.

4 For Page Range, make sure that All Pages in Document is selected. The radio button is filled when the option is selected.

To apply page transitions to a range of pages, select the Pages Range option and enter the start and end page numbers of the page range. To apply page transitions to the pages selected in the Pages tab, you must select the pages before choosing the Set Page Transitions command in the Options menu.

5 Select a page transition effect from the Effect menu. We chose Glitter Right-Down.

6 Set the speed of the transition—slow, medium, or fast. We chose Medium.

💡 *To preview your transition effect, click OK to close the Set Transitions dialog box and to apply your choices, and then choose Window > Full Screen View. To move from page to page, press the Enter key or Return key. To exit the full-screen view, press the Esc key. To return to the Set Transitions dialog box, choose Set Page Transitions from the Options menu of the Pages tab.*

Now you'll set the speed at which the viewer moves from page to page.

Setting the "page turning" speed

1 In the Set Transitions dialog box, select the AutoFlip option. If you don't select this option, the user will need to press Enter or the spacebar to move through the presentation.

2 Enter a number of seconds for the current page to be displayed. You can type in a number or choose a number from the pop-up menu. We chose **3** seconds.

3 Click OK to apply your changes.

4 Choose File > Save to save your work.

5 To preview your work, click the First Page button on the status bar to return to page 1 of the document, and then choose Window > Full Screen View.

Glitter Right-Down page transition

6 When you are finished, press the Esc key to exit full-screen view.

You can experiment with different transitions, transition speeds, and rates of moving through the presentation.

If you want your presentation to run continuously, cycling from the end back to the beginning automatically, choose Edit > Preferences (Windows) or Acrobat > Preferences (Mac OS), and select Full Screen in the left panel of the Preferences dialog box. Check the Loop after Last Page option. This option is a system setting rather than a setting that is saved with the PDF file. You'll need to be sure that you set this option on the system on which you display your presentation.

Adding sound to page transitions

You can add sound to your Adobe PDF file to enhance page transitions, or to provide audio commentary where necessary. Any sound file that you add is embedded in the PDF document in a cross-platform format that plays on both Windows and Mac OS.

In this part of the lesson, you'll add the sound of champagne pouring into a glass to the third page of the presentation to enhance the page turning effect.

1 In the Pages panel, click the third page thumbnail.

2 Choose Page Properties from the Options menu.

3 In the Page Properties dialog box, click the Actions tab.

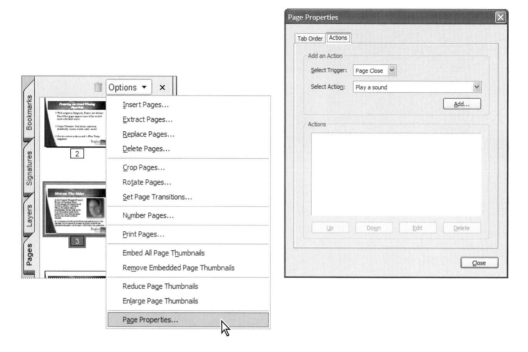

4 Under Add an Action, choose Page Close from the Select Trigger menu. This ensures that the sound that you add will play whenever page 3 is closed.

5 From the Select Action menu, choose Play a Sound, and then click Add.

Now you'll choose the sound file to add.

6 In the Select Sound File dialog box, select the pourwine.wav file and click Select.

7 Click Close to close the Properties dialog box.

8 Choose File > Save to save your work, and then choose Window > Full Screen View to hear the sound. The sound will play as you move from page 3 to page 4 of the presentation.

You can also preview the sound file by selecting the page 3 thumbnail in the Pages panel.

9 When you are finished, press the Esc key to exit full-screen view, and then choose File > Close to close the Invite1.pdf file.

Setting the Full Screen preferences

Now you'll look at some of the system preferences that affect how your presentation displays. The Full Screen preferences let you define whether a presentation loops—that is, whether it plays continually from beginning to end and back to the beginning.

The Full Screen preferences also allow you to set default transitions and other full-screen options to be applied to presentations for which no presentation options are set.

Looping a presentation

1 In Acrobat Professional, choose Edit > Preferences (Windows) or Acrobat > Preferences (Mac OS), and select Full Screen in the left panel of the Preferences dialog box.

2 Under Full Screen Navigation, click in the check box next to the Loop After Last Page option. This plays the presentation continuously.

3 Click OK to apply your preferences.

4 To see the effect of your changes, choose File > Open, and open the Invite1.pdf file in the Lesson13 folder.

The file opens in full-screen view and plays continuously.

5 Press the Esc key when you are finished, and choose File > Close and close Invite1.pdf.

Setting default Full Screen preferences

You can also set options to be applied to PDF files viewed in full-screen mode when the creator of the PDF file didn't specify any full-screen options. You'll set default full-screen navigation and appearance options and see their effect on the original winery presentation for which no full-screen options were defined.

1 In Acrobat Professional, choose Edit > Preferences (Windows) or Acrobat > Preferences (Mac OS), and select Full Screen in the left panel of the Preferences dialog box.

2 Under Full Screen Navigation, click in the Advance Every check box to select the option. A check mark appears when the option is selected. After you select the option, you can enter a value for the number of seconds that the current page remains open. We chose **10** seconds.

Setting this value gives you control over how quickly the presentation moves along.

3 From the Default Transition menu, you can choose not to use any transitions (No Transition) or select a transition from the pop-up menu. (We chose Fly in from Bottom.)

4 Click OK to apply your preferences.

5 To see the effect of your changes, choose File > Open, and open the Invite.pdf file in the Lesson13 folder.

6 Choose Window > Full Screen View.

The file displays in full-screen view, but with the transition of your choice and a ten-second delay between page turning.

7 Press the Esc key when you are finished and close the Invite.pdf file.

Adding pages to your presentation

No matter how well prepared you are, at some point someone will ask you to add or change a page in your presentation. With Acrobat Professional that's not a problem. In this section, you'll update the invitation page by replacing the current page with a new page and you'll check that the page transitions and special effects are still in place.

Imagine that you're at the sales convention, and your colleague calls to say that you need to change the date of the wine tasting featured in your presentation. You can convert the replacement PowerPoint page to Adobe PDF. (You learned how to do that in Lesson 3, "Converting Microsoft Office Files.") Then you simply replace the old page with the new one in a couple of easy steps.

1 Choose File > Open, and open the Invite1.pdf file. Press Esc to exit Full Screen view.

2 Click the Last Page button (▶▌) on the status bar to go to page 4 of the presentation.

Now you'll replace the existing page 4 with the new page 4 that contains the updated information on the time and place of the tasting.

3 Choose Document > Pages > Replace.

4 In the Select File with New Pages dialog box, select the file NewPage.pdf in the Lesson13 folder and click Select.

5 In the Replace Pages dialog box, under Original, make sure that 4 is entered in the two Replace Pages text boxes. Because the replacement file contains only one page, leave the Replacement section as is, and click OK. Click Yes to clear the message box.

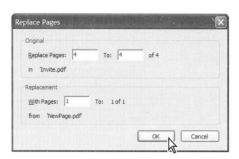

6 Choose File > Save As, name the file **Invite2.pdf** and save it in the Lesson13 folder.

Just to be sure, you'll check that the page transitions and sound effects are still in place.

7 Choose Window > Full Screen View and page through the presentation to make sure that the page transitions and the sound effect in the presentation are working correctly. You'll see that the page transitions have been inherited by the replacement page.

That's all there is to it. You're ready to display your updated presentation.

8 When you're finished, press Esc, close any open files, and exit Acrobat Professional.

Review questions

1 Where do you set the opening view for a PDF document?

2 How do you add page transitions to a PDF document?

3 How can a user of a PDF file override opening view settings?

4 How do you make a presentation loop continuously?

Review answers

1 As the creator of a PDF document, you set the opening view of your document using the Initial View settings in the Document Properties dialog box. To access these settings, choose File > Document Properties, and choose Initial View in the left pane.

2 You can add page transitions in two places. You can use the Full Screen preferences to add page transitions to all PDF documents that you view in full-screen view on your system. You can also use the Set Page Transitions command in the Options menu of the Pages panel to add page transitions to an individual PDF document.

3 A user can set system preferences to override a document's opening view settings. The Full Screen preferences override the document's opening view settings.

4 The option to make a presentation play continuously, looping after the last page, is set in the Full Screen preferences.

Lesson 14

14 Working with Pictures and Images

There are many ways Acrobat Professional can help you manage pictures and images. You can export images from a PDF file so you can re-use the images. You can use the image viewer plug-in to view multimedia slide shows and eCards created with Adobe Photoshop Album. You can use the Picture Tasks plug-in to export JPEG files. You can use Acrobat Professional to convert JPEG files from your digital camera into editable Adobe PDF files that you can build into a slide show.

In this lesson, you'll do the following:

• Export images from an Adobe PDF file in JPEG format.

• Copy images and text to the clipboard.

• Use the Picture Tasks plug-in to export, edit, and print pictures using your desktop printer.

• Convert JPEG files from your digital camera to Adobe PDF files and edit the photos in Acrobat Professional.

• Use the Acrobat header and footer feature to add text to your pictures.

• Create Adobe PDF "slide shows" using your PDF picture files.

This lesson will take about 45 minutes to complete.

If needed, remove the previous lesson folder from your hard drive, and copy the Lesson14 folder onto it.

Note: Windows users may need to unlock the lesson files before using them. For information, see "Copying the Classroom in a Book files" on page 3.

All the photographic images used in this lesson, except for the Clarity Ad, are copyright SBR Associates, 2003.

Getting started

The document that you'll work with in this first part of the lesson is the advertisement for Clarifying Lotion. You'll export the background image to a JPEG file so that you can re-use it in other projects.

1 Start Acrobat Professional.

2 Choose File > Open, and select the ClarityAd.pdf file in the Lesson14 folder. Click Open.

3 Choose Advanced > Export All Images.

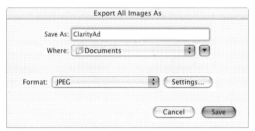

4 In the Export All Images As dialog box, navigate to the Lesson14 folder.

5 Open the Save as Type (Windows) or Format (Mac OS) menu to see the image formats to which you can export images. Make sure that JPEG is selected.

You can export images in JPEG, PNG, TIFF, or JPEG2000 format. For this lesson, you'll use the JPEG format. You'll also use the default conversion settings. (You click the Settings button to change the conversion settings. For information on changing the conversion settings, see "Conversion settings for image files" in the Complete Acrobat 6.0 Help.)

6 Click Save to export all the images in the ClarityAd.pdf file to the Lesson14 folder.

7 Choose File > Close, and close the ClarityAd.pdf file.

Now you'll look at the images that you've exported.

8 From your desktop, navigate to the Lesson14 folder and open it. You'll see two JPEG files—ClarityAd_Page_1_Image_0001.jpg and ClarityAd_Page_1_Image_0002.jpg.

9 Double-click the file ClarityAd_Page_1_Image_0001.jpg to open it. This is the file that contains the background image. (The ClarityAd_Page_1_Image_0002.jpg is an overlay of the bottle of lotion.)

You can import this JPEG file into any image editing application, such as Adobe Photoshop or Adobe Illustrator. The file is fully editable.

Note: The JPEG file should open in Windows Picture and Fax Viewer or Preview, depending on the default image viewing application you have loaded on your system.

When you're finished, close the ClarityAd_Page_1_Image_0001.jpg file and the program you used to view the file.

Copying images to the clipboard

In addition to exporting images in an image file format, you can also copy images or a combination of images and text to the clipboard for re-use in other applications using the Snapshot tool.

First you'll open the advertisement for Clarifying Lotion again.

1 Choose File > Open. Select the ClarityAd.pdf file in the Lesson14 folder, and click Open.

2 Click the Snapshot tool ( ) on the toolbar, and drag to select the headline text and the model's face.

Drag with the Snapshot tool to select text and image . . . which are copied to the clipboard.

The colors in the selected area are reversed momentarily, and a message box advises you that the image has been copied to the clipboard.

3 Click OK to close the message box.

If you select the wrong area with the Snapshot tool, you can start over by clicking outside the selected area and redrawing your selection.

4 On Windows, choose Window > Clipboard Viewer to display the Clipboard. On Mac OS, in the Finder, choose Edit > Show Clipboard.

The Snapshot tool allows you to copy both text and image. However, the resulting image is in bitmap format and the text is not editable.

5 When you are finished, close the clipboard and the ClarityAd.pdf file without saving any changes.

💡 *On Windows, you can create a PDF file from a clipboard image using the File > Create PDF > From Clipboard Image command.*

Exporting, editing, and printing pictures

Increasingly people are using digital cameras and email to send pictures electronically. Acrobat Professional has a new feature, the Picture Tasks plug-in, to help you capture these pictures, edit, and print them either to your own printer or send them to a professional print service.

In this part of the lesson, you'll open an eCard prepared using Adobe Photoshop Album and extract a picture (as a JPEG file) from it.

1 In Acrobat Professional, choose File > Open. Select the GoodLuck.pdf file in the Lesson14 folder, and click Open.

The eCard opens in full-screen view and the two pages of the greeting card display in sequence. After both pages of the card have displayed, the card is displayed in the Acrobat Professional document window.

2 Click OK to close the message box that tells that the document was created using the Adobe Photoshop family of products and that you can access special tools that allow you to work with pictures in the document by clicking the Picture Tasks button.

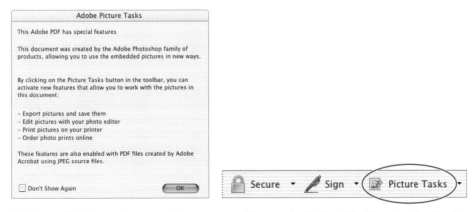

The Picture Tasks button is present when you open a file created with the Adobe Photoshop family of products or when you open a PDF file created by Acrobat using a JPEG source file.

3 If the Adobe Photoshop Album dialog box appears, click its Close button.

4 Click the Picture Tasks button (⬚) on the Acrobat Professional toolbar to open the How To window.

The links in this How To window lead you through tasks related to pictures in the document window.

Exporting pictures with the Picture Tasks feature

In this part of the lesson you'll use the picture task links in the How To window to export (or save) a copy of the night heron picture in JPEG format so that you can use the image outside of the eCard.

1 In the How To window, click the Export Pictures link.

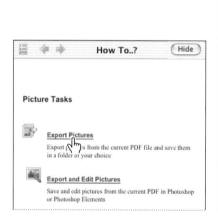
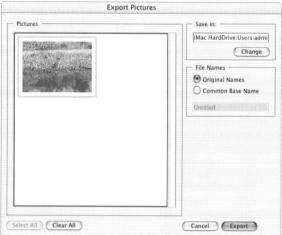

Clicking this link opens the Export Pictures dialog box where you name your picture and choose where to save it. This eCard only has one picture, but if you had received a document containing several pictures, all would be displayed in the Pictures area, and you could select which one or ones you wanted to save and re-use. Because you have only one picture, the heron picture is selected automatically.

2 Click the Change button to select a folder in which to save the picture. Navigate to the Lesson14 folder and click OK or Choose.

3 For File Name, select Common Base Name. Select the "Untitled" text, and name the picture. We entered **NightHeron**.

The Common Base Name option lets you save multiple files using a common name. For example, if your document contained several bird pictures, you could use the Common Base Name, Bird, and then the pictures would be saved with the names Bird1, Bird2, etc.

4 Click Export. (The Export button will not be available unless you have a picture selected in the Pictures area.)

You can easily import the resulting JPEG file into any photo editing program or print it to your desktop printer.

5 To view your exported JPEG file, navigate to the Lesson14 folder and double-click the NightHeron1.jpg file to open it. (You may want to minimize the Acrobat Professional application.) When you are finished, click the Close button to close the JPEG file, and close your viewer application.

Note: The JPEG file should open in Windows Picture and Fax Viewer or Preview, depending on the default image viewing application you have loaded on your system.

Editing and printing with the Picture Tasks feature

If you have an image editing program on your computer, such as Adobe Photoshop Elements, Adobe Photoshop, or Microsoft PictureIt, you can export and edit the picture in the eCard. From Acrobat, simply click the Export and Edit Pictures link in the How To window and follow the on-screen prompts to export the picture into your favorite editing program. Your image editing program is launched automatically, and your image displayed.

Note: You can't import the edited image back into the Acrobat file.

The Picture Tasks plug-in also makes printing pictures easy. You can use the Print Pictures link to print pictures to your desktop printer, or you can use the Order Prints Online link to send your pictures to Adobe or third-party photo finishers.

First you'll see how simple it is to print to your desktop printer.

1 If you minimized the Acrobat Professional application window, restore it to full size.

2 Click the Print Pictures link in the How To window.

3 In the Select Pictures dialog box, click Next. If you had more than one picture, you would select the pictures that you want to print in this window.

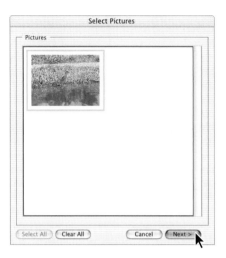

4 Make sure that the correct printer page size is selected in the Layout Sizes menu. We chose **US Letter (8.5 x 11)**.

5 In the Print Sizes list, select the size of print you want. We chose **3.5 x 5** inches.

6 Then we entered 4 for the Use Each Photo option, and pressed Enter or Return to preview the layout.

This combination of settings prints four photographs per page. You can change any of the settings on this page and preview your print sheet before sending the file to your printer.

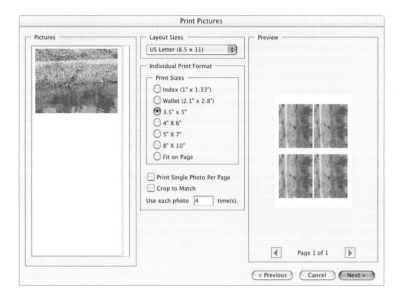

7 When you are satisfied with your print selection and size, click Next to go to your Print dialog box. If you have a color desktop printer, make sure that your printer is selected in the Printer menu, and then you can go ahead and print the images. If you don't have a color printer, or if you don't want to print the pictures, you can click the Cancel button in your Print dialog box to exit the process.

If you don't have a desktop color printer, or if you want professional-quality pictures, you can equally easily send your pictures to an online photo finisher using the Order Prints Online link in the How To window.

8 When you are finished, choose File > Close, and close the GoodLuck.pdf file.

9 Click the Hide button to close the How To window.

Working with digital camera pictures

Most digital cameras store images in JPEG format because this format allows you to store a large number of images in a relatively small space. But what do you do with your images after you download them from the camera onto your computer system? You can certainly store and view them as JPEG files. You can email JPEG files to your friends. But unless your digital camera came with user-friendly image editing software, or unless you have third-party software such as Adobe Photoshop Elements, Adobe Photoshop, or Adobe Photoshop Album, your JPEG files often end up under-viewed and under-used.

If you don't have image editing software on your computer system, or if you haven't learned the image editing software provided with your digital camera, you can use Acrobat Professional to create interesting presentations that you can easily share with your friends and relatives.

The JPEG file format allows you to save a lot of data in a small file space. Unfortunately, you lose image quality each time you re-save a JPEG file. TIFF is an excellent file format for preserving image quality, but TIFF files are very large. Consider editing your images in TIFF format and then saving the final images in JPEG format.

Converting JPEG images to Adobe PDF

In the earlier parts of this lesson, you converted images in Adobe PDF to JPEG format so that you could edit them or re-use them in other applications. In this part of the lesson, you'll convert the JPEG files that you get from your digital camera into Adobe PDF files. Once you have a PDF file, you can crop the image, rotate it, add text and edit it just as you would any other PDF file. And because you're not working with a JPEG file during this editing process, saving the file won't downgrade the image. If you don't have an image editing program, or if you're not confident working in your image editing program, Acrobat provides an easy way to edit and share your digital photographs.

In this part of the lesson, you'll convert a JPEG image file to an Adobe PDF file, crop the file and add text before emailing it to friends.

First you'll preview the JPEG image that you'll be working with.

1 Open the Lesson14 folder, and double-click the Windsor.jpg file to open it.

This is a photograph of part of Windsor Castle in Great Britain. You'll crop the image to reduce the amount of garden in the foreground, and you'll add an identifying message.

2 When you've finished reviewing the JPEG image file, close the file and the viewing application.

Now you'll convert the JPEG file to Adobe PDF.

3 In Acrobat Professional, click the Create PDF button (🖉) on the toolbar, and choose From File from the menu.

4 In the Open dialog box, select the Windsor.jpg file in the Lesson14 folder, and choose JPEG from the File of Type (Windows) or Show (Mac OS) menu. For this lesson, you'll use the default conversion settings. If you want to learn more about the settings, see "Conversion settings for image files" in the Complete Acrobat 6.0 Help.

5 Click Open to complete the conversion of the JPEG file to Adobe PDF.

6 If necessary, click OK to close the Picture Tasks dialog box.

7 Choose File > Save As, name the file **Windsor1.pdf** and save it in the Lesson14 folder.

That's all there is to converting your JPEG files to Adobe PDF.

Cropping your Adobe PDF pictures

1 Click the Fit Page () button so that you can see the entire image.

The image has a lot of garden in the foreground and a path with an unattractive handrail. You'll crop the photograph to reduce the amount of garden and eliminate the handrail.

2 Choose Tools > Advanced Editing > Crop Tool. Your pointer changes to a plus sign (-¦-).

3 Position the pointer over the top left corner of the photograph, and drag to define the cropping area. We dragged from the top left of the picture to the right edge, just above the white bush.

4 Double-click inside the cropping area to open the Crop Pages dialog box. Notice that the units for the cropped page size are given in inches.

Before you fine tune the crop area, you'll change the page units from inches to points to give yourself better control over the position of the crop box.

5 Click Cancel to close the Crop Pages dialog box without making any changes.

6 Choose Edit > Preferences (Windows) or Acrobat > Preferences (Mac OS), and select Units in the left pane of the Preferences dialog box.

7 From the Page Units menu, chose Points.

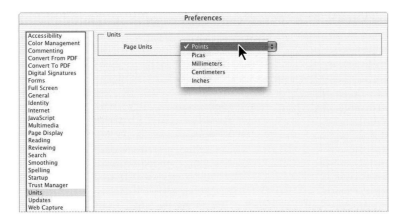

8 Click OK to apply the change.

Now you'll open the Crop Pages dialog box again and fine tune your crop area.

9 Double-click in the crop area (somewhere over the stone tower) to re-open the Crop Pages dialog box.

10 Adjust the cropping area in this box by clicking the up and down arrows in the top, left, right, and bottom text boxes or type in values. You can drag the Crop Pages dialog box by its title bar if you can't see the crop margins clearly. We typed in the values: Top **0** pt, Left **5** pt, Right **40** pt, Bottom **250** pt to remove some of the white space to the right and left, as well as minimize the garden area.

Note: The Remove White Margins option crops the page so that the margins are minimal. This option is useful for trimming the edges of presentation slides saved as PDF files.

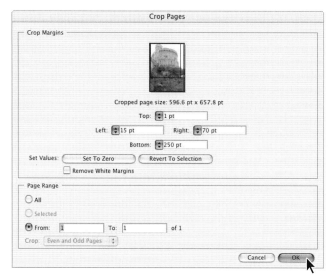

11 Click OK to crop the photograph.

💡 *If you crop a PDF image and don't like the result, you can undo the crop operation by immediately choosing Edit > Undo Crop Pages.*

12 Click the Hand tool, and choose File > Save to save your changes.

Note: We recommend that you reset your page units to inches using the method outlined in Steps 6 through 8.

Adding a personal message

You can use the header and footer feature of Acrobat Professional to identify your picture or add a personal message. For this picture, you'll add a header in the top right of the picture.

1 Choose Document > Add Headers & Footers, and click the Header tab in the dialog box to add text at the top of the page.

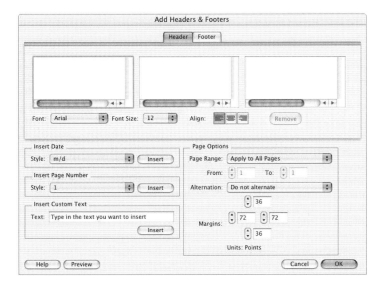

2 In the text box under Insert Custom Text (at the bottom of the dialog box), enter the text **Windsor Castle, Round Tower — May, 2002**, and click Insert.

3 Choose a font from the Font menu. We chose **Arial.**

4 Choose a font size. We chose **14** pt.

5 Click one of the Align buttons (▤) to align the message text. We chose to place our message in the top right corner of the photograph.

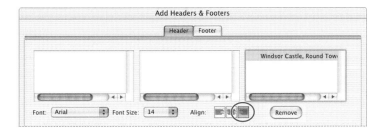

Clicking the Center Align button (▤) centers the message at the top of the photograph, clicking the Left Align button (▤) places the caption at the top left corner of the photograph.

You can adjust the distance of the caption from the top of the page using the Margins values located under Page Options in this dialog box. Notice that the current value for the top margin is 36 points, so your caption will be one half inch from the top of the photo. (72 points = 1 inch, 36 points = 1/2 inch.) You can change the distance of the caption from the top of the photograph by increasing or decreasing the value of the top margin. Similarly, you can increase or decrease the distance of the caption from the right edge of the photograph by increasing or decreasing the value of the right margin. The bottom margin value is used for footers only.

6 Click the Preview button at the bottom of the Add Headers & Footers dialog box to see what your finished photograph looks like. Click OK to return to the Add Headers & Footers dialog box.

7 When you are happy with the position and text of your message, click OK in the Add Headers and Footers dialog box to apply the heading.

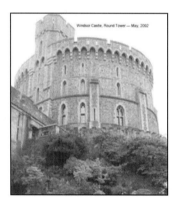

8 Choose File > Save As, and save your finished photograph as **Windsor2.pdf** in the Lesson14 folder.

Changing the color of message text

It was easy to add message text to the Windsor Castle photograph because the expanse of sky made a good background for adding black text. Supposing, however, that you wanted to add a message at the bottom of the photograph. Black text might be hard to read against the background of foliage. In this section of the lesson, you'll see how you can change the color of the message text.

In this part of the lesson, you'll simply change the color of the text in the message that you already created. If you wanted to experiment on your own, you could open the Windsor1.pdf, add a message as a footer, and then change the color of the footer. (To add a footer, choose Document > Headers & Footers, and click the Footer tab. The steps for adding a footer are virtually identical to those for adding a header in "Adding a personal message" on page 391.)

1 With the Windsor2.pdf file open, choose Tools > Advanced Editing > TouchUp Text Tool ( ).

2 Click in the text message that you just added. A text box surrounds the message area. You can edit any text within this bounding box.

3 Drag across the entire line of text to select it all, right-click (Windows) or Control-click (Mac OS), and choose Properties from the context menu.

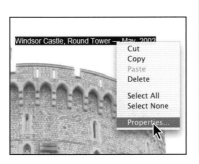
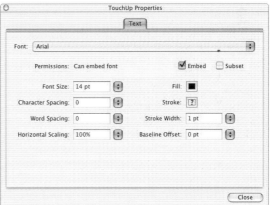

You can change a number of font attributes, including the font, the font size, and the color in the Touchup Properties dialog box. You'll just change the font color.

4 In the Touchup Properties dialog box, click the Fill box to open the color palette, and choose a color. We chose blue.

5 Click Close to apply your changes to the message color, and click outside the message text to see your changes.

For more information on using the Touchup Properties dialog box, see Lesson 7, "Modifying Adobe PDF Files."

6 Choose File > Save As, and save your finished photograph as **Windsor3.pdf** in the Lesson14 folder.

Now that you've cropped your photograph and added identifying text, you can email it to friends.

Emailing pictures from Acrobat

1 Click the Email button ( ) on the Acrobat toolbar to open a new message window in your default email application. Your photograph is automatically attached to a new email message window. All you have to do is fill in the recipient information and add a message and a subject line, and you're ready to send your edited photograph.

For more information on emailing from Acrobat, see Lesson 8, "Using Acrobat Professional in a Document Review Cycle."

2 When you're finished, close your email application and close the Windsor3.pdf file.

Setting up a slide show

You've learned how to convert a JPEG file to Adobe PDF and edit the file. You can also assemble your favorite JPEG pictures and convert them into one Adobe PDF file. You can easily edit, reorganize, and even delete pages in the PDF file. You can add page transitions and sound to convert your photographs into a slide show. You can show the slide show on your computer system, or you can create a CD and share it with others. (For more information on setting up a slide show or presentation, see Lesson 13.)

In this part of the lesson, you'll consolidate a series of photographs of orchids, rotate pages as necessary, add page transitions, and set the document to open in full-screen view.

 These JPEG files are quite large, as is the consolidated Adobe PDF file. If the memory on your computer system is limited, use just a few of the JPEG files instead of using all of them.

First you'll consolidate the JPEG files.

1 Choose File > Create PDF > From Multiple Files.

2 Under Add Files, click the Browse button (Windows) or Choose button (Mac OS).

3 In the Open dialog box, navigate to the Lessons14\Orchid folder and select all the JPEG files. Click the first file and Ctrl-click (Windows) or Command-click (Mac OS) to add other files to the selection.

4 When you have all the files selected, click Add.

5 Look at the files in the Files to Combine window. If necessary, highlight files and use the Move Up and Move Down buttons to arrange the files in numerical order, with file 100-1331.jpg at the top of the list and 100-1338.jpg at the bottom.

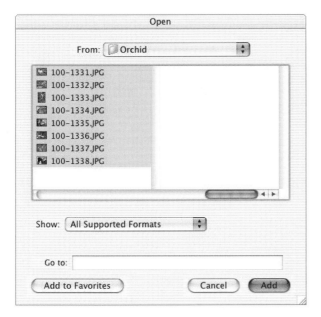

Note: Because of file size limitations on the lesson CD, the file size of these images has been reduced to 3.5 x 5 inches and the resolution to 144 dpi.

6 Click OK to convert and consolidate the files.

A message box shows the progress of the conversion, and when the conversion is complete, the consolidated Adobe PDF file opens automatically with the name Binder1.pdf.

7 If necessary, click Close to close the Adobe Picture Tasks dialog box.

8 Choose File > Save As, and save your file as **Orchids.pdf** in the Lesson14 folder.

Now you'll page through your PDF file to make sure that you have the pictures that you want.

9 Click the Fit Page button (⬜) so that you can see the entire image.

10 Click the Next Page button (▶) until you get the picture of the dog (page 8 in our file). This dog definitely isn't an orchid, so you'll delete the page.

11 Chose Document > Pages > Delete. Make sure that you are deleting only the page on which the dog picture occurs (page 8), and click OK. Click Yes to clear the warning box.

12 Click the First Page button (◀) to go to the beginning of the file.

As you paged through the file, you probably noticed that many of the pictures are wrongly oriented for the slide show. You'll rotate these pages. Because there are so many pages to rotate, you'll use the page thumbnails to rotate several pages at once.

💡 *The toolbar has two buttons—Rotate Clockwise (⬜) and Rotate Counterclockwise (⬜). These buttons change the on-screen view, but the change in rotation is not saved in the PDF file. To change the rotation permanently, you must use the Rotate command.*

13 Click the Pages tab to display the page thumbnails for the file.

14 Select the first picture to rotate. We selected the page 1 thumbnail. Then Ctrl-click (Windows) or Command-click (Mac OS) to add the page thumbnails of other pages that need to be rotated to the selection. We added pages 2 and 6 to the selection.

15 Click the Options button at the top of the Pages panel, and choose Rotate Pages from the menu.

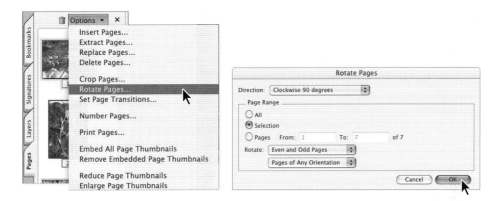

16 For Direction, choose Clockwise 90 degrees. Make sure that the Selection option is chosen, and click OK to rotate the pages.

17 Use the Next Page button to page through the file and check that the orientation of all the pictures is correct.

Now you'll add a page transition effect and set the number of seconds that each picture is displayed.

18 From the Options menu in the Pages panel, choose Set Page Transitions.

19 From the Effect menu, choose a transition effect. We chose **Cover Left Down**.

20 Choose a speed for the transition. We chose **Medium**.

21 Click the check box for the AutoFlip option. (If you don't select this option, and you set your slide show to run in full-screen view, the user will have to press Enter to move from page to page.) Then enter the number of seconds you want each picture to display. We entered **3** seconds.

22 For Page Range, we chose **All Pages in Document**. Then click OK.

23 Click the First Page button (◄) on the status bar to return to the beginning of the file.

Now you're ready to preview your slide show, but if you reset your Full Screen preferences in Lesson 13 to ignore all transitions, you'll need to reset these preferences before you can view your page transitions.

24 Choose Edit > Preferences (Windows) or Acrobat > Preferences (Mac OS), and choose Full Screen in the left pane. Deselect the Ignore All Transitions option, and click OK.

25 Preview your slide show by choosing Window > Full Screen View.

26 Press the Esc key to exit the full-screen view.

27 When you have finished previewing your slide show, choose File > Close, and save and close your work.

In this section, you've set the page transitions and the amount of time each picture displays. If you want this file or slide show to open automatically in full-screen view, you'll need to set the initial view for the file. The steps for doing this are the same as described in Lesson 13, "Preparing Presentations." Lesson 13 also describes how to add sound to your slide show.

Review questions

1 How can you export images from a PDF file?

2 Can you add text messages to your pictures?

3 How do you crop pictures in Acrobat?

4 What's the best way to print pictures?

Review answers

1 There are several ways in which you can export images from a PDF file so that you can re-use the images in an image-editing program.

• You can use the Export All Images command to export images using an image file format such as JPEG, PNG, TIFF, or JPEG2000.

• You can use the Snapshot tool to copy an image to the clipboard. Images copied in this way are copied as bitmap images.

• You can use the Export Pictures link or the Export and Edit Pictures link in the Picture Tasks How To window to export your pictures as JPEG files.

2 Yes. You can use the Add Headers and Footers feature in Acrobat to add text to your pictures.

3 You use the Crop tool to crop pictures.

4 If your pictures were created using the Adobe Photoshop family of products or by converting a JPEG source file to Adobe PDF using Acrobat, you can use the Picture Task Print Pictures link to print pictures to your desktop printer. You can also use the Order Prints Online link to send your pictures to Adobe or third-party photo finishers.

Lesson 15

15 | Working with eBooks

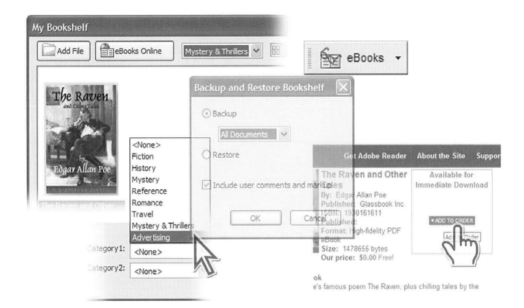

You can use Acrobat Professional as a vehicle for purchasing and borrowing eBooks, as well as for reading eBooks. The My Bookshelf window makes it easy to manage your eBook collection.

In this lesson, you'll learn how to do the following:

• Activate Acrobat Professional as an eBook reader.

• Download a free eBook.

• Set preferences for reading eBooks.

• Check the meaning of a word using the Look Up feature.

• Manage the eBooks on your bookshelf.

If needed, remove the previous lesson folder from your hard drive, and copy the Lesson15 folder onto it.

If you are working on Mac OS, you must have Mac OS, Version 10.2.4 or later installed to complete this lesson.

Note: Windows users may need to unlock the lesson files before using them. For information, see "Copying the Classroom in a Book files" on page 3.

Getting started

Adobe eBook PDF files are PDF files that have been specially packaged to protect the copyright of the author or publisher. You will typically buy eBooks from online bookstores, borrow them from online lenders, or exchange them with other users. Before you can read an eBook file, you must have a license. The license is usually provided by the seller. Also, you must activate Acrobat Professional as an eBook reader.

You can send an eBook to any computer or device in much the same way as you would send any PDF file. The receiving device must also have an activated eBook reader installed. If a recipient attempts to open an eBook file for which they don't have a license, they will be prompted to obtain a license.

Activating Acrobat Professional as an eBook reader

Note: The steps for activating Acrobat Professional as an eBook reader may vary from the steps given below. Please use the activation steps given in this lesson as a guide, but always follow the on-screen directions if they differ from the steps given here.

Before you can use Acrobat Professional to purchase or read eBooks, you must activate the application. If you plan on using multiple devices, such as your laptop and desktop systems and PDAs, you must activate each device separately.

If you want to read eBooks on a Palm OS handheld device, download and activate Adobe Reader for your handheld device. See the Complete Acrobat 6.0 Help for information on how to do this.

You can create an eBook account when you first install Acrobat. If you didn't do so, you'll create an eBook account and activate Acrobat as an eBook reader in the first part of this lesson. If you already have an eBook account you can skip this section and go on to "Adding the eBooks button to the toolbar" on page 407.

1 Be sure you are connected to the Internet.

2 Open Acrobat.

3 In Acrobat, choose Advanced > eBook Web Services > Adobe DRM Activator. Close any warning dialog boxes.

To activate your eBook reader software, you need an Adobe ID and password or a Microsoft.Net Passport ID and password. Follow the on-screen prompts to register as a new user if you don't have these IDs already. On Windows, you may have to select the I Prefer Not to Sign in Using Microsoft .NET Passport option before proceeding.

Note: The process for setting up an eBook account and activating Acrobat may vary depending on your operating system and the type of ID you use. Use the following steps as a guideline, but if in doubt, follow your on-screen prompts. The following steps assume you are establishing a new Adobe ID and that you have not activated Acrobat as an eBook reader.

4 Click the Sign Up for an Adobe ID button. Clear any warning boxes.

5 Select your country of residence from the menu. We selected **United States**. Click Continue.

6 Enter your first name, last name, and email address.

7 Create your Adobe ID and password. Re-enter your password in the Confirm password box, and enter a password hint to help you remember your password.

8 When you have completed the required fields (required fields are marked with an asterisk), click Save Changes.

Acrobat takes you to the Adobe store.

9 Close your browser.

Adding the eBooks button to the toolbar

The eBook button on the Acrobat toolbar offers an easy way to get books online and open the My Bookshelf window where you manage your eBooks.

1 If necessary, maximize the Acrobat window.

2 To add the eBooks button to your Acrobat toolbar, choose View > Task Buttons > eBooks. The eBooks button is present on the toolbar when the option is checked in the Task Buttons menu.

Now you're ready to download your first eBook.

Activating your profile

1 Click the eBooks button () on the Acrobat toolbar, and choose Get eBooks Online.

Acrobat launches your browser.

2 You may be asked to activate Adobe Reader or Adobe Acrobat again before continuing. If so, click Yes. If you aren't asked to activate Acrobat again or sign in, go on to step 2 in the next section, "Downloading your first eBook" on page 408.

3 Acrobat Professional opens your browser and returns you to the Adobe DRM Activator page.

This time, you'll sign in.

4 Enter your Adobe ID and password, and click the Sign In button. Clear any warning dialog boxes.

Now you'll activate your profile.

5 Enter your first name, last name, and email address, and click the Create Profile button.

6 Click the Activate button.

7 A dialog box shows the progress of the activation.

8 Sign out and close your browser.

Downloading your first eBook

1 In Acrobat, click the eBooks button () on the toolbar., and choose Get eBooks Online.

Acrobat takes you to the eBook mall.

2 Navigate to the free eBook downloads available from Adobe Systems by typing the following URL into the Address box of your browser window, and pressing enter:

http://ebookstore.adobe.com/store/

We recommend that you download *The Raven and Other Tales* by Edgar Allan Poe, because it is relatively short.

3 Click the book image, and click the Add to Order button.

Note that the book is free, despite the "Purchase Confirmed" header. You will not be charged for this download.

 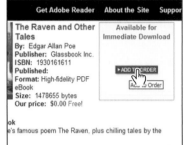

4 Click the Click Here to Download Your eBook button.

A dialog box shows the progress of the download.

Note: By default eBooks are saved in the My Documents/My eBooks directory on Windows 2000 and later and in the Documents:Ebooks folder on Mac OS.

5 Click OK to open the eBook.

Note: If you are redirected to the DRM Activator, follow the directions for activating Acrobat Professional again.

6 Click the Fit Page button (▢) on the Acrobat toolbar to view the entire page.

7 Use the Next Page button (▶) and the Previous Page button (◀) on the status bar to page through the book.

Looking at eBook permissions

eBook permissions control how often you can print and copy an eBook and when a borrowed eBook expires.

1 Choose File > Document Properties, and click Security in the left pane.

2 Click the Show Details button to see the level of permission set by the book publisher.

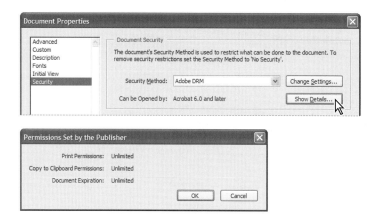

The publisher has placed no restrictions on the printing or copying of content, and there is no time limitation on the use of the book.

3 Click OK, and click OK again to return to the eBook.

Reading an eBook

You can page through an eBook just as you can page through any other PDF file. But you have several additional features to enhance your reading experience.

Smoothing text

You can set the Acrobat preferences to smooth text, line art, and images, which is helpful when you're reading large text sizes or you have a high-contrast between the background and text or image. You can also elect to use CoolType to improve readability, especially with handheld devices and laptops.

1 Choose Edit > Preferences (Windows) or Acrobat > Preferences (Mac OS), and select Smoothing in the left pane.

The default is to smooth text, line art, and images. Leave these options selected.

2 To improve on-screen readability, select the Use Cool Type option, and select the text display that looks best to you. Click the Next button to see additional displays.

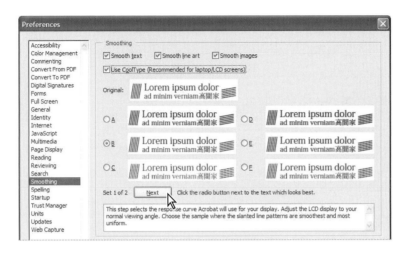

3 When you've found the best display, click OK to apply your changes.

Reading out loud

Depending on your system, you may be able to use the read out loud feature for pages or for the entire book.

1 With your eBook open, navigate to page 5 by dragging across the page number in the page number box on the status bar, typing in 5, and pressing enter or return.

2 On the Acrobat toolbar, choose View > Read Out Loud > Read This Page Only.

If you have the necessary software, the page will be read to you.

3 To stop the reading out loud, choose View > Read Out Loud > Pause or Stop or press Shift+Ctrl+E (Windows) or Shift+Command+E (Mac OS).

You set the preferences for volume, type of voice, pitch, reading order, etc. in the Reading preferences. For more information on setting these preferences, see Lesson 16, "Making Documents Accessible and Flexible."

You determine whether your eBook is automatically opened to the last page viewed in the Startup preferences.

Checking the meaning of words

If you're reading an eBook on your laptop or handheld device, you may not have a dictionary close by. But if you have a connection to the Internet, you can simply select a word and Acrobat will automatically launch your browser to check the meaning of the word. On page 5 of the eBook, you might be unsure of the meaning of nepenthe.

You'll use the Look Up feature to check the meaning of nepenthe. You'll find the word on the second or third line from the bottom of the page.

1 Select the Select Text tool ([T]) on the Acrobat toolbar, and drag across the word **nepenthe**.

2 Right-click (Windows) or Control-click (Mac OS), and choose Look Up "nepenthe" in the context menu.

3 Acrobat launches your browser and takes you automatically to dictionary.reference.com where the word and its meaning are displayed.

4 Close your browser when you are finished reading the information about nepenthe.

Adding notes to eBooks

You can add notes and highlight text in your eBooks, just as you can with any other PDF document.

You just checked the meaning of the word "nepenthe," so now you'll add a note reminding yourself of the meaning.

1 Choose Tools > Commenting > Show Commenting Toolbar.

2 Select the Note tool (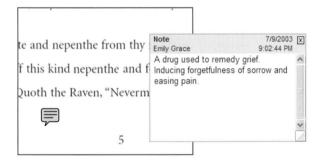) on the Commenting toolbar, and click towards the bottom of the page to add a note.

3 In the open note, type in your reminder. We typed in:

A drug used to remedy grief.

Inducing forgetfulness of sorrow and easing pain.

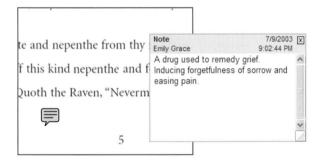

4 Click the Close button on the note to close the note.

You can use all the text markup tools and commenting tools to annotate your eBook, as described in Lesson 8, "Using Acrobat Professional in a Document Review Cycle."

5 Choose File > Save As, and save the file using the same name and folder as were used for the eBook. If necessary, click Replace.

6 Choose File > Close to close your eBook.

In the next part of the lesson, you'll look at how you manage eBooks on your system.

Managing your eBooks

You manage your eBooks in the My Bookshelf window. You can also add and manage non-eBook files in this bookshelf. For example, you might have a collection of reports that you'd like to be able to categorize according to department or subject. You can do that easily by using the My Bookshelf window to assign categories to the reports. In this part of the lesson, you'll add two documents that you used in earlier lessons.

1 To open the My Bookshelf window, click the eBook button and choose My Bookshelf from the menu.

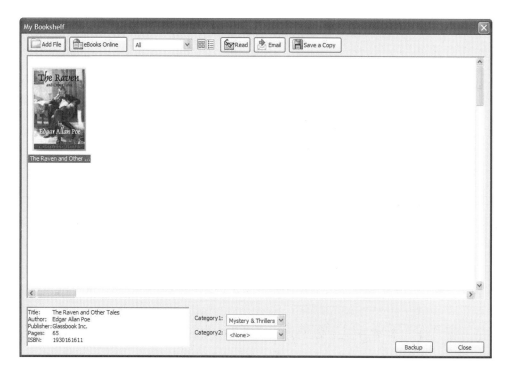

Notice that information about your eBook is displayed in the bottom left of the window. The Category 1 menu shows that the eBook is assigned to the Mystery & Thrillers category.

Now you'll assign another category to the book.

2 Click the arrow to open the Category 2 menu, and choose a second category. We chose **Fiction**.

Later in the lesson, you'll use these category labels to sort your files. Now though, you'll add two more files to your bookshelf.

Adding PDF files to your bookshelf

1 Click the Add File button on the My Bookshelf toolbar, and select Lotion.pdf in the Lesson15 folder. Click Add.

2 Repeat step 1 to add CustCareEB.pdf from the Lesson15 folder.

You should now have three icons on your bookshelf.

Changing the bookshelf display

By default, eBooks and PDF files on your bookshelf are displayed as thumbnails (small images). You'll change the display to a listing of title, author, access information, and category.

1 Click the Detail View button ( ) on the My Bookshelf toolbar.

2 When you're finished reviewing the information on the files, click the Thumbnail View button ( ) to return to the pictorial view.

Now you'll add category information for the two PDF files that you just added.

Using category information

1 Click the icon for the Clarity advertisement. Notice that the category is None.

You can add categories to the category list and you can edit categories that you add. You can't edit the predefined categories. You'll add a category to assign to the files that you've added, and you'll see how you can assign categories and use the category labels to organize your bookshelf display.

First you'll add a category.

2 Click the arrow to open the All menu at the top of the My Bookshelf window, and choose Edit Categories. You may need to scroll down the menu.

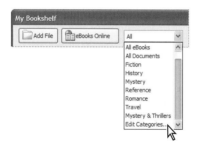

3 Enter the name of your new category. We typed in **Advertising**. Then click Add to add the name to the category list.

4 Click OK to return to the My Bookshelf window.

Now you'll assign the two PDF files that you added to this new category.

5 Select the icon for the Lotion.pdf file in the bookshelf, and click the arrow to open the Category 1 menu. Select Advertising.

6 Repeat step 5 for the CustCareEB.pdf file that you added.

Now you'll see how easy it is to sort files by category.

7 Click the arrow to open the Edit Categories menu at the top of the My Bookshelf window, and choose Mystery & Thrillers.

The only image displayed is that of the *The Raven and Other Tales.*

8 Click the arrow again to open the menu, and choose Advertising.

The two images displayed are those of the two PDF files that you added. Categories make it easy to keep track of the different types of books and files you have on your bookshelf.

9 Click the arrow again to open the menu, and choose All.

Backing up your eBooks.

Especially if you start buying eBooks, you'll want to think about backing up your collection. You can back up your collection with one click of a button from your bookshelf.

1 Click the Backup button at the bottom of the My Bookshelf window, and make sure that the Backup option is selected.

2 Click the arrow to open the menu, and choose which categories to back up. We choose **All documents** because our shelf has PDF files as well as eBooks.

3 Make sure that the Include User Comments and Markup option is checked so that you back up any comment that you have added.

4 Click OK.

5 Choose a folder in which to store your backups (or click New Folder to create a folder), and click OK (Windows) or Choose (Mac OS) to complete the process.

6 To close the bookshelf, click the Close button. Then exit or quit Acrobat.

You can email an eBook from the My Bookshelf window by clicking the Email button on the toolbar. Acrobat automatically opens your email application and attaches the eBook or PDF file that is currently selected.

You can also save a copy of an eBook or PDF file in the My Bookshelf window by clicking the Save a Copy button on the toolbar. You can only save a copy if the publisher permissions allow you to do so.

Borrowing eBooks from an online library

You can borrow, or "check out," eBooks from an eBook library in the same way that you borrow printed books. Borrowed eBooks expire at the end of the loan period and are returned, or "checked in," automatically, so you never have to worry about overdue fees. Because some online libraries limit the number of eBooks that you can borrow at a time, you may want to return a borrowed eBook before it is due. Borrowed eBooks appear in My Bookshelf with a Time-out icon displayed next to the thumbnail of the book. You can click the Time-out icon to view when the eBook expires.

To borrow an eBook from an online library:

1. Locate and select the book you want to borrow.

2. Follow the prompts to complete the download process.

To return an eBook to an online library:

1. Connect to the Internet.

2. Click the Time-out icon next to the eBook thumbnail.

3. In the Document Expiration dialog box, do one of the following:

• Click Return to Lender.

• Right-click (Windows) or Control-click (Mac OS) and select Return to Lender.

–From the Complete Acrobat 6.0 Help.

Review questions

1 Can you read an eBook using Acrobat Professional without activating it as an eBook reader?

2 How can you add notes to an eBook or highlight text?

3 How can you add a category for managing your eBooks?

Review answers

1 No. You must activate Acrobat Professional as an eBook reader before you can download and read eBooks.

2 You can use text mark up and commenting tools on eBooks, just as you can on conventional Adobe PDF files. To save any text mark ups and comments, choose File Save As, and save the eBook under a modified name or replace the original copy.

3 Click the arrow for the Category menu at the top of the My Bookshelf window, and choose Edit Categories. In the next dialog box, enter the name of your new category, and click Add and then click OK.

Lesson 16

16 | Making Documents Accessible and Flexible

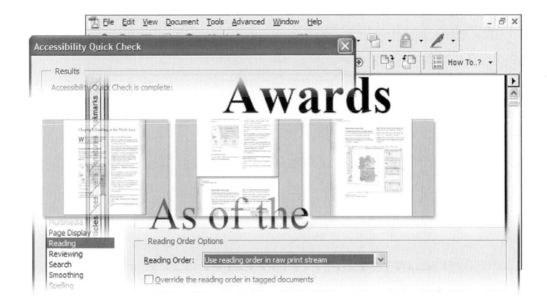

The accessibility and flexibility of your Adobe PDF files determines how easily vision- and motion-impaired users and users of hand-held devices and ebook readers can access the content of your files and reuse the content. You control the accessibility and flexibility of your Adobe PDF files through the amount of structure you build into the source file and the method you use to create the Adobe PDF file.

In this lesson, you'll do the following:

• Review an accessible, tagged PDF file.

• Check a PDF file for accessibility and make it accessible.

• Reflow a document.

• Learn to scroll through a document automatically.

• Review keyboard shortcuts.

• Review the Acrobat features that make it easier for vision- and motor-impaired users to work with Adobe PDF files.

• Change your on-screen display to enhance readability.

This lesson will take about 30 minutes to complete.

If needed, remove the previous lesson folder from your hard drive, and copy the Lesson16 folder onto it.

Note: Windows users may need to unlock the lesson files before using them. For information, see "Copying the Classroom in a Book files" on page 3.

Getting started

In this lesson, you'll look at what constitute flexible and accessible documents, and you'll look at the preferences and features that make it easier for motion- and vision-impaired users to work with Adobe PDF files.

In the first part of the lesson, you'll examine a tagged PDF document and see how easy it is to reflow the document and extract content. Then you'll examine an unstructured document and make it accessible.

In the second part of the lesson, you'll look at the Acrobat 6.0 Professional features that make it easier for motion- and vision-impaired users to access PDF files.

About flexibility

An Adobe PDF file is considered to be flexible when the content can be easily reused— that is, content can be reflowed for viewing on non-traditional monitors, such as hand-held devices, and tables, text, and graphics can be exported for use in other applications. The degree of flexibility of a PDF file depends on the underlying logical structure of the document.

About accessibility

Many people with vision and motor impairments use computers, and Acrobat Professional has a number of features that make it easier for these users to work with Adobe PDF documents. These features include:

• Automatic scrolling.

• Keyboard shortcuts.

• Supports for several screen reader applications, including the text-to-speech engines built-in to Windows and Mac OS platforms.

• Enhanced on-screen visibility.

About structure

For Adobe PDF files to be flexible and accessible they must have structure, and Adobe PDF files support three levels of structure—unstructured, structured, and tagged. Structured PDF files have some structure, but are not as flexible or accessible as tagged PDF files. Unstructured PDF files have no structure, although you can add limited structure even to unstructured files, as you will see later in this lesson. (PDF files created with early versions of Acrobat may not have structure.)The more structure a file has, the more efficiently and reliably its content can be reused.

Structure is built-in to a document when the creator of the document defines headers, columns, adds navigation aids such as bookmarks, and adds alternative text description for graphics, for example. In many cases, documents are automatically given logical structure and tags when they are converted to Adobe PDF. When you create Adobe PDF from Microsoft Office files (2000 and XP) or from files created in later versions of Adobe FrameMaker, InDesign, or PageMaker, or when you create Adobe PDF using Web Capture, the resulting PDF files are tagged. The most built-in structure is obtained when you create a document that has defined structure and convert that document to give tagged PDF files.

Understanding how structure types affect flexibility

A key distinction of the three levels of structure is the presence or lack of a logical structure tree that supports and informs the author's content.

Unstructured Adobe PDF files *Do not have a logical structure tree. All content is treated as a single unit without any hierarchies or relationships.*

You can save unstructured files to other formats, such as RTF, usually with good results. The resulting files retain the author's text and recognize paragraphs as paragraphs. All other formatting, including formatting for basic text, tables, and lists, is lost.

Structured Adobe PDF files *Have logical structure trees that refer to the author's content in a natural reading order.*

Like unstructured files, structured files retain all the text and paragraphs when you convert them, but also recognize and incorporate basic text formatting, such as font attributes. Structured (but untagged) file conversions do not recognize lists or tables. For example, you can create structured PDF files from files you create with Adobe FrameMakerSGML 6.0 or FrameMaker 7.0 running in Structured mode.

Tagged Adobe PDF files *Include a logical structure and a set of defined relationships and dependencies among the various elements, plus additional information that permits reflow. You cannot view or edit tags in Acrobat Professional 6.0. If your work requires you to work directly with PDF tags, you should upgrade to Adobe Acrobat Professional 6.0.*

Tagged files recognize tables, formatted lists, and tables of contents. Tagged files also recognize which content blocks belong to the different stories. Furthermore, tagged files contain text-formatting information such as Unicode values of characters, spacing between words, and the recognition of soft and hard hyphens.

If you want to reflow an Adobe PDF document, especially to a handheld device or to create Web pages, you must start with a tagged file. (See "Creating new, tagged Adobe PDF documents" in the online Help.) A tagged structure also affects how reliably a screen reader works with the file, producing results that are distinctly superior to those of the other two types.

–From the Complete Acrobat 6.0 Help.

Looking at accessible documents

The accessibility of an Adobe PDF document depends on the built-in document structure, and the best built-in structure is obtained when you create a document that has defined structure and when you convert that document to give tagged PDF files.

In the first part of this lesson, you'll examine a tagged PDF file created by converting a Microsoft Word document using PDFMaker on Windows.

Working with a tagged Adobe PDF file

You'll look at the accessibility and flexibility of a tagged PDF file that was created from a Word file.

1 Choose File > Open, and open the Tag_Wines.pdf file in the Lesson16 folder.

2 Choose File > Save As, and save the file as **Tag_Wines1.pdf** in the Lesson16 folder.

First you'll look at the accessibility of the Tag_Wines1.pdf file.

Checking for accessibility

1 Choose Advanced > Accessibility > Quick Check.

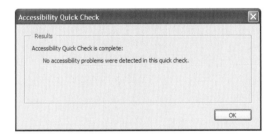

The message box indicated that the document has no accessibility issues.

2 Click OK to close the message box.

💡 *You can add security to your PDF files and still make them accessible. The 128-bit encryption offered by Acrobat 6.0 Professional prevents users from copying and pasting text from a PDF file while still providing access to assistive technology. You can also modify security settings on older PDF documents to make them accessible without compromising security by using the Enable Content Access for the Visually Impaired option.*

Now you'll take a quick look at how flexible a tagged PDF file is. First you'll reflow the PDF file and then you'll save the contents of the PDF file as accessible text.

Reflowing a PDF file

First, you'll adjust the size of your document window to mimic the smaller screen of a hand-held device.

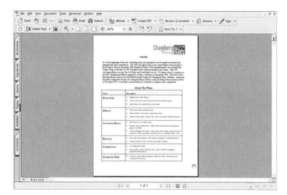

Reduce the size of the document window.

1 Click the Windows minimize button to reduce the size of the document pane, or position the pointer over the bottom corner of the application window and drag until the document pane is the desired size. We made our Acrobat window about 50% smaller.

2 Click the Actual Size button ( ) in the Acrobat toolbar to display the document at 100%.

3 Choose View > Reflow.

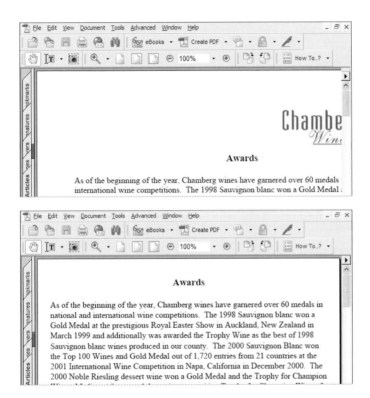

The content of the document is reflowed to accommodate the smaller document screen. Note that you can read an entire line of text without using the horizontal scroll bar.

When you reflow text, artifacts such as page numbers and page headers often drop out because they are no longer relevant to the page display. Text is reflowed one page at a time, and you cannot save the document in the reflowed state. Later in this lesson, you'll reflow a document that was created without structure.

Now, you'll examine the effect of changing the magnification.

4 Click the arrow next to the magnification box on the toolbar, and choose 400% from the menu.

5 Scroll down the page to see how the text reflows. Again, because the text is reflowed, you don't have to use the horizontal scroll bar to move back and forth across the page to read the enlarged text. The text is automatically contained within the document pane.

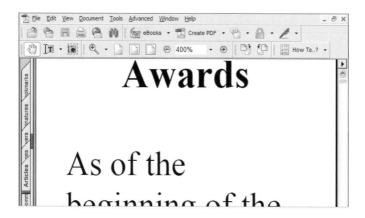

Note: If the magnification is too great and the screen area is too small, you may start to lose text, such as the wine names in the first column of the table. Reduce the magnification or increase the document window size.

6 When you've finished viewing the reflowed text, maximize the Acrobat document window and click the Fit Page button (⬚) on the toolbar to view the entire page of the PDF file.

Now, you'll see how efficiently Acrobat saves the contents of a tagged document for reuse in another application.

Saving as accessible text

1 Choose File > Save As, and in the Save As dialog box, choose Text (Accessible) for Save as Type (Windows) or Format (Mac OS), and click Save.

By default, your file is saved with the same file name and in the same folder, but with a .txt extension.

2 Minimize the Acrobat Professional window using the Windows or Mac OS controls, and navigate to the Lesson16 folder.

3 Double-click on the Tag_Wines1.txt file to open the file in any simple text editor that you have on your system.

Notice how the format of the table is translated into a format that is easily interpreted by a screen reader.

4 When you have finished examining the accessible text, exit or quit your text editor and the Tag_Wines.txt file and maximize the Acrobat Professional window.

5 In Acrobat, choose File > Close to close the Tag_Wines1.pdf file.

With Acrobat Professional you can make documents more readily accessible to all types of users. But Acrobat also offers tools to make it easier for motion- and vision-impaired users to access PDF files.

About automatic scrolling

When you're reading a long document, the Acrobat automatic scrolling feature saves a lot of keystroke and mouse actions. You can control the speed of the scrolling, you can scroll backwards and forward, and you can exit automatic scrolling with single keystrokes.

Now, you'll test the automatic scroll feature.

1 Choose File > Open, and open the AI_ch01.pdf file.

2 Choose View > Automatically Scroll.

3 You can set the rate of scrolling using the number keys on your keyboard. The higher the number, the faster the rate of scrolling. To exit automatic scrolling, press the Esc key.

About keyboard shortcuts

Many keyboard shortcuts are listed to the right of the menu command. Also, many tools can be selected with a single keystroke, but before these keyboard shortcuts are available, you may have to change your General preferences.

1 Move your pointer over the Select Text tool on the toolbar and notice that the tooltip is Select Text Tool. Do not select the Select Text tool; keep the Hand tool selected.

2 If you don't see a keyboard shortcut in the tooltip, choose Edit > Preferences (Windows) or Acrobat > Preferences (Mac OS), and select General in the left pane.

3 Click the check box for the Use Single Key Accelerators to Access Tools option. The option is on when the check box contains a check mark.

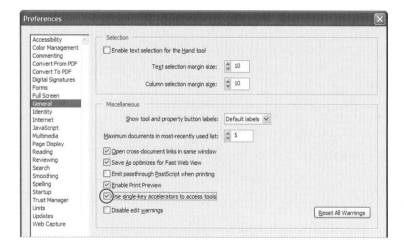

4 Click OK to apply your change.

5 Move your pointer over the Select Text tool again, and notice that the tooltip now contains the name of the tool plus the keyboard shortcut, V. Again, don't select the Select Text tool.

6 Move the pointer into the document pane, and press the V key on your keyboard. The pointer changes from the Hand tool ( ) to the Select Text tool ( ).

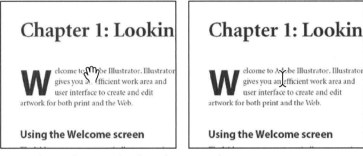

Pointer changes from Hand tool to Select Text tool.

7 Press H on your keyboard to select the Hand tool again.

A list of the keyboard shortcuts that are not displayed next to the associated command or tooltip is available in the Complete Acrobat 6.0 Professional Help.

Note: Acrobat keyboard shortcuts may differ from standard Windows shortcuts. More keyboard shortcuts are available on Windows than on Mac OS.

Setting reading out loud preferences

After you have installed your screen reader or similar application and set it up to work with Acrobat Professional, you can set preferences in Acrobat that control the volume, pitch, and speed of the speech; the nature of the voice; and the reading order.

Note: Newer systems (both Windows and Mac OS platforms) have built-in text-to-speech engines.

In this section, you'll look at the preferences that affect the reading out loud of Adobe PDF documents. Unless you have text-to-speech software on your system, you do not need to set these preferences.

1 To determine if your system has text-to-speech software, click the page number box on the Acrobat status bar, type in 1, and press Enter or Return. This takes you to the first page of chapter1.

2 Choose View > Read Out Loud > Read This Page Only. If your system has text-to-speech software, you will hear page 1 read aloud. To stop the reading, press Shift+Ctrl+E (Windows) or Shift+Command+E (Mac OS).

If you don't have text-to-speech software on your system, go to "Making files accessible" on page 437. If you do have the appropriate software, you can experiment with the following reading options.

3 Choose Edit > Preferences (Windows) or Acrobat > Preferences (Mac OS), and select Reading in the left pane.

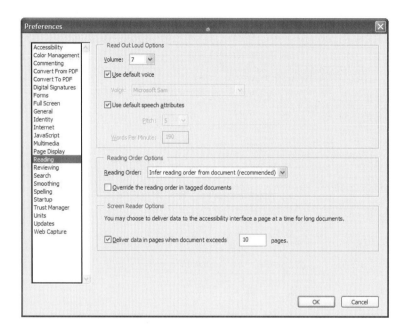

• You can control the volume, pitch, speed, and voice used. If you use the default voice, you cannot change the pitch and speed of delivery.

• If your system has limited memory, you may wish to reduce the number of pages before data is delivered by page. The default value is 10 pages.

4 You need to click OK in the Preferences dialog box to apply any changes that you make. Or click Cancel to exit the Preferences dialog box without making any changes.

You set the reading order options in General preferences.

Looking at the reading order

A well-designed, accessible online document will have a logical reading order. As you saw earlier in this lesson, you can check the accessibility of any document. Now, you'll look at the accessibility of this printed guide that has been converted to a PDF file. This PDF file was designed as a print delivery mechanism, so no attempt was made to make it accessible.

1 Choose Advanced > Accessibility > Quick Check. The message box indicates that the document is unstructured and that it might be necessary to change the reading order.

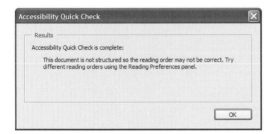

2 Click OK to close the message box.

You'll check the effect of changing the reading order preferences.

3 Click the Next Page button (▶) on the status bar to go to page 2.

4 Choose View > Read Out Loud > Read This Page Only.

5 As you listen to the reading, notice that the left column of text is read first, followed by the caption of the illustration, followed by the right column of text. Unfortunately, the reading of the caption after the end of the left column breaks the logical flow. You'll fix this by changing the reading order preferences.

6 Choose Edit > Preferences (Windows) or Acrobat > Preferences (Mac OS), and select Reading in the left pane.

7 From the Reading Order menu, choose Use Reading Order in Raw Print Stream to use the word order in the PDF document's print instructions. Click OK to apply the change.

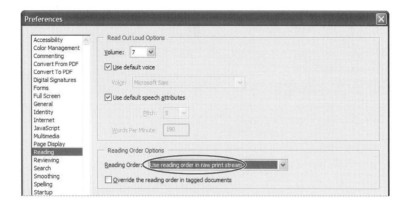

8 Choose View > Read Out Loud > Read This Page Only.

This time as you listen to the reading, notice that the left column is read first, followed by the right column, followed by the caption of the illustration. This is a more logical reading order.

If you are going to be using the text-to-speech function, you should restore the recommended reading order preference (Infer Reading Order From Document).

Making files accessible

As you saw earlier in this lesson, if the document you are reading is accessible, you can zoom in to magnify the view and then reflow text so that you don't have to scroll back and forth across the page when you magnify the view.

1 Choose View, but notice that the Reflow command is dimmed. The document cannot be reflowed because it has no structure.

2 Click the Next Page button on the status bar to go to page 3 of the document.

3 From the magnification menu on the toolbar, choose 400%. Even with a two-column format, you have to use the horizontal scroll bar to read across the column.

Now, you'll make the file accessible and reflow the text for easier viewing at higher magnifications.

4 Choose Advanced > Accessibility > Add Tags to Document.

5 If necessary, click OK to close any message box warning of difficulties.

6 When the process is complete (and it may take a few seconds), choose File > Save As, and save the file as Access_AI_ch01.pdf in the Lesson16 folder.

7 Choose View > Reflow.

Using tools and commands

Tools change the function of your mouse pointer to let you create, select, and modify objects. Commands, meanwhile, let you perform different tasks on objects

The text immediately reflows to fill the width of the screen at 400% magnification. Again, you can read entire lines of text without having to use the horizontal scroll bar.

8 When you are finished, click the Fit Page button (▣) on the toolbar and the Single Page button (▢) on the status bar to view the entire page.

Note: Remember, when you reflow text, artifacts such as page numbers and page headers often drop out because they are no longer relevant to the page display. You cannot save the document in the reflowed state.

Changing the on-screen display

In addition to the options for enhancing on-screen display available in Windows and Mac OS, you can adjust the color of text and background and you can smooth text.

Changing background color

Now you'll experiment with changing the color of the background. Note that these changes affect only the on-screen display on your own system; they do not affect the printed document, nor are they saved with the document for display on systems other than your own.

1 Choose Edit > Preferences (Windows) or Acrobat > Preferences (Mac OS), and select Accessibility in the left pane.

2 Click the check box to select the Replace Document Colors option.

3 On Windows, select Custom Color.

4 Click the Page Background color square to open the color panel.

5 You can select a color from the color picker or you can select a custom color. We choose pale gray.

6 Click OK to apply your changes.

7 You can leave your background color as is, or return it to white.

You can change the background color of form fields and the color of form fields when your pointer moves over them in the Forms preferences. You can change the background color, which is black by default, for full-screen presentations in the Full Screen preferences. You can change the color of the underline used by the spell check feature to identify misspelled words in the Spelling preferences.

Smoothing text

Acrobat allows you to smooth text, line art, and images to improve on-screen readability, especially with larger text sizes. If you use a laptop or if you have an LCD screen, you can also choose to use CoolType to optimize your display quality. For information on smoothing text, see Lesson 15, "Working with eBooks."

Magnifying bookmark text

You can increase the text size used in bookmark labels.

1 Click the Bookmarks tab to open the Bookmarks pane.

2 Choose Text Size > Large from the Options menu of the bookmarks panel.

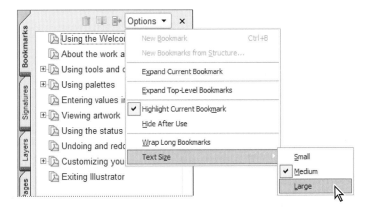

3 When you're finished, close the file and exit or quit Acrobat.

You should experiment with screen display options and other accessibility controls to find a combination that best suits your needs.

Review questions

1 Can you make an unstructured document accessible?

2 What is the difference between changing the magnification when viewing a standard PDF file and changing the magnification when viewing a reflowed PDF file?

3 Where do you turn keyboard shortcuts on or off?

4 How do you check whether or not a file is accessible?

Review answers

1 You can often improve the accessibility of an unstructured document by choosing the Advanced > Accessibility > Make Accessible command. If you can't improve the accessibility sufficiently, try saving the PDF file in accessible text format.

2 When you change the magnification when viewing a standard PDF file, you may need to use the horizontal scroll bars to read the full width of a line of text. When you change the magnification when viewing a reflowed PDF file, the text is reflowed to fit in the visible area; you never have to scroll horizontally to view text.

3 You turn keyboard shortcuts on or off in the General preferences, using the Use Single-Key Accelerators to Access Tools option.

4 Choose Advanced > Accessibility > Quick Check.

Lesson 17

17 Creating Multimedia Presentations

PDF is the perfect format for delivery of multimedia presentations. Whether you use PDF to deliver a presentation, or you distribute a PDF presentation across your entire organization, it is the complete solution for delivering interactive content, including movies and sounds.

In this lesson you will learn how to do the following:

• Add and embed movies and animations to PDF files.

• Add and embed sounds into PDF documents.

• Control movies and sounds through buttons and page actions.

• Control transitions and timing of presentations using Full Screen mode.

If needed, remove the previous lesson folder from your hard drive, and copy the Lesson17 folder onto your hard drive.

Note: Windows users may need to unlock the lesson files before using them. For information see "Copying the Classroom in a Book files" on page 3.

This lesson involves multimedia content that can be shared across multiple computer platforms, and uses several cross-platform formats for the sound and movie files. To view the animated .swf files included in this lesson, your computer needs to have the free Flash player installed, available at www.macromedia.com. To view the movie files used in this lesson, your computer needs to have the free QuickTime Player installed, this Windows and Macintosh movie player is available at www.apple.com/quicktime.

Getting started

In this lesson you'll work on a multimedia tour of the Freedom Trail, which is a National Park that consists of a collection of historic locations in Boston, Massachusetts. The tour visits eight locations, and each location has its own separate page on which you will add a multimedia element, such as a sound or movie file. You will control the sounds, movies and animations using buttons and page actions. You will also add navigational buttons for users to easily move through the document, as it will be presented in the full screen viewing mode, which hides all the menus and palettes.

1 Start Adobe Acrobat 6 Professional.

2 To see what the finished file looks like, open the file FreedomTrail_end.pdf. Your menu bars will be hidden when you open this file because it includes instructions to open into a Full Screen mode. Use the navigational buttons in the document to move through each page.

3 When you have finished examining the completed PDF file, choose Ctrl+L to return to a view that shows all your menus. You can keep this file open for reference while you work on this exercise, or you can close the file by choosing File > Close.

💡 *You can also use the Esc key to leave the full screen mode, but this option can be disabled in Preferences.*

4 Choose File > Open and choose the file FreedomTrail_start.pdf in the Lesson17 folder.

Adding an interactive animation

If the advanced editing toolbar is not open, open it now via View > Toolbars > Advanced Editing. You will use this toolbar to add movies, animations and sounds to your PDF presentation.

1 If necessary, navigate to page one. Choose the Movie tool (▤) from the Advanced Editing toolbar.

The Movie tool and the Sound tool (◀) share the same position on the Advanced Editing toolbar. If the Sound tool is visible, click the arrow to the right of the Sound tool and choose the Movie tool (▦) from the menu that appears. To see both the Movie tool and the Sound tool at the same time, choose Expand this button, which adds both tools to the Advanced Editing toolbar, so they are both visible at the same time.

2 Using the Movie tool (▦), click and drag a rectangle that completely encloses the tan box on the upper left side of first page. This box has been placed for you to use as a guide. After you release the mouse, the Add Movie window appears.

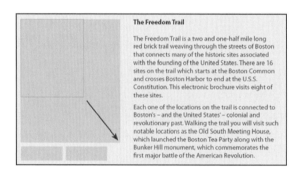

3 In the Add Movie window, select the Acrobat 6 Compatible Media radio button. Click Browse (Windows) or Choose (Mac OS). In the Select Movie File dialog box, choose the file named opening_animation.swf file that is located in the movies folder in the Lesson17 folder. Click the Select button.

After selecting the file, choose the following options in the Add Movie Window:

• Deselect Snap to content proportions

• Select Embed content in document

• Select Retrieve Poster from Movie

Note: When selecting the movie or animated movie files on a Windows computer, it may be necessary to select "Most Common Formats" from the Files of Type drop-down menu, when browsing for the files to input.

Then click OK. The animated movie file appears in the box you created with the Movie tool.

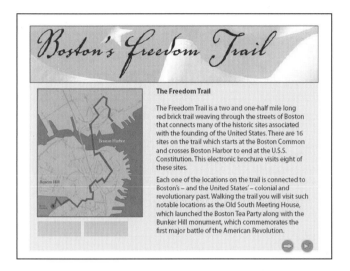

4 If necessary, change the position of the movie file by clicking and holding down on the center of the movie file, and dragging it to the desired location. To adjust the dimensions of the movie file proportionally, shift-click the handles in the corner of the movie file and drag toward the center of the movie to reduce the size, or away from the center to enlarge the size.

Always use the Shift key when resizing a movie or animation file to ensure that it remains proportional. Clicking and dragging without the Shift key may cause the movie or animation to become distorted.

5 Choose the Hand tool (🖐) from the Basic toolbar, and move the cursor over the animated map. The cursor changes to a pointing finger (👆) to indicate that the content is interactive. Click on the center of the Flash animation. The animated map will play. The animation also includes audio. If you cannot hear the audio, you may need to adjust the sound controls on your computer.

To stop an animated movie file, an action must be created that specifically tells Acrobat to stop the playback. Without an action stopping the playback, the file will continue to play, even after navigating to another page. It is advisable to always create an action that allows a user to stop a movie, animation or sound file. This is described in Adding an Action to Stop the Animation *later in this lesson.*

Adding a button

1 Choose the Button tool (■) from the Advanced Editing toolbar. Move your cursor to the upper left corner of the box that is positioned below and to the left of the animated map. Click and drag from the upper left corner of the box to the lower right corner. The Button Properties window opens after you release the mouse.

2 In the Button Properties window, choose the General tab and enter the button name **Start Introduction**. The button name is used by Acrobat to identify this button. The name is not visible to users and does not appear on the button itself.

3 Click on the Options tab in the Button Properties window and enter the Label name of **Start Introduction**. The label name appears on the face of the button, and is the text that is visible to the viewer.

4 Click the Actions tab in the Button Properties window. For the Select Trigger option, keep the default selection of Mouse Up. This indicates that when the mouse is clicked and released, the action will occur. For the Select Action option, choose Play Media (Acrobat 6 Compatible) and then click the Add button. The Play Media (Acrobat 6 Compatible) window will open.

5 In the Play Media (Acrobat 6 Compatible) window, leave the Operation to Perform option set to Play and in the Associated Annotation section of the window, choose Annotation from opening_animation.swf which is listed under Page 1. Click OK in the Play Media (Acrobat 6 Compatible) window and then click the Close button in the Button Properties window.

6 Choose the Hand tool () and test your button by clicking the Start Introduction button.

Adding an action to stop the animation

1 Choose the Button tool (■). Move your cursor to the upper left corner of the box that is positioned to the right of the Start Introduction button you created in the previous step. Click and drag from the upper left corner of the box to the lower right corner. The Button Properties window opens after you release the mouse. Choose the General tab and name the button **Stop Introduction**. For Tooltip, enter **Click to stop movie**.

2 Choose the Options tab in the Button Properties window. In the Label field type the words **Stop Introduction**.

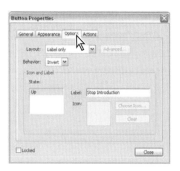

3 Choose the Actions tab in the Button Properties window and keep the Select Trigger option as Mouse Up. Choose Play Media (Acrobat 6 Compatible) from the Select Action options and click Add. The Play Media (Acrobat 6 Compatible) window opens.

Even though you are selecting Play Media as the action, this action is also used to stop a movie. It is also used any time you want to start, stop, pause, resume or re-start a movie, sound or animation.

4 In the Play Media (Acrobat 6 Compatible) window, choose Stop from the Operation to Perform list and in the Associated Annotation portion of the window, choose Annotation from opening_animation.swf, which is listed under Page 1. Click OK and then click the Close button in the Button Properties Window.

5 Choose the Hand tool (✋) and click the Start Introduction button. After the animation starts to play, click the Stop Introduction button to stop the animation. Here you have used the Stop and Start actions. Acrobat 6 Professional also includes actions for pausing and resuming the play of sounds and movies.

If the Stop or Start Introduction buttons do not provide the desired results, you can edit their actions by choosing the Button tool (▪) and double-clicking either button and choosing the Actions tab, then selecting the action to be changed and clicking the Edit button. You may need to edit the action if the Stop Introduction button does not actually stop the media from playing. Because the default Play Media action is to play rather than stop a media element, you may accidentally set the Stop Introduction action to Play rather than Stop.

Adding a show/hide field

Form fields, such as buttons, can be set to appear only when they are needed. For example, you can have a form field that only appears if a certain checkbox or button is selected or when the mouse is in a certain location. Here you will use two overlapping images that have been placed in the PDF as buttons. One of the two images appears when you click a button, and disappears when you click a second button.

1 Navigate to page two. Select the Zoom In tool (🔍). Click and drag a box around both the map and buttons below the map, so that both the map and buttons are visible in the document window.

The red circle on the map with the number 1 in its center will be made to appear and disappear based upon which button is selected. You will start by making the circle hidden by default, and then require the viewer to click the Show Location button for the circle to appear.

2 Choose the Button tool (▪) and move the cursor over the map, a field called boston common location. Red handles around the corners appear when you move your cursor over this field, indicating that it will be selected if you click. Double click on the boston common location button field to open the Button Properties window.

3 In the Button Properties window, choose the General tab and select Hidden from the Form Field drop-down menu. Click the Close button.

4 Select the Hand tool (✋). The red circle showing the location of the Boston Common along the trail is now hidden from view.

5 Choose the Select Object tool (▸). Use this tool to edit all types of form fields, or use a specific form tool to only edit form fields of a certain type. Double-click the Show Location button. The Button Properties window appears.

6 In the Button Properties window, choose the Actions tab. For Select Action choose Show/hide a field. Leave the Select Trigger set to Mouse Up and click the Add button.

7 In the Show/Hide Field window, choose the Show radio button on the right side of the window. From the list of fields, choose boston common location and click OK to close the Show/Hide Field window, then click Close to close the Button Properties window.

8 Choose the Hand tool and click on the Show Location button. The red circle appears on the trail map, showing the location of the Boston Common.

9 Choose the Select Object tool (▶) and double-click the Hide Location button, which is located immediately to the right of the Show Location button.

10 In the Button Properties window, choose the Actions tab in the Button Properties window. Leave the Select Trigger as Mouse Up. For Select Action, pull down the menu and choose Show/hide a field Click the Add button. The Show/Hide Field window appears.

11 In the Show/Hide Field window, choose the Hide radio button on the right side of the window. Choose boston common location from the list of available form fields, and click OK. Click Close to close the button properties window.

12 Choose the Hand tool and alternate between selecting the Show Location and Hide Location button.

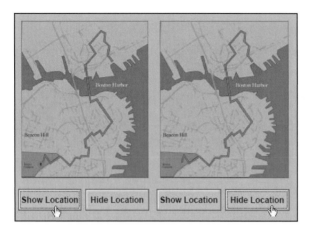

💡 *If buttons do not work as expected, use the Select Object tool and right-click (Windows) or Ctrl-click (Mac OS) and choose Properties. Confirm that the actions applied to the buttons are correct under the Actions tab.*

Adding a movie clip and controlling it with buttons

1 Choose View > Fit Page or click the Fit Page button (▯).

2 If necessary, open the Advanced Editing toolbar by clicking the Advanced Editing task button or choose View > Toolbars > Advanced Editing.

3 Choose the Movie tool (▣) from the Advanced Editing toolbar. Both the Sound tool (◄») and the Movie tool are located in the same position in the toolbar. To change from the Sound tool to the movie tool, click on the Sound tool and select the Movie tool from the menu that appears.

4 Using the Movie tool, click and drag to create a frame in the empty space on the page, immediately to the right of the Play Multimedia and Stop Multimedia buttons. After you have created the frame, the Add Movie window appears.

Note: You may see a brief dialog box informing you that Acrobat is initializing the authoring system.

5 In the Add Movie window, choose the Acrobat 6 Compatible Media radio button and click the Browse button (Windows) or Choose button (Mac OS) to select the movie file. Navigate to the Lesson17 folder and choose Boston_Common.mov from the movies folder. Click the Select button, then click the OK button to close the Add Movie window. The movie is added to your page.

6 If necessary, move the file by clicking and dragging it so that it is positioned to the right of the Play and Stop buttons, and above the navigational buttons. The movie file should not be resting on top of any other content.

7 Choose the Hand tool (🖑) and move the cursor over the movie. The cursor changes to a pointing finger (👆) to indicate that the content is interactive. Click on the center of the movie file and the movie will play.

8 Choose the Select Object tool and double-click on the Play Multimedia button positioned to the left of the movie. Click the Actions tab and, from the Select Action, pull-down menu, choose Play Media (Acrobat 6 Compatible). Leave the Select Trigger set at Mouse Up and click the Add button. The Play Media (Acrobat 6 Compatible) window opens.

9 In the Play Media window, choose Annotation from Boston_Common.mov from the list of Associated Annotations and leave the Operation to Perform option set to Play. Click OK, then click Close to shut the Button Properties window.

You can test your first button if you wish, however we will be adding a stop action to the second button so users can have the option of stopping the movie.

10 Double-click the Stop Multimedia button and choose the Actions tab in the Button Properties window that appears. Keep the default Select Trigger set to Mouse Up. From the Select Action pull down menu, choose Play Media (Acrobat 6 Compatible) and then click the Add button. The Play Media (Acrobat 6 Compatible) window opens.

11 In the Play Media (Acrobat 6 Compatible) window select Stop from the Operation to Perform options and choose Annotation from Boston_Common.mov from the list of Associated Annotations and click OK. Click the Close button to close the Button Properties window.

12 Choose the Hand tool () and click the Play Multimedia and Stop Multimedia buttons to start and stop the movie.

Adding, aligning and duplicating navigational buttons

1 Click the Next Page button in the lower right corner of the document. Note that the button has an action that takes you to another page. Return to page 2.

2 Choose the Button tool (■) from the Advanced Editing toolbar. Click and drag a square to the left of the Next Page button that is approximately the same size as the other two buttons.

When you finish drawing the frame for the button, the Button Properties window opens. Click the General tab and enter the name for the button as **Previous Page**.

3 In the Button Properties window, click the Appearance tab. Click the Fill color swatch and choose No Color from the available colors. This sets the fill color of the button to be transparent.

4 Click the Options tab and in the Layout menu choose Icon Only.

5 For the Behavior option choose Push. The three separate options appear in the State portion of the window after choosing Push for the Behavior options: Up, Down, and Rollover.

6 If it's not already selected, click the Up state and then click the Choose Icon button to select a graphic that will be positioned on the button as it is up. In the Choose Icon window that appears, click the Browse button and navigate to the buttons folder in the Lesson17 folder and choose previous_page.pdf to use as the button, then click Select. A preview of the button appears in the Choose Icon window. Click OK to confirm the selection of this graphic.

7 Choose the Rollover state and click the Choose Icon button to select a graphic that will be positioned on the button as the mouse rolls over the button. In the Choose Icon window that appears, click the Browse button and if necessary, navigate to the buttons folder in the Lesson17 folder, choose previous_page_rollover.pdf. A preview of the button appears in the Choose Icon window. Click OK to confirm the selection of this graphic.

8 Click on the Actions tab to assign an action to this button. Choose Execute a menu item from the Select Action menu. Note that the menu choices may extend both above and below the menu selection, so you may need to scroll up in the menu to locate the Execute a menu item choice. Leave the Select Trigger option set to Mouse Up and click the Add button. The Menu Item Selection window appears.

In the Menu Item Selection window, choose View > Go To > Previous Page (Windows), or from the menu, select View > Go To > Previous Page (Mac OS), then click OK. Click Close to close the Button Properties window.

9 Select the Hand tool and click on the Previous Page button you created in the previous steps. Return to page 2.

Adding a first page button

1 Choose the Button tool (■) from the Advanced Editing toolbar. Click and drag a square to the left of the Previous Page button that is approximately the same size as the other two buttons. When you finish drawing the frame for the button, the Button Properties window opens. Click the General tab and enter the name for the button as **First Page**.

2 In the Button Properties window, click the Appearance tab. Click the Fill Color swatch and choose No Color from the available colors. This sets the background color of the button to be transparent.

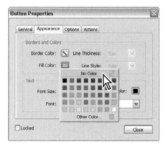

3 Click the Options tab and in the Layout menu choose Icon Only.

4 For the Behavior option choose Push. Note that three separate options appear in the State portion of the window after choosing Push for the Behavior options: Up, Down, and Rollover.

5 Click the Up state and then click Choose Icon to select a graphic that will be positioned on the button as it is up. In the Choose Icon window that appears, click the Browse button and navigate to the buttons folder in the Lesson17 folder and choose first_page.pdf. A preview of the button appears in the Choose Icon window. Click OK to confirm the selection of this graphic.

6 Choose the Rollover state and click Choose Icon to select a graphic that will be positioned on the button as the mouse rolls over the button. In the Choose Icon window that appears, click the Browse button and navigate to the buttons folder in the Lesson17 folder and choose first_page_rollover.pdf to use as the button and click Select. A preview of the button appears in the Choose Icon window. Click OK to confirm the selection of this graphic.

7 Click on the Actions tab to assign an action to this button. Choose Execute a menu item from the Select Action menu. Note that the menu choices may extend both above and below the menu selection, so you may need to scroll up in the menu to locate this choice. Leave the Select Trigger option set to Mouse Up and click the Add button and the Menu Item Selection window appears.

In the Menu Item Selection window, choose View > Go To > First Page (Windows) or from the menu, select View > Go To > First Page (Mac OS), then click OK.

8 Choose Close on the Buttons Property Window.

9 Choose the Hand tool (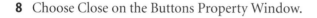). Click on the buttons to change from one page to another.

Aligning buttons

1 Choose the Select Object tool (⬉).

2 Shift-click to select each of the buttons.

3 Right-click (Windows) or Ctrl-click (Mac OS) on any button and choose Align > Bottom from the pop-up menu.

4 The buttons all align with the bottom of the button on which you Right-click (Windows) or Ctrl-click (Mac OS).

Duplicating buttons

1 On page 2, confirm the four navigational buttons in the lower right corner are selected. If necessary, Shift-click each button to select them all with the Select Object tool.

2 Right-click (Windows) or Ctrl-click (Mac OS) on any of the four buttons, making certain that they remain selected.

3 Choose Duplicate from the contextual menu

4 In the Duplicate Field window, enter in the From textbox **3** and in the To textbox **9**. Click OK.

5 Click on the Hand tool and begin navigating through the document, using the buttons you've created.

Adding a sound file and adding two actions to one button

1 Navigate to page 3. If the Advanced Editing toolbar is not currently visible, choose View > Toolbars > Advanced Editing.

2 Select the Sound tool (◀») and draw a small square at the bottom of the page on the white area near the edge. The size and exact location are not critically important, as the box will be hidden from view.

 Remember that both the Sound tool (◀») and the Movie tool (▣) are located in the same position in the toolbar. To change from the Movie tool to the Sound tool, you may need to click on arrow to the right of the Movie tool and select the Sound tool from the menu that appears. To make both tools visible at the same time, click on either tool and choose Expand this Button from the menu that appears.

3 In the Add Sound window, choose the following options:

• Acrobat 6 Compatible media

• Embed content in document

Then click the Browse button to identify the location of the Sound file that you are adding to the presentation. Navigate to the sound file Statehouse_audioclip.wav in the audio folder in the Lesson17 folder, and click Select to choose the file. Click OK to close the Add Sound window.

4 Double click the frame that was created in the previous step. Note that the frame containing the sound contains a border.

5 In the Multimedia Properties window, click the Appearance tab and choose Invisible Rectangle from the Border Type drop-down menu. This removes the black border around the perimeter of the frame containing the sound, making the sound border invisible on the PDF page. Click the Close button to shut the Multimedia Properties window.

Adding multiple actions to one button

Because the sound and movie files are added to this page separately, you will add two actions to a single button to cause both the sound and the movie to play at the same time.

1 Choose the Select Object tool (⬆) and double-click the Play Multimedia button. The Button Properties window appears.

2 Click on the Actions tab. For Select Trigger, keep the default setting of Mouse Up and for Select Action choose Play Media (Acrobat 6 Compatible). Click the Add button.

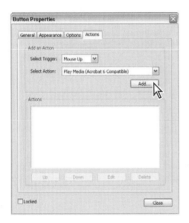

3 In the Play Media (Acrobat 6 Compatible) window, choose Play as the Operation to Perform. Choose Annotation from Statehouse_audioclip.wav from the list of Associated Annotations and click OK.

Do not close the Button Properties window, as you will add another action for this button. The second action will also be a Play Media (Acrobat 6 Compatible) action, and will also occur when the mouse is clicked and released, so do not change these settings.

4 Click the Add button and choose Annotation from Statehouse.mov from the list of Associated Annotations in the Play Media (Acrobat 6 Compatible) window. Click OK and then click the Close button in the Button Properties window.

5 Choose the Hand tool and click the Play Multimedia button to play both the sound clip and movie clip simultaneously.

Creating page actions to stop multimedia clips

In the previous section, you controlled both sound and movie elements through a button action. You can also use other methods for starting or stopping a sound or movie files. Here you will create an action to cause a movie to play when a page is opened. When the page closes, you will have the movie stop playing.

When you play either sound or movie files in Acrobat, they continue to play until the file has reached its end or an action tells it to stop. For example, if you start playing the movie files on page 3, and then move to a different page before the movie is complete, it will continue playing even after you move to the other page.

1 Open the Pages panel by clicking the Pages tab on the left side of the screen or choose View > Navigation Tabs > Pages.

2 In the Pages panel, right-click (Windows) or Ctrl-click (Mac OS) the page 3 thumbnail. From the context menu that appears, choose Page Properties.

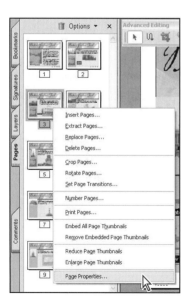

3 Click on the Actions tab in the Page Properties window. For Select Trigger, choose Page Close and for Select Action choose Play Media (Acrobat 6 Compatible) then click the Add button. The Play Media (Acrobat 6 Compatible) window appears.

4 In the Play Media window, choose Stop from the Operation to Perform menu and then choose Annotation from Statehouse.mov from the list of Associated Annotations. After making these selections, click OK. This action stops the movie from playing whenever the page is closed.

5 In the Page Properties window, choose the Select Trigger of Page Close and the Select Action as Play Media (Acrobat 6 Compatible) and then click Add. Choose Stop for the Operation to Perform and choose Annotation from Statehouse_audioclip.wav as the sound file that will be affected by this action. Click OK, and then click Close to close the Page Properties window.

6 Choose the Hand tool (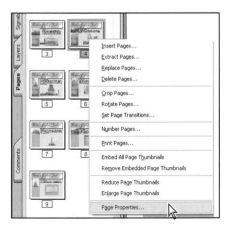) and click the Play Multimedia button. As the multimedia clips are playing, click on the next page button. Both the sound and movie files stop playing after you navigate to another page of the document.

Creating page actions to start multimedia clips

Just as you created a page action that stopped movie and sound files, you can also create a page action which plays a multimedia clip when a page is opened.

1 Navigate to page four. A movie file has already been placed on the page for you.

2 Open the Pages panel by clicking its tab on the left side of the screen or choosing View > Navigation Tabs > Pages and Right-click (Windows) or Ctrl-click (Mac OS) on the page thumbnail representing page four. Choose Page Properties from the context menu. The Page Properties window appears.

3 Click on the Actions tab and set the Select Trigger option to Page Open. Choose Play Media (Acrobat 6 Compatible) and then click the Add button. The Play Media (Acrobat 6 Compatible) window opens. Choose Play as the Operation to Perform. From the Associated Annotations list choose Annotation from Granary.mov and click OK, then click Close to close the Page Properties window.

4 Choose the Hand tool (🖐). Using either the navigational buttons in this document, or the previous page button, navigate to page 3, then return to page 4 to see the movie clip automatically start playing.

Opening a movie clip in a floating window

1 Navigate to page 5. This page already includes a movie file along with a button to play the movie. This movie plays in the default location, in its current frame located on the document page. You will change the movie so that it plays in a separate window.

2 Choose the Select Object tool (▶) and double-click the movie frame. In the Multimedia Properties window that opens, choose the Settings tab. Select rendition from Old _South.mov from the list of renditions, then click the Edit Rendition button.

Note: You may need to scroll to locate this object.

3 In the Rendition Settings window, choose the Playback Location tab. For Playback Location, change the current setting of In Document to Floating Window and keep this window open.

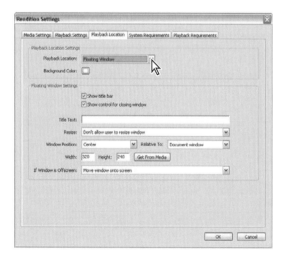

4 In the Floating Window Settings at the bottom of the window, click the Get From Media button to set the size of the window based upon the size of the movie file.

5 Choose the Playback Settings tab and select the Show Player Controls option. This allows viewers to pause, rewind and adjust the sound volume of the movie file as it is playing in the floating window. Click OK to close the Renditions Settings window.

6 Click the Close button to close the Multimedia Properties window.

7 Choose the Hand tool () and click the Play Multimedia button to see the movie play in a separate window.

Creating a full screen presentation with transitions

Here you will view your PDF document without all of the tools and menus by using the Full Screen viewing mode. You will also create transitions that vary how the screen changes from one page to the next.

1 Open the Pages panel. Shift-click to select both page 1 and page 2. Right-click (Windows) or Ctrl-click (Mac OS) on the thumbnail of either page. Choose Set Page Transitions from the context menu that appears.

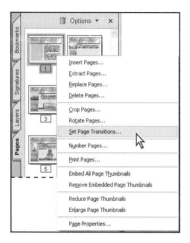

2 In the Set Transitions window, choose Fade from the Effect options. Check the Auto Flip checkbox, and choose 30 Seconds from the After drop-down menu. In the Page Range portion of this window, confirm that the option Pages selected in Pages panel is selected, and then click OK.

These choices will cause this page to fade into these pages whenever the document is viewed using the Full Screen mode. Also, if the first page is not changed manually, it will automatically move to the next page after 30 seconds.

3 In the Pages panel, right-click on the page thumbnail for Page 3. From the context menu, choose Set Page Transitions and from the Effect options, choose Random Transition. In the Page Range portion of the window, choose Pages Range and enter from 3 to 9. Click OK after entering these settings.

4 Navigate to the first page of the document. To view the presentation using the Full Screen mode, choose Window > Full Screen View. Wait 30 seconds to test the automatic transition, or click the Next Page button to view the Fade effect as the page transitions from page 1 to page 2. To exit Full Screen viewing mode, use the Esc (Escape) Key on the upper left corner of your keyboard, or press Ctrl+L.

5 To set the entire document to always open in the Full Screen viewing mode, choose File > Document Properties and select the Initial View option. In the Window Options portion of this window, check Open in Full Screen Mode and then click OK.

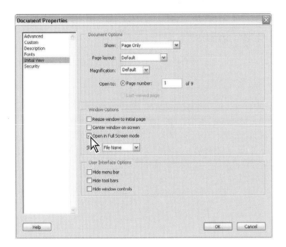

6 Save your PDF presentation file, close the document and then reopen it. The file then opens directly into the Full Screen mode.

On your own

1 On pages 6-9 add the following

• Sound files for each page.

• Play buttons for the movie and sound clips on each page.

• Show/hide buttons for the map on each page.

2 Explore the full screen preferences by choosing Edit > Preferences (Windows) or Acrobat > Preferences (Mac) and selecting Full Screen.

• You can override the page transitions so that they use those set in the preferences, and not those set in the file.

• If you do not want to use the Escape key to leave the Full Screen mode, deselect Escape key exits.

• Choose Loop after last page to have the file return to the first page after viewing the last page in a file.

3 Change the movie rendition settings to have the movie files play in their own window. Try having the movie files play both with and without a visible controller.

Review questions

1 Why would you convert an existing presentation to Adobe PDF? Why would you create a new multimedia presentation using the Sound and Movie tools of Adobe Acrobat 6 Professional?

2 Are you able to automatically start playing sound and movie files, and how would this be useful?

3 How can you make a form field, such as a button, invisible? Why would you do this?

Review answers

1 As a universal file format, Adobe PDF files are not limited by the software on the recipient's computer or the fonts used when creating a file. Typical presentation software files, such as PowerPoint, require the recipient of a presentation to have the presentation software on their computer, along with the same fonts used when the file was created. Presentations delivered as an Adobe PDF can be viewed by users on many computer systems—including Palm, Windows, Macintosh and various forms of Unix.

2 Movie and sound files can be started based upon a number of actions. These can include a page being opened or closed, or the mouse being moved to a certain location on the page. You can even have sounds or movies play because the viewer has moved their cursor to a certain form field. These automatic actions are helpful for delivering presentations or presenting information about a document, with minimal effort on the part of the viewer.

3 Set a Button Field's properties to Hidden to keep it from displaying or printing. Buttons and form fields can be made visible or invisible for both on-screen and printing purposes. This can be useful if you want a button to be visible on screen, but not print. For multimedia purposes, you can have buttons that are not visible until a certain action occurs. Clicking on a portion of the document can cause a graphic or text to appear on the page.

Lesson 18

18 | Using Acrobat's Engineering and Technical Features

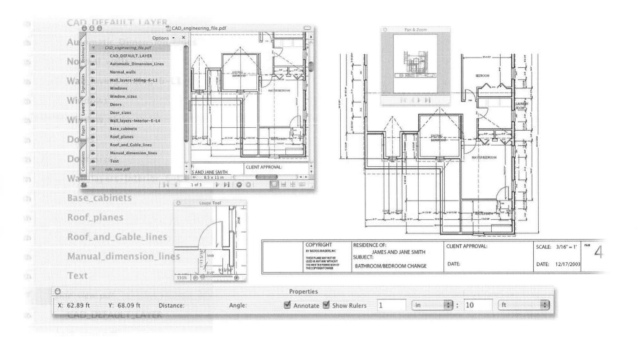

Adobe Acrobat Professional 6.0 lets you share technical drawings with clients and colleagues while maintaining control over your valuable documents. You can clearly communicate project needs using special review and commenting tools that are designed for the needs of technical professionals.

In this lesson you will learn how to do the following:

- Merge separate PDF documents into one consolidated file.

- Use Layers created in an AutoCAD drawing.

- Work with Acrobat's measuring tools.

- Use navigational tools to easily move through PDF documents.

If needed, remove the previous lesson folder from your hard drive, and copy the Lesson18 folder onto your hard drive.

Note: Windows users may need to unlock the lesson files before using them. For information, see "Copying the Classroom in a Book files" on page 3.

Getting started

In this lesson you'll work on the architectural plans for a home remodeling project that is adding three new rooms to a home. You will combine three independent PDF files, work with the layers from the AutoCAD file, add measurements, comments and use special navigational tools that make it easy to view technical illustrations.

1 Start Adobe Acrobat Professional 6.0.

2 To see what the finished file looks like, open the file engineering_end.pdf. Notice the document contains several pages including different views of this construction project.

3 You can keep this file open for reference while you work on this exercise, or you can close the file by choosing File > Close.

Merging documents

You will start by combining three separate Computer Aided Design (CAD) drawing files into one single PDF file. Sharing these files as PDF allows those who do not have specialized design software to view the drawings. And rather than having users open three separate files, they will have all the files they need in one document.

1 Choose File > Open and navigate to the Lesson18 folder. Choose the file rear.pdf and click the Open button.

2 Click the Pages tab along the right side of the document window, or choose View > Navigation Tabs > Pages.

3 In the Pages panel, choose Options > Insert Pages. The Select File to Insert window appears.

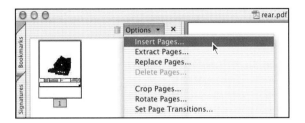

4 If necessary, navigate to the Lesson18 folder. Click once to select the file side.pdf. Ctrl-click (Windows) or Command-click (Mac OS) the floorplan.pdf. Both the side.pdf and the floorplan.pdf file should be selected.

5 Click the Select button. The Insert Pages window opens.

6 In the Insert Pages window, confirm the pages are being inserted After Page 1, then click OK.

7 The PDF file now includes three pages showing the different views of the building project.

Enhanced navigation tools: pan & zoom

Using the Pan & Zoom window, it is easy to focus on important portions of your documents.

1 Navigate to page 3, the floorplan view of the construction project.

2 Choose View > Fit Page.

3 Choose Tools > Zoom > Pan & Zoom Window. The Pan & Zoom window opens. If necessary, move this window to the side of the window so that the architectural plans are also visible.

4 In the Pan & Zoom window, notice the red box surrounding the frame. Click the handle in the upper left corner of the red box. Drag the handle straight down, until the top line of the red frame is aligned with the top portion of the drawing.

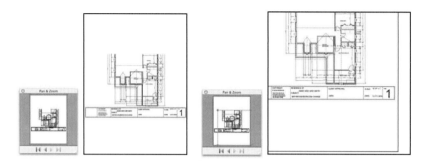

5 In the Pan & Zoom window, click and drag the lower left corner handle up and to the right. Stop when the bottom of the red frame is aligned with the bottom of the drawing.

6 Continuing to work in the Pan & Zoom window, click the handle in the upper right corner of the red box surrounding the Pan & Zoom window. Drag down and to the left. Stop when the focus of the document window is on the Master Bath.

Maintain a view that allows you to see this entire room. If necessary, click and drag the center of the red box in the Pan and Zoom window to reposition the visible portion of the page. You will be measuring several items in this area.

7 Click on the Close button in the upper corner of the Pan and Zoom window to close it.

Working with layers

This document was created using AutoCAD. Adobe Acrobat Professional 6.0 is able to preserve layers from AutoCAD and Visio files, which can be enabled or disabled for viewing. This makes it easier to focus on the information in your file that is most relevant.

1 Click the Layers tab or choose View > Navigation Tabs > Layers to open the Layers panel.

2 If necessary, in the Layers panel, click the plus sign (+) (Windows) or triangle (▶) (Mac OS) located to the left of the floorplan section. This makes all the layers in this section available for modification.

If you can already see a number of layers visible under the heading floorplan, do not click, as this will hide the layers for this portion of the PDF document.

3 In the Layers panel, click the Eye icon (👁) located to the left of the layer name for each of the following layers:

• Automatic Dimension Lines

• Window sizes

• Door sizes

• Roof Planes

All the text, lines and other elements on these layers are now hidden from view.

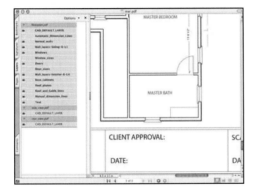

💡 *The Eye icon (👁) in the Layers panel is used to represent layers that are visible. If the icon is not visible and a layer's objects are hidden, you can make a layer visible by clicking in the first column of the layer's panel, to the left of the layer name. By default, layers that are not visible do not print.*

About Acrobat layers

Information can be stored on different layers of an Adobe PDF document. The layers that appear in the PDF document are based on the layers created in the original application. You can examine the layers and show or hide the content associated with each layer using the Layers tab in the Navigation panel.

You can select or copy content in a layered Adobe PDF document using a selection tool, such as the Select Text tool, or the Snapshot tool. You can edit content using a touch-up tool. These tools recognize and select any content that is visible, regardless of whether the content is on a selected layer.

If the content that you edit or delete is associated with one layer, the content of the layer reflects the change. If the content that you edit or delete is associated with more than one layer, the content in all the layers reflects the change. For example, if you want to change a title and byline that appear on the same line on the first page of a document, and the title and byline are on two different visible layers, editing the content on one layer changes the content on both layers.

You can add content, such as review comments, stamps, or form fields, to layered documents just as you would to any other PDF document. However, the content is not added to a specific layer, even if that layer is selected when the content is added. Rather, the content is added to the entire document.

—From the Complete Acrobat 6.0 Help

Changing layer attributes

Using the Layers panel, you can control which layers are visible when a document is opened, and whether individual layers print.

1 Right-click (Windows) or Ctrl-click (Mac OS) the Base_cabinets layer and choose Properties. The Layer Properties window opens.

2 In the Layer Properties window, for Default state, choose Off. For Print, choose Never Prints. Leave the other settings in this window unchanged, and click OK.

Using measuring tools

You will add some measurements to this file, helping to clarify the size of some of the windows in the drawing. Additionally, you will have Acrobat calculate both the area and perimeter of portions of the construction project.

Using rulers and the distance tool

1 Choose View > Rulers to display rulers on the top and side of the document window.

2 Position your cursor over the horizontal ruler across the top of the document window. Click in the window and drag downward, stopping when the ruler guide is aligned with the top of the window on the right side in the Master Bath.

3 Click and drag a second ruler guide from the rulers at the top of the page, positioning the second guide along the bottom of the same window

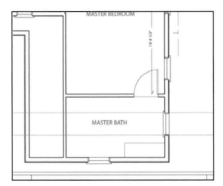

The guides extend to the ruler, allowing you to measure the distance or confirm alignment with other objects. Acrobat also provides automatic measuring tools that can calculate the measurement for you.

4 Choose View > Toolbars > Measuring. The Measuring toolbar appears.

5 Click the Distance tool (↔), and the Properties toolbar is displayed.

6 In the Properties toolbar, set the scale for the drawing by changing the 1 in : 1 in to 1 in : **10.75** ft.

7 Click once on the top of the window on the right side of the Master Bath, then click once on the bottom of the same window. Hold down the Shift key while clicking to keep the line straight.

The size of the opening is displayed in the Properties toolbar as approximately 2.5 ft.

8 In the Properties toolbar, click the Annotate checkbox. Repeat the process of measuring the window with the Distance tool (↦). Acrobat creates an annotation showing the distance of the area you have measured. The distance is displayed when you roll your cursor over the annotation.

9 Repeat this process to measure the window along the bottom side of the drawing.

Measuring perimeter and area

1 Using the Layers panel, click to turn off the following layers so they are not visible:

- Doors

- Roof and gable lines

2 If necessary, scroll up so the Master Bedroom is entirely visible.

3 Choose the Perimeter tool (⌐↴) and click in the upper left corner of the Master Bedroom. Proceed to click in all four corners of the room, moving counter-clockwise to the bottom left corner, the bottom right corner and the upper right corner. Hold down the Shift key to maintain a straight line as you click in each corner.

4 Move the cursor to the starting point—the upper left corner—and double-click. The perimeter of the room is displayed in the Properties toolbar.

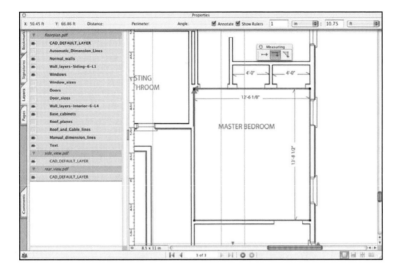

5 Choose the Area tool ( ). Click once in the upper left hand corner of the Master Bedroom, then in a counterclockwise direction, click one time in each of the three remaining corners. Move the cursor over the original starting point, until the crosshair also display a small open circle ( ). Click to complete the measurement of the area of this room.

6 The area of the room is displayed in the Properties toolbar.

7 Click the Close button in the upper corner of the Properties toolbar and the measuring toolbar to close these toolbars.

Enhanced navigation tools: loupe

1 Switch to the side view of the house on page two of the document.

2 Choose View > Fit Page.

3 Choose the Loupe tool ( ) from the Zoom toolbar or choose Tools > Zoom > Loupe.

4 On the bottom row of the house's windows, locate the window in the center that is shorter than the other four. Click once in its center. The Loupe window opens, showing a magnified view of this window.

5 Along the bottom of the Loupe tool click and drag the slider to the right, increasing the magnification. Stop when the window fills the Loupe window.

Use the Loupe tool to view specific portions of your documents at a higher magnification, while maintaining a separate zoom level in the document window.

6 Close the Loupe Tool window.

Using the cloud annotation tool

On technical drawings and illustrations with many straight lines, traditional notes and comments may not be clearly visible. Acrobat solves this problem with the Cloud annotation tool.

Notice that the small window, which you magnified with the Loupe tool, contains four small panes in its top row, and four below. All the other windows in this construction project only contain three panes in each row. You will add a comment for the designer, suggesting a change in the number of panes in this window.

1 Choose the Cloud Annotation tool ( ) by choosing Tools > Advanced Commenting > Drawing > Cloud or click the tool in the Drawing toolbar.

2 Click once in the upper left corner of this window, then travel in a counterclockwise direction and click in the lower left corner, and then the lower right corner of the window. Move to the upper right corner, and double click. This completes the annotation.

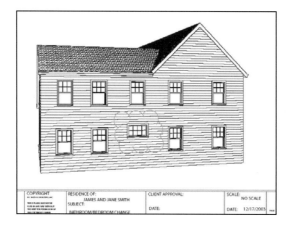

3 Choose the Hand tool (<img_1 image>) and Right-click (Windows) or Ctrl-click (Mac OS) inside the cloud and choose Properties. The Polygon Properties window appears.

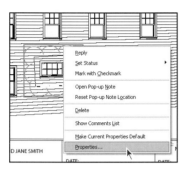

4 In the Appearance Tab, choose Cloudy 1 from the Style drop-down. Increase the thickness to 2 by clicking the upward facing arrow. Notice the annotation changes appearance to reflect these modifications.

5 Click the Close button to close the Polygon Properties window. Click anywhere on the page outside of the annotation to deselect the annotation.

Preparing engineering documents for distribution

Acrobat includes a variety of tools to make it easier for your audience to read and navigate through your documents, and for you to secure your projects from editing or unauthorized viewing.

Cropping pages

This document includes a large amount of empty space on both the top and bottom of the document. Before distributing the file, you will crop it so that the drawings are easier to view and navigate.

1 Choose View > Fit Page or click the Fit Page button (▣).

2 Choose the Crop tool (✄) from the Advanced Editing toolbar, or choose Tools > Advanced Editing > Crop tool. Your cursor changes to a plus sign (-¦-).

3 Position your cursor below and to the left of the project information, along the left edge of the document itself. Click and drag up and to the right, creating a box that completely encloses the entire drawing on the page.

4 Tap the Return or Enter key on your keyboard. The Crop Pages window opens. In the Page Range section of this window, select All, then click OK.

The white area surrounding the drawings is no longer displayed.

Set Initial view to show layers panel and page

Because this document contains layers that might need to be enabled or disabled, you will set the document to open with the Layers panel visible. This makes it easier for viewers to take advantage of the document layers.

1 Choose File > Document Properties.

2 Click the Initial View option along the left side of the Document Properties window.

3 From the Show drop-down, at the top of the window, choose Layers panel and Page. Keep this window open.

Set security to no changes

1 Click the Security option along the left side of the window.

2 From the Security Method drop-down, choose Password Security. The Password Security-Settings window opens.

3 From the Compatibility drop-down, choose Acrobat 6.0 and later.

💡 *The Acrobat 6.0 and later compatibility setting requires users to have either Adobe Reader 6.0 (or later) or Adobe Acrobat 6.0 (or later). It provides access to more advanced file features. If you need to have your documents accessed by users with older versions of Adobe Acrobat or Adobe Reader, you can always choose an earlier version under the Compatibility setting.*

4 Click the Require a password to open the document checkbox, and for Document Open Password enter **engineering123**.

5 Click the checkbox for Use a password to restrict printing and editing of the document and its security settings. For Permissions Password enter **cad789**.

6 For Permissions, set the following:

• Printing Allowed: Choose low resolution (150dpi).

• Changes Allowed: Choose Commenting, filling in form fields, and signing.

7 Confirm that Enable copying of text, images, and other content is not checked.

8 Select the checkbox to select Enable text access for screen reader devices for the visually impaired, and also select the checkbox for Enable plaintext metadata.

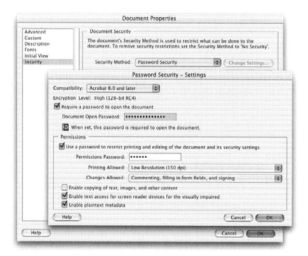

9 Click OK to close the Password Security-Settings window. Confirm the passwords when requested.

Acrobat informs you that Password settings are fully supported by all Adobe products, such as the Adobe Reader, but recipients using some non-Adobe products may be able to bypass some of the Password Security settings. Click OK to close this window. If necessary, click OK to confirm that the security options you've selected will not take effect until the file is saved. Click OK to close the Document Properties window.

10 Choose File > Save As. Navigate to your Lesson18 folder and enter the name **engineering_finished.pdf**. Click the Save button to save the file, then choose File > Close.

💡 *Adobe Acrobat Professional 6.0 can also work with large-format documents, including ARCH, ISO, JIS, and ANSI.*

Comparing documents

Two separate cover letters have been written at different times to accompany this project. Only one of these letters is correct. You will use Acrobat to highlight the differences between the two letters, allowing you to determine which one should be used.

1 If necessary, close any open documents by choosing File > Close.

2 Choose Document > Compare Documents. The Compare Documents window opens.

3 In the Compare (older document) portion of the window, click the Choose button and navigate to the Lesson18 folder and select Client_letter2.pdf. Click Open, and you are returned to the Compare Documents window.

4 In the To (newer document) portion of the window, click the Choose button and navigate to the Lesson18 folder and select Client_letter1.pdf. Click Open, and you are returned to the Compare Documents window.

5 In the Compare Documents window, choose the Textual differences radio button and also select Side by Side report. Leave the other settings unchanged, and click OK.

6 Acrobat opens a new document with the one letter on the left side of the window, and the other letter on the right side of the window. The initial page provides an overview of the number of words that match or do not match, which provides an understanding of how substantially different the documents are.

7 Scroll down to see the actual letters presented side-by-side. Acrobat underlines words that have been added in one document, and strikes-through those words that have been removed. This provides a clear view of how the document has been changed.

8 Close the document by choosing File > Close.

Congratulations! You have finished this lesson.

On your own

1 Using the Pages panel, merge the file Client_letter1.pdf into the engineering_finished.pdf file. Because you added security to the engineering file, you will need to use the Document Properties window to remove the security settings before integrating the files.

2 Using the Distance Tool and a ratio of 1 in : 8 ft., measure the distance between each of the windows on the side of the house. Annotate these measurements.

3 Using the floorplan and the Layers panel, locate all the layers displaying text, and disable these layers for viewing when the document is initially opened using the layers Properties option.

Review questions

1 Where do layers in an Adobe PDF file originate? How are they added into the file?

2 What tools exist to help navigate large documents?

3 How is the Cloud Annotation tool useful for technical drawings and illustrations?

Review answers

1 Layers come from the authoring program, such as AutoCAD, Visio, Adobe Illustrator, or Adobe InDesign. They are created in these programs and exported as a component of the PDF at the time the PDF file is generated. Layers are not added to a PDF file using Acrobat, but you can merge multiple layers together and edit attributes of the layers, including whether they are visible or print.

2 Acrobat Professional includes both a Loupe tool to focus on smaller portions of a document, and a Pan & Zoom window to easily change the focus of the document window. The Crop tool can be used to remove unnecessary borders around the perimeter of a document.

3 Because the Cloud Annotation tool, by default, does not use any straight lines, the comments it creates are more visible on documents containing many straight lines. You can change the properties of these comments to adjust the color, thickness, opacity and cloud style to make them even more visible in your documents.

Lesson 19

19 | Creating PDF Forms

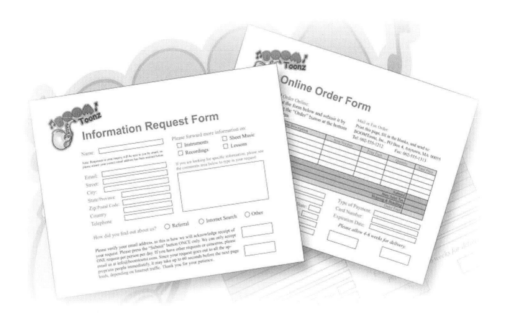

Using Adobe Acrobat 6 Professional you can create dynamic PDF forms to capture and share information electronically.

In this lesson you will learn how to do the following:

- Convert paper forms to PDF and create electronic PDF forms.

- Add form fields including text, numbers, check boxes and lists.

- Validate and calculate form data.

- Import and export form data.

If needed, remove the previous lesson folder from your hard drive, and copy the Lesson19 folder onto your hard drive.

Note: Windows users may need to unlock the lesson files before using them. For information, see "Copying the Classroom in a Book files" on page 3.

Getting started

In this lesson you'll work on two forms for a fictitious music supply business. You'll start by taking an existing paper form and converting it to a PDF. You'll then work with an existing PDF file.

1 Start Adobe Acrobat.

2 To see what the finished file looks like, navigate to the Lesson19 folder and open the file info_end.pdf.

3 When you have finished examining the completed PDF file, you can keep the file open for reference while you work on this exercise, or you can close the file by choosing File > Close.

Converting paper forms to pdf forms

With Acrobat you can create electronic forms or convert your paper forms to Adobe PDF files. You will start by opening a paper form that has already been scanned for you and you will convert it to PDF. You will then add fields to the document, using Adobe Acrobat 6 Professional, to turn the file into an interactive form.

1 Choose File > Create PDF > From File. Navigate to the Lesson19 folder and locate the file info_start.tif.

2 Click Open.

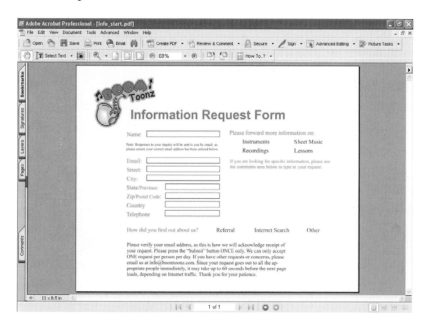

3 After the document appears, choose File > Save. Name the file info.pdf and save it in the Lesson19 folder.

4 Choose Tools > Advanced Editing > Forms > Show Forms Toolbar to access the tools for creating an electronic form.

Adding text fields

Users will use text fields to enter letters and numbers that provide information, such as their name or telephone number. Text fields are represented by boxes on the form, and are created using the Text Field tool.

1 From the Forms toolbar, choose the Text Field tool ().

2 Move your cursor to the box next to the area titled Name.

3 Position the crosshair at the upper left corner of the box. Click-drag downward and to the right to trace the box. The Text Field Properties dialog box opens after you have finished drawing the region for the field.

4 Choose the General tab and set the following:

- For Name, type **Name**.

- For Tooltip, type **Enter your name here**.

Tooltips appear when the cursor is placed over a form field. They provide contextual help or information.

Leave the other settings in this tab at their default values. The Name field is used to apply names to each form field, such as address or phone number. You will use this information about each form field to understand the data if it is exported. The names of form fields should be descriptive.

5 Choose the Appearance tab and for Font Size choose 10. This sets the size of the text as it is entered into this field by the user. Leave the other settings in this tab at their default values.

6 Choose the Options tab and for Alignment, select Center. Leave the other settings in this tab at their default values.

7 Click the Close button to close the Text Field Properties dialog box.

8 Choose the Hand tool (🖐) and click within the Name field you created. Enter your name, and note that the text appears in the form field, using the attributes you applied.

Formatting multiple form fields

Here you will create the other text fields on this page, and then format them at the same time.

1 Choose the Text Field tool.

2 Using the process from the previous step, create text fields for each of the following fields. Be certain to name each field appropriately in the General tab of the Text Field Properties window:

• Email

• Street

• City

• State/Province

• ZIP code/Postal Code

• Country

• Phone

Note: It is not necessary to close the Text Field Properties window after creating and naming each field.

3 Position your cursor over the Email field and hold down the Ctrl key (Windows) or Command (Mac OS). Click to select the Email field. While continuing to hold down Ctrl or Command keys, click and select the Street, City, State/Province, ZIP code, Country and Telephone fields. Right-click (Windows) or Ctrl-click (Mac OS) on any of the selected fields and choose Properties to open the Text Field Properties dialog box.

4 Choose the Appearance tab and for Font Size choose 10. This sets the size of the text as it is entered into this field by the user. Leave the other settings in this tab at their default values. Do not close the dialog box.

5 Choose the Options tab and for Alignment, select Center. Leave the other settings in this tab at their default values.

6 Click the Close button to close the Text Field Properties dialog box.

7 Choose the Hand tool (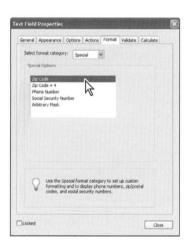) and click within the Email field you created. Enter your email address. Also enter information in the other fields by either clicking within them or using the Tab key to move from one field to another. The formatting attributes you specified are applied to the text.

Adding special format restrictions

You can use special formatting to restrict the type of data that is entered, or convert information into a specific format. You can set fields to accept only numbers, or conform to special formats such as those used with ZIP codes or telephone numbers.

1 Choose the Select Object tool (k) from the Advanced Editing toolbar. Double-click the ZIP code field you created in the previous section.

2 Choose the Format tab and select Special from the Select format category. Choose Zip Code from the list of available formatting choices. This will restrict the user's entry to a five-digit numerical value. Click the Close button to close the window.

3 Double-click the Phone field you created in the previous section.

4 Choose the Format tab and select Special from the Select format category.

5 Under the Special Options header, choose Phone Number. This will restrict the user's entry to a 10-digit numerical value, and will display the field according to conventional North American telephone numbers.

6 Click the Close button to close the window.

Adding check boxes

Check boxes are useful for responses that allow one or more selections. You will use check boxes to allow users to select multiple items from a list of products.

1 From the Forms toolbar, select the Check Box tool (☑).

2 Position your cursor to the left of the word Instruments on the upper right side of the form. Click-drag downward and to the right to draw a small box that is approximately the same height as the letter I in the word Instruments. When you release the cursor, the Check Box Properties dialog box opens.

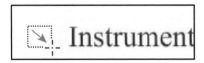

3 Click the General tab of the Check Box Properties and set the following:

• For Name, type **Instruments**.
• For Tooltip, type **Select to receive more information**.

Leave the other settings in the General tab unchanged, do not close this dialog box.

4 Click the Options tab and for Check Box Style, choose Check. Leave the selection for Check box is checked by default deselected. Readers will need to check this box if they wish to make the selection. Click the Close button.

5 If necessary, select the check box you created in the previous steps. Zoom-in on the check box, by using Ctrl + (Windows) or Cmd + (Mac OS). With the Select Object tool, hold down the Ctrl (Windows) key or Option (Mac) key and drag the checkbox downward. While dragging it, continue to hold down the Ctrl or Option key and then also hold the Shift key to maintain the alignment of the duplicate copy. Once the duplicate copy is in place, release the mouse first and then release the keys from the keyboard.

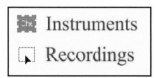

6 Double-click the duplicated field and choose the General tab in the Check Box Properties window. Change the name to **Recordings**, then click the Close button.

7 Using the Select Object tool (▶) Shift-click to select both check boxes. Hold down the Ctrl (Windows) key or Option (Mac OS) key and drag copies of these boxes to the right. You can hold down the Shift key while duplicating to create a duplicate aligned with the original. The duplicate copies should be positioned next to the words Sheet Music and Lessons.

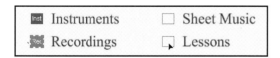

8 Choose Edit > Deselect and double-click separately on each of the two check boxes you've copied. In the General tab of the Check Box Properties dialog box, name the duplicated check boxes **Sheet Music** and **Lessons**.

Creating a multi-line text field

You can establish form fields that allow for more than one line of text to be entered. To accommodate multiple lines of text you will create a larger text field and adjust the properties of the field to allow for additional lines of text to be entered.

1 Choose the Text Field tool (▭). Click and drag a text field that fills all the available space under the sentence that begins "If you are looking for specific information… ." The Text Field Properties window opens after you create the text field. Keep this window open.

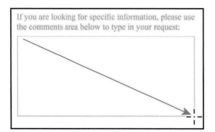

2 Click the General tab of the Text Field Properties dialog box. For Name, enter **Specifics** and for Tooltip, enter **Place your special requests here**. Do not change the other settings within the General tab, and keep the Text Field Properties window open.

3 Choose the Appearance tab and set the following:

- For Border Color, hold down on the swatch to the right and choose Black.
- For Fill Color, hold down on the swatch to the right and choose White.
- From the Line Thickness drop-down menu choose Thin.
- From the Line Style drop-down menu choose Solid.
- Set Font Size to Auto.

Leave the other settings in this tab at their default values, and do not close the window.

💡 *The Auto setting for Font Size allows Acrobat to increase or decrease the size of text as it is entered into a field. With this option, Acrobat changes the font size based upon the amount of space available within the field. If you prefer to use a specific size rather than a variable font size, you can also enter a specific size for the text.*

4 Choose the Options tab and for Alignment, choose Left. Then click the Multi-line checkbox. This allows the text to expand beyond one line as it is entered. Leave the other settings in this tab at their default values.

5 Click the Close button to close the Text Field Properties window.

Adding radio buttons

Next you will add radio buttons to allow users to indicate how they learned about this company.

1 From the Forms toolbar, select the Radio Button Tool (◉).

2 Position your cursor to the left of the word Referral. Click and drag downward and to the right to create a small radio button. The radio button should be approximately the same height as the letter R in the word Referral. The Radio Button Properties window opens after you finish drawing the button.

3 Choose the General tab of the Radio Button Properties dialog box, and for Name, enter **Learned About Us From** and for Tooltip, enter **Tell us how you learned about BoomToonz**. Leave the other settings in this tab unchanged, and keep the Radio Button Properties window open.

4 Choose the Appearance tab and set the following:

• For Border Color, hold down on the swatch to the right and choose Black.

• For Fill Color, hold down on the swatch to the right and choose White.

• From the Line Thickness drop-down menu choose Thin.

• From the Line Style drop-down menu choose Inset.

Leave the other settings unchanged, and keep the window open.

5 Choose the Options tab and for Button Style, choose Circle. For Export Value, type **Referral**. Leave the other settings unchanged, and click the Close button to close the window.

6 Using the Radio Button tool (⊙) select the Referral radio button. Hold down Ctrl (Windows) or Option (Mac) and drag the button to the right. While continuing to hold down the Ctrl or Option key, also press the Shift key while dragging the field to the right. Place the copy of the radio button to the left of the words Internet Search.

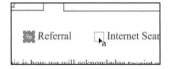

Note: It may be helpful to increase the magnification of the radio button before duplicating. Use either the Zoom-in tool or Ctrl + (Windows) or Command + (Mac OS).

💡 *Using the shift key along with either the Ctrl (Windows) or Option (Mac OS) you can duplicate form fields and have the duplicated fields remain in alignment with the original fields. The shift key constrains movement to keep the copy positioned on the same vertical or horizontal path as the original.*

7 Repeating the process in step 6, duplicate the original radio button and place the duplicated button adjacent to the word "Other."

8 Continuing to use the radio button tool, right-click (Windows) or Ctrl-click (Mac OS) on the radio button you duplicated and placed adjacent to the words "Internet Search." Choose Properties from the contextual menu and the Radio Button Properties window opens. Choose the Options tab and for Export Value, type **Internet Search**. Leave the other settings unchanged, and click the Close button to close the window.

9 Repeating the process in step 8, right-click (Windows) or Ctrl-click (Mac OS) on the radio button you duplicated and placed adjacent to the word "Other" and choose Properties. In the Radio Button Properties window, choose the Options tab and for Export Value, type **Other**. Leave the other settings unchanged, and click the Close button to close the window.

💡 *Because several choices are available, and you only want one answer, you will use a radio button. If you want to give users the choice of selecting multiple options all at once, you can use check boxes instead of radio buttons.*

Adding print and reset buttons

With Adobe Acrobat 6 Professional you can create buttons that enhance the functionality of PDF forms. Here you will create two buttons that can be used to clear the data from the form fields and also to print the form.

1 From the Forms Toolbar, select the Button tool (▮).

2 Move your cursor to the blank area below the radio button "Other." Click and drag downward and to the right to draw a box that covers the top half of the empty space. The Button Properties window opens when you release the mouse. Keep this window open.

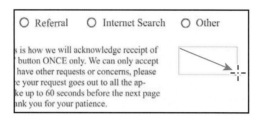

3 Choose the General tab and for Name, enter **Print**. For Tooltip enter **Click to submit form**. Leave the other settings in this tab at their default values, and keep the window open.

4 Choose the Appearance tab of the Button Properties dialog box.

- Click on the swatch to the right of Border Color and choose a light red color.
- Click on the swatch to the right of Fill Color and choose a dark red color.
- From the Line Thickness drop-down menu, choose Medium.
- From the Line Style drop-down menu, choose Beveled.
- From the Font Size drop-down menu, choose 14.
- Click on the swatch to the right of Text Color and choose White.
- In the Font drop-down menu, choose Helvetica Bold.

Leave the other settings in this tab unchanged, and keep the window open.

5 Click the Options tab and set the following:

- For Layout, choose Label only.

- For Behavior, choose Invert.

- For Label, enter **Print**.

Leave the other settings in this tab unchanged, and keep the window open.

6 Choose the Actions tab and for Select Trigger, choose Mouse Up. For Select Action, choose Execute a Menu Item, then click Add. The Menu Item Selection window appears.

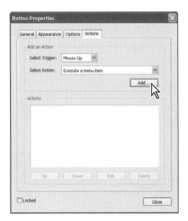

7 In the Menu Item Selection window, choose File > Print. Click OK to accept this action and close the Menu Item Selection window (Windows) or choose File > Print then click OK (Mac OS).

8 Click the Close button to close the Button Properties window.

To create a reset button

1 If necessary, choose the Button tool (■) from the Forms Toolbar.

💡 *You can use the Grid to help you align buttons and form fields. Choose View > Grid to make the grid visible, or to hide it. You can set the size of the grid by choosing Edit > Preferences > Units & Guides.*

2 Position the cursor under the Print button created in the previous step. You will create a similarly sized button by positioning below the lower left corner of the Print button. Click and drag down and to the right, creating a box that is approximately the same size as the Print button. When you release the mouse, the Button Properties window opens.

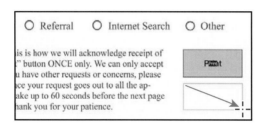

3 In the General tab locate the Name textbox and enter **Clear** and enter **Click to reset form** in the Tooltip text field. Leave the other settings in the General tab unchanged, and do not close the window.

4 Choose the Appearance tab of the Button Properties dialog box.

• Click on the swatch to the right of Border Color and choose a light red color.

• Click on the swatch to the right of Fill Color and choose a dark red color.

• From the Line Thickness drop-down menu, choose Medium.

• From the Line Style drop-down menu, choose Beveled.

• From the Font Size drop-down menu, choose 14.

• Click on the swatch to the right of Text Color and choose White.

• In the Font drop-down menu, choose Helvetica Bold.

5 Select the Options tab and make the following selections:

• From the Layout drop-down menu, choose Label only.

• From the Behavior drop-down menu, choose Invert.

• In the Label textbox, type **Clear**.

Leave the other settings in the Options tab unchanged, and leave the window open.

6 Click the Actions tab and choose Mouse Up from the Select Trigger drop-down menu. Choose Reset a Form from the Select Action choices, and click the Add button. The Reset a Form window opens.

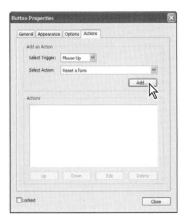

7 In the Reset a Form window, confirm that all the fields are selected. If necessary, click Select All to choose all the fields that will be reset. Click OK to close this window, then click Close to close the Button Properties window.

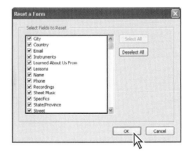

8 From the Toolbar, select the Hand tool ().

9 Enter the requested information into each of the form fields you have not yet completed. You will use this information in the next section, so keep the form open after you have filled in the fields, check boxes and radio buttons.

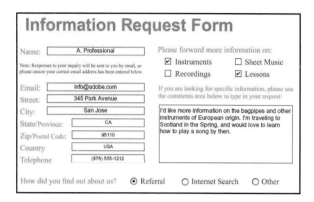

Exporting form data

Adobe Acrobat 6 Professional can be used to extract data from PDF forms. Because the form data that is entered is independent of the form itself, the form data can be submitted into a database, sent as an email or simply extracted and saved as a separate file. You will extract the form data from the information request form, and then transfer the information into an electronic order form.

1 Choose Advanced > Forms > Export Forms Data...

2 In the Export Form Data As dialog box, navigate to your Lesson19 folder.

3 Confirm that the Save as Type is set to Acrobat FDF files (*fdf), enter **information** as the file name, then click Save. This is an open format that Adobe has developed for storing forms data. The information is extracted from the PDF and saved in the location you specify. Later in this lesson, we will import the form data into another PDF form that you will create.

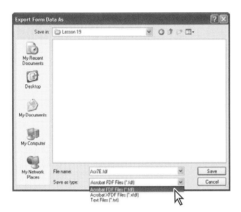

The process of extracting the data can be more automated and transparent to the end-user. We discuss submitting forms data later in this lesson.

4 Choose File > Save to save the file. Choose File > Close.

Creating an electronic order form

By adding form fields to existing PDF documents you make them interactive and allow for data capture. Here you will use a form that was created using Adobe InDesign CS— but it could have been created using any other software package and then converted to PDF. You'll be adding interactivity and the ability to capture the form data using Acrobat 6 Professional.

1 Choose File > Open and navigate to the Lesson19 folder. Choose the file order_start. pdf.

2 To see what the finished file looks like, navigate to the Lesson19 folder and select the file order_end.pdf, click Open.

3 When you have finished examining the completed file, you can keep the file open for reference while you work or you can close the file by choosing File > Close.

4 If necessary, choose Tools > Advanced Editing > Forms > Show Forms Toolbar to access the Forms Toolbar and its tools for creating electronic forms.

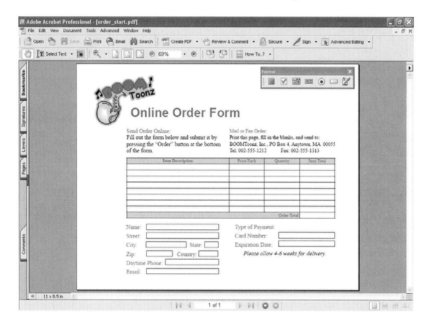

Adding combo boxes

Use combo boxes to create pull-down menus from which users can select a response or choose a specific item. Here you will create a list of musical instruments that can be purchased from BoomToonz.

1 From the Forms Toolbar, select the Combo Box tool (▤).

2 Move your cursor to the first column under the heading Item Description.

3 Position the cursor approximately one third of the way across the first empty cell in this column. Click and drag down and to the right, creating a box that covers the middle one third of the cell. The Text Field Properties window opens after you have completed drawing the box. Keep this window open.

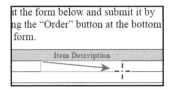

4 Choose the General tab. For Name, enter **Item** and for Tooltip, enter **Choose first item**. Leave the other settings unchanged and keep the window open.

5 Choose the Appearance tab. For Font Size, select 10 and leave the other settings in this tab unchanged. Keep this window open.

6 Choose the Options tab. In the Item textbox, enter **Make Selection**, and then click the Add button.

7 Return to the Item textbox and enter **bagpipes**, then click the Add button. Repeat this procedure for the following items:

- **drums**
- **guitar**
- **saxophone**
- **trombone**
- **tuba**

Confirm that Make Selection remains highlighted, as the highlighted text is used as the default selection. Leave the other settings in this tab unchanged.

7 Click Close to close the Combo Box Properties dialog box.

Duplicating fields

1 If necessary, select the combo box you created in the previous section using either the Combo Box tool (⊞) or the Select Item tool (▸).

2 Right-click (Window) or Ctrl-click (Mac OS) and choose Create Multiple Copies. The Create Multiple Copies of Fields window appears.

3 For Copy selected fields down, enter **8**. For Copy selected fields across, enter **1**. If necessary, click the Preview checkbox to view the duplicate fields.

You can use the Overall Size (All Fields) to adjust the amount of space between each field affected by the duplication. Additionally, use the Overall Position (All Fields) to move the field being duplicated and all of the copies. If all the fields are either too high or too low within each cell, click the Down or Up button to move the fields on the page. Click the OK button to close the window.

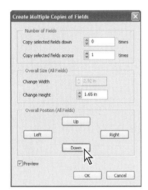 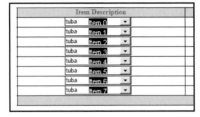

4 Double-click the original form field that was duplicated, and click the General tab. Note that Adobe Acrobat added a period and number following the form field name. When fields are duplicated using this method, Acrobat automatically renames each field so that it is unique by adding a consecutive number at the end of each form field name. Because of this, it is not necessary to rename each of the duplicate fields—all the time-consuming work has been accomplished for you.

5 Click Close to close the Combo Box Properties Box.

After duplicating form fields, the individual fields can be moved using the Selection tool (▸).

Validating text/numeric fields

To ensure that correct information is entered into form fields, use Acrobat's field validation feature. For example, if a response needs to be a number with a value between 10 and 20, you can restrict entries to only these numbers. Here you will limit the price of instruments to no more than $1,000.

1 From the Forms toolbar, select the Text Field tool (▭).

2 Move your cursor to the second column from the left, with the heading of Price Each in the Order Form table.

3 Position the crosshair at the upper left corner of the first empty cell at the top of this column. Click and drag downward and to the right to create a field that completely fills the cell. The Text Field Properties window opens when you complete drawing the field.

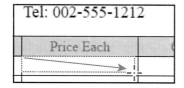

4 Click the General tab of the Text Field Properties window. For Name, enter **Price** and for Tooltip, enter **Price per item**. Leave the other settings in this tab unchanged, and keep the window open.

5 Click the Appearance tab and for Font Size, choose 10. Leave the other settings in this tab unchanged, and keep the window open.

6 Click the Options tab and for Alignment, choose Center. Leave the other settings in this tab unchanged, and keep the window open.

7 Click the Format tab and set the following:

- For Select format category, choose Number.
- For Decimal Places, choose 2.
- For Separator Style, choose 1,234.56 (the default).
- For Currency Symbol, choose Dollar ($).

Leave the other settings unchanged, and keep the window open.

8 Click the Validate tab, then choose the radio button to select "Field value is in range." In the range fields, type the following:

- From: **0**
- To: **1000**

9 Click the Close button to close the Text Field Properties window.

10 Right-click (Windows) or Ctrl-click (Mac OS) the text field you have just created, and choose Create Multiple Copies from the contextual menu. The Create Multiple Copies of Fields window opens.

11 In the Create Multiple Copies of Fields window, choose the following:

• For Copy selected fields down, enter **8**

• For Copy selected fields across, enter **1**

Leave the other settings in this dialog box unchanged, and click OK.

More numeric fields

Another method for ensuring that data entered into numeric form fields is appropriate is through formatting. By specifying a field's contents as a number, you can prevent users from entering letters or any other characters.

1 If necessary, select the Text Field Tool.

2 Move the cursor to the third column, with the heading Quantity.

3 Select all the fields in this column by Ctrl-clicking (Windows) or Cmd-clicking (Mac OS) each one of them. Right-click (Windows) or Ctrl-click (Mac OS) on any of the selected fields, and choose the Properties command from the contextual menu. The Text Field Properties window opens.

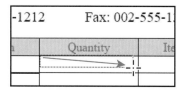

💡 *Be careful not to click or drag while holding down the Ctrl key (Windows). Ctrl-clicking is used to select multiple fields while Ctrl-clicking and dragging duplicates fields.*

4 Click the Appearance tab and for Font Size, choose 10. Leave the other settings in this tab unchanged, and keep the window open.

5 Click the Options tab and for Alignment, choose Center. Leave the other settings in this tab unchanged, and keep the window open. Leave the other settings in this tab unchanged, and click the Close button to close the window.

6 Select Quantity 0. Right-click (Windows) or Ctrl-click (Mac OS) and choose Properties. The Text Field Properties window opens. Click the Format tab and set the following:

• For Select format category, choose Number.

• For Decimal Places, choose 0.

• For Separator Style, choose 1,234.56 (the default).

• For Currency Symbol, choose None.

Leave the other settings in this tab unchanged, and click the Close button to close the window. The other Quantity fields have been formatted for you.

Calculating numeric fields

In addition to verifying and formatting form data, Acrobat can be used to calculate values used in form fields. For your PDF order form, you will calculate the cost for each item, based on the quantity that has been ordered. You will then have Acrobat calculate the total cost of all items that have been ordered.

1 If necessary, select the Text Field Tool.

2 Move your cursor over the top most field in the Item Total column, Total 0.

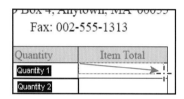

3 Right-click (Windows) or Ctrl-click (Mac OS) and choose Properties. The Text Field Properties window opens.

4 Click the Calculate tab and set the following:

• Select the Value is the radio button, which is the second from the top.
• Choose product (x) of the following fields:
• Press the Pick button. The Field Select window displays a listing of fields that can be used in the calculation. In the Field Selection window, check the boxes to the left of Price 0 and Quantity 0. Click the OK button to close the Field Select window and the Close button to close the Text Field Properties window.

5 Right-click (Windows) or Ctrl-click (Mac OS) the Total 1 field, which is the second field from the top in the Item Total column. Choose Properties.

6 Repeat step 4 to establish the calculation for this field, changing the fields selected in the Field Selection window to Price 1 and Quantity 1.

7 Repeat steps 5 and 6 to format the Total 2 through Total 7 fields so that they include the appropriate calculation. Each Total field should include a calculation that is the product of the Price and Quantity in its row.

Do not format the last field in this column Order Total, as it will perform a different calculation.

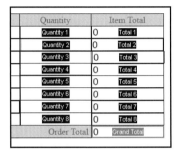

8 Right-click the Order Total field and choose Properties. Click the Calculate tab. You will establish a calculation that adds the totals on each line to create the entire cost of the order. In the Calculate tab, set the following:

• Select the Value is the radio button, which is the second from the top.

• Choose sum (+) of the following fields:

• Press the Pick button. The Field Selection window displays a listing of fields that can be used in the calculation. In the Field Selection window, check the boxes to the left of all of the Total fields, Total 0 through Total 7. After selecting the fields, click the OK button to close the Field Select window and the Close button to close the Text Field Properties window.

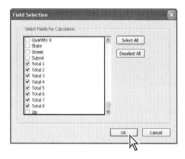

Formatting a date field

1 Right-click (Windows) or Ctrl-click (Mac OS) the Expiration Date field and choose Properties from the context menu. The Text Field Properties window opens.

2 Click the Format tab.

3 Choose Date, from the Select format category drop-down list.

4 Choose mm/yy, from the list of date formatting options.

5 Click the Close button to close the Text Field Properties window.

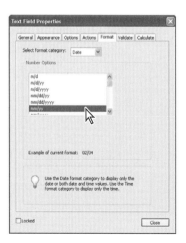

Adding a submit button

As you discovered in the information request form you created earlier in this chapter, buttons can add functionality to electronic forms, making it easy to print or reset a form. Here you will explore creating a submit button.

Because every organization has different needs and security concerns relating to electronic data, Acrobat supports a variety of methods for extracting data from PDF forms and routing it electronically. In our example, we will create a button that will submit data to a fictitious URL. Because we are not actually submitting the data to an on-line server, the data will not leave your computer.

If you have a server that is capable of receiving data from electronic forms, such as those posted on the Internet, you can use PDF forms to submit data to your own server. For example, you can use Perl, CGI, ASP or JSP scripts to route form data created from PDF files. The routed form data can be sent via Email or entered automatically into a database.

For additional information on routing form data, you may want to read Real World Adobe Acrobat 6 *or* Creating PDF Forms. *Both books are published by Adobe Press and available from your favorite bookseller.*

1 From the Forms Toolbar choose the Select Object tool (￼). Move the cursor over the Reset button.

2 Ctrl-click and drag (Windows) or Option-click and drag (Mac OS) the Reset button, dragging the duplicate button directly to the left. Release the mouse, and then the Ctrl or Option key, when the left edge of the duplicate button is aligned with the word Expiration.

￼ *While dragging the copy of the button, you can hold down the Shift key to keep the copy of the button aligned with the original.*

3 Position the cursor over the duplicated button and Right-click (Window) or Ctrl-click (Mac OS) and select Properties from the contextual menu. Be certain to select the copy and not the original when choosing Properties. The Button Properties window opens.

4 Click the General tab of the Button Properties window. For Name, enter **Submit** and for Tooltip, enter **Click to submit form**. Leave the other settings unchanged, and keep the window open.

5 Click the Options tab and set the following:

- For Layout, choose Label only.

- For Behavior, choose Invert.

- For Label, type Submit.

Leave the other settings unchanged, and keep the window open.

6 Click the Actions tab and set the following:

• For Select Trigger, choose Mouse Up.

• For Select Action, choose Submit a Form.

Click the Add button, the Submit Form Selection window appears.

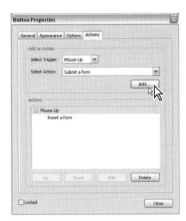

7 In the Submit Form Selections window, leave the URL empty.

This is the location where you would enter the Internet address of any script or server that would receive and route your form data.

8 In the Export Format portion of the window, choose HTML.

About Acrobat form data

Acrobat can submit data from PDF forms in a variety of formats:

• FDF exports as an FDF file. You can choose to export the form fields data, comments, incremental changes to the PDF, or all three. The Incremental Changes to the PDF option is useful for exporting a digital signature in a way that is easily read and reconstructed by a server.

***Note:** If the server returns data to the user in FDF, or XFDF formats, the server's URL must end with the #FDF suffix, for example, http://myserver/cgi-bin/myscript#FDF.*

• HTML exports as an HTML file.

• XFDF exports as an XML file. You can choose to export the form fields data, comments, or both.

• PDF exports the entire PDF file that is your form. Although this creates a larger file than the FDF option, it is useful for preserving digital signatures.

—From the Complete Acrobat 6.0 Help.

9 In the Field Selection portion of the window, choose specific fields you want to submit if you only want a portion of the form submitted. Or choose All Fields to submit all the fields from the form. Also choose whether you want dates converted to a standard format.

10 Click OK, do not close the Button Properties window.

11 In the Button Properties window click on Submit a form, then press the Up arrow. This causes this action to occur first.

Buttons may contain multiple actions. The sequence in which they occur is decided by their order in the Actions portion of the Buttons Property window.

12 Click the Close button to close the Button Properties window.

When you test the Submit button, you will receive an alert message from Acrobat because you have not specified an actual location where the form data can be sent. If you have a database administrator, and information technology professional or an Internet Service Provider that hosts your web server, they can establish an address where you can submit your forms data for testing purposes.

Importing form data

Just as data can be submitted and extracted from PDF files, it can also be imported. You will import the form data from the Information Request form that you completed earlier in the lesson.

1 Select the Hand tool ( ).

2 Choose Advanced > Forms > Import Forms Data. The Select File Containing Form Data window opens.

3 Navigate to the Lesson19 folder and choose information.fdf. This is the file you exported earlier in this lesson.

4 Click the Select button.

5 The fields in the order form that share the same name as those in the "Information Request" form are automatically populated with the form data that you imported.

Fields must share the same name, including capitalization, to input correctly.

Using automatically calculated form fields

To complete the testing of the order form, you will select several items, enter their price and quantity.

1 If necessary, select the Hand tool (🖑).

2 In the first row of the order form, choose drums from the Item Description column. Enter a price of 10 and a quantity of 2. Tap the Enter or Return key on your keyboard.

Note that Acrobat automatically calculated the total price for these items based upon the quantity and the cost per item that you specified. The calculation occurred immediately after your cursor left the field. Whether you click in another field, use the Enter or Return key or use the Tab key, Acrobat completes the calculation when you finish entering the data necessary for the calculation.

Item Description		Price Each	Quantity	Item Total
drums	▾	$10.00	2	$20.00
Make Selection	▾			$0.00
Make Selection	▾			$0.00

3 In the second row of the order form, choose guitar from the Item Description column. Enter a price of 20 and a quantity of 1. Tap the Return or Enter key on your keyboard.

Note the Order total at the bottom of the form now reflects the cost of these two lines of the order. As items are added to the order, the total will continue to update and reflect any changes to the order.

Item Description		Price Each	Quantity	Item Total
drums	▾	$10.00	2	$20.00
guitar	▾	$20.00	1	$20.00
Make Selection	▾			$0.00
Make Selection	▾			$0.00
Make Selection	▾			$0.00
Make Selection	▾			$0.00
Make Selection	▾			$0.00
Make Selection	▾			$0.00
			Order Total	$40.00

4 Choose File > Save As and save your file as **order.pdf** in the Lesson19 folder.

Congratulations! You have completed the lesson.

On your own

Open the Information Request form you completed in the first part of this lesson, and enable the Grid by choosing View > Grid. If necessary, choose Edit > Preferences and choose Units and Guides to change the Grid increments and use the grid to align the left and right sides of the form.

Open the order form you created. Using the Select Object tool, Ctrl-click (Windows) or Cmd-click (Mac OS) to select the fields Name, Street, City and ZIP. Right-click (Windows) or Ctrl-click (Mac OS) and from the contextual menu that appears, choose Align > Left.

In the Pages panel of the Order form, right-click (Windows) or Ctrl-click (Mac OS) the page thumbnail for the first page. Choose Page Properties from the contextual menu. In the Page Properties window, click the Tab Order tab and choose Use Row Order to have the form tab move naturally from left to right.

Review questions

1 Why would you use Adobe PDF forms?

2 What options exist for presenting users with several choices from which they can choose when completing a form?

3 Can you separate form data from the PDF itself?

Review answers

1 With Adobe PDF forms you can maintain the look and feel of existing forms. Users making the transition from paper to electronic forms will maintain familiarity with the appearance of the forms. Because PDF forms can be viewed and completed using the free Adobe Reader, they are the perfect option for placing forms on line.

2 Acrobat provides several options for presenting various choices. Combo boxes provide a drop-down list of choices, from which a user can select one. Use radio buttons when there are several options, but only one option can be selected. For options that allow several choices, use check boxes or list boxes, as these allow for more than one choice. For more information, see "Elements of an Adobe PDF Form" in the Complete Acrobat 6.0 Help.

3 Form data can be extracted manually and saved using the Advanced > Forms > Export Form Data command. Using a submit action, which can be attached to a button, the data can be routed to a script that will send the form information into a database or direct it to an email address.

Lesson 20

20 Using Adobe Acrobat for Professional Publishing

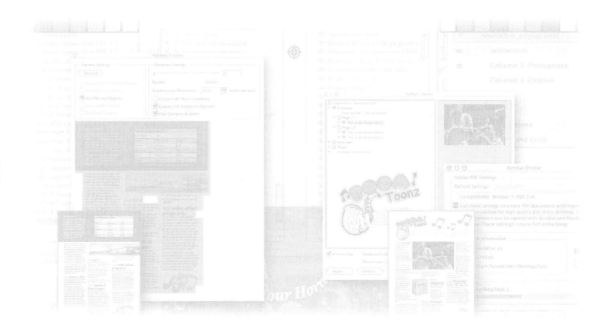

Use Adobe Acrobat Professional 6.0 to create high-quality PDF files. Acrobat's specialized prepress tools allow you to check color separations, preflight PDF files to check for quality concerns before printing, adjust how transparent objects are imaged, and color-separate PDF files.

In this lesson you will learn how to do the following:

- Create Adobe PDF files suitable for high resolution printing.
- Preflight Adobe PDF files to check for quality and consistency.
- Use layers from Adobe Illustrator and Adobe InDesign.
- Check how transparent objects impact a page.
- Use Acrobat to generate color separations.

If needed, remove the previous lesson folder from your hard drive, and copy the Lesson20 folder onto your hard drive.

Note: Windows users may need to unlock the lesson files before using them. For information see "Copying the Classroom in a Book files" on page 3.

Getting started

In this lesson you'll convert an Adobe PostScript file to a high quality PDF file using Adobe Acrobat Distiller 6.0. You will then check the file using Acrobat's preflight tools and view its color separations. You will also work with a file that contains transparency and layers, and generate a color separated proof.

1 Start Adobe Acrobat Professional 6.0.

2 To see what the finished file looks like, open the file newsletter_end.pdf. This two page PDF file is a full-color brochure that will be delivered to a printer, where it will be color separated to either a film imagesetter or a computer-to-plate device.

3 When you have finished examining the completed PDF file, you can keep this file open for reference while you work on this exercise, or you can close the file by choosing File > Close.

About Adobe PostScript files

Adobe PostScript is a page description language that is used by software applications to provide imaging instructions to output devices, such as laser printers, ink jet printers, along with high resolution imagesetters and platesetters. These imaging devices use the PostScript information to determine how text and graphics are plotted onto a page.

Instead of sending the PostScript imaging information directly to an output device, you can have it saved on your computer's hard drive. These files are sometimes called print-to-disk files, or .prn, because the printing information is stored on the hard disk instead of being sent to a printer. Adobe PostScript files are a special type of print-to-disk file, because they contain high quality imaging information. PostScript files are typically designated by a .ps file extension on the end of their name.

To create a PostScript file

1. Choose File > Print.

2. In the print window, select a PostScript print driver, such as the AdobePDF printer.

You can also use other PostScript print drivers to create PostScript files. You can obtain the latest Adobe PostScript print driver for both Windows and Macintosh computers at the downloads section of Adobe.com.

3. Choose the Print to file check box (Windows) or select Save as File check box in the Output Options section and choose PostScript as the format (Mac OS).

4. Click OK (Windows) or Save (Mac OS), name the file and specify the location where it should be saved.

Creating PDF files for print & prepress

You will start by converting an Adobe PostScript file to PDF using Acrobat Distiller. Acrobat Distiller converts PostScript files and EPS files to PDF. The quality and size of the PDF file are determined by the settings that you specify.

1 Choose Advanced > Acrobat Distiller. Acrobat Distiller starts and a window opens.

2 From the Default Settings drop-down, choose Press Quality. This establishes the kind of PDF file that will be created.

3 In the Acrobat Distiller window, choose File > Open. Navigate to the Lesson20 folder and choose newsletter.ps.

4 Click Open. The PostScript file is processed by Acrobat Distiller and is converted into an Adobe PDF file.

Acrobat Distiller creates a new file called newsletter.pdf. You will use this file you have created in the next exercise.

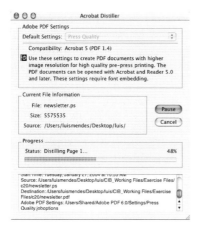

5 From the Acrobat Distiller window, choose File > Close.

There are several PDF settings that can be used to create PDF files that are generally suitable for high resolution printing and publishing.

• **High Quality** *creates PDF files for high-quality output. This set of options downsamples color and gray-scale images at 300 ppi and monochrome images at 1200 ppi, does not embed subsets of fonts used in the document, prints to a higher image resolution, and uses other settings to preserve the maximum amount of information about the original document. These PDF files can be opened in Acrobat 5.0 and Acrobat Reader 5.0 and later.*

• **PDF/X-1a** *checks incoming jobs for PDF/X1-a compliance, and creates PDF files only if compliant. PDF/X1-a is an ISO standard for graphic content exchange. PDF/X-1a requires all fonts to be embedded, the appropriate PDF boxes to be specified, and color to appear as either CMYK or spot colors. PDF files that meet PDF/X-1a requirements are targeted to a specific output condition (for example, web offset printing according to SWOP).*

• **PDF/X-3** *checks incoming jobs for PDF/X-3 compliance, and creates PDF files only if compliant. Like PDF/X1-a, PDF/X-3 is an ISO standard for graphic content exchange. The main difference is that PDF/X-3 supports device-independent color.*

• **Press Quality** *creates PDF files for high-quality print production, for example, on an imagesetter or platesetter. In this case, file size is not a consideration. The objective is to maintain all the information in a PDF file that a commercial printer or prepress service provider needs to print the document correctly. This set of options downsamples color and grayscale images at 300 ppi and monochrome images at 1200 ppi, embeds subsets of all fonts used in the document, prints to a higher image resolution, does not automatically rotate pages based on the orientation of the text or DSC comments, and uses other settings to preserve the maximum amount of information about the original document. Print jobs with fonts that cannot be embedded will fail. These PDF files can be opened in Acrobat 5.0 and Acrobat Reader 5.0 and later.*

Note: *Before creating an Adobe PDF file to send to a commercial printer or prepress service provider, find out what the output resolution and other settings should be, or ask for a .joboptions file with the recommended settings. You may need to customize the Adobe PDF settings for a particular provider and then provide a .joboptions file of your own.*

—From the Complete Acrobat 6.0 Help

Preflighting

Preflighting a document checks the file's content against a set of standards to determine whether the file is suitable for print publishing. Preflighting does not correct documents, but it does alert you to concerns such as fonts that are not embedded in a PDF document, colors that may not print correctly, or other objects that may not print as intended.

1 Open Adobe Acrobat Professional.

2 Choose File > Open and navigate to the Lesson20 folder. Choose newsletter.pdf and click Open.

Note: A completed file newletter_end.pdf has been provided for you to use if you did not have access to Acrobat Distiller to complete the previous exercise. If necessary, use this file instead. Be certain to use either newsletter.pdf or newsletter_end.pdf for this exercise.

3 Choose Document > Preflight. The Preflight: Profiles window opens.

Preflight analyzes the contents of a PDF and compares the results against a set of values that are defined within a profile. Acrobat reports any items within the document that are listed within the profile.

4 Select the Not supported in PostScript 3 profile and then click Analyze.

5 In the Preflight: Results window, review the information presented. Under the Problems heading, the profile used to assess the file is displayed. Because there were no problems when the file was compared against the profile, Acrobat displays a message "No problems found" under this section.

Acrobat confirms that this file should print successfully on a PostScript Level 3 output device—the most current version of PostScript used by a variety of printers and plotters.

6 Click the Done button in the Preflight: Results window.

7 In the Preflight: Profiles window, select the List all images profile and then click Analyze. The Preflight: Results window opens.

Examining the quality of the images used in a PDF file helps identify possible quality concerns before the file is printed. Acrobat's Preflight capability can also be used to examine the resolution used in graphics located in a PDF.

8 In the Preflight: Results window, a list of all images in the file is displayed under the Problems heading.

Items displayed under the Problems heading in the Preflight: Results window are not always "Problems." This is where Acrobat displays any items that meet the criteria of an analysis—or search—of a PDF file. In this example, the images listed are not all problematic—but because the PDF profile looked for images, this is what is displayed under the Problems heading.

9 Click the plus sign (+) (Windows) or the triangle (▶) (Mac OS) immediately to the left of the designation This is an image object under the Page: 1 section of the Preflight: Results window. This displays the resolution of the image.

This image is approximately 200 pixels per inch (ppi). This resolution is appropriate for printing to a laser printer, high speed copier and many newspapers. But this does not contain enough information for most high quality commercial printing methods.

💡 *If your print service provider has suggested that you provide images of a certain resolution, use the Preflight option to confirm the resolution of graphics that are used within a PDF.*

10 Choose Activate Snap in the bottom left of Preflight: Results window. Use this option to have Acrobat identify specific objects that have been identified as a result of a Preflight search.

11 Click the This is an image object under the Page: 1 heading. This image is displayed to the right side of the Preflight: Results window, because Active Snap is selected.

12 Click the Done button to close the Preflight: Results window. Keep the Preflight: Profiles window open.

Creating a custom preflight profile

The default preflight profiles provide a good foundation for identifying possible concerns within a PDF file. Acrobat can also search for nearly 100 criteria within PDF files based upon custom profiles that you create. You will develop criteria that will search for Red Green Blue (RGB) color elements. Because these colors do not align directly with the colors used in the printing process, they can be problematic when used in PDF files that are intended for use in graphics and prepress.

1 In the Preflight: Profiles window, click the Edit button. The Preflight: Edit profiles window opens.

2 At the bottom of the Profiles list, which is the first column, click the New Profile button. The Preflight: Edit profiles window opens.

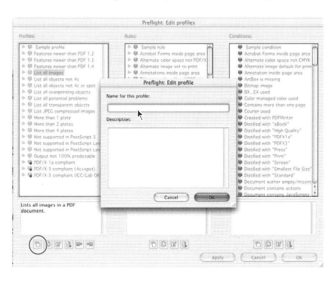

3 In the Preflight: Edit profiles window, for the Name for this profile enter **RGB Color used in document**. For Description, enter **Identifies objects that use RGB color in the PDF file**. Click OK. The new profile is listed in the Profiles column of the Preflight: Edit profiles window.

4 Confirm the new profile is selected in the Profiles column. In the Rules column, scroll to locate the Uses RGB Color rule. Click once to choose this rule, then click the Assign (≪) arrows to assign this rule to the profile you created.

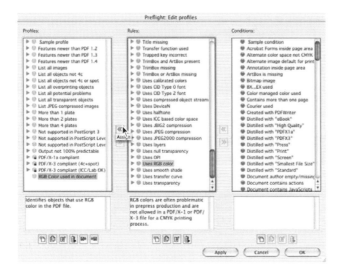

5 Click OK to close the Preflight: Edit profiles window.

6 In the Preflight: Profiles windows, double-click the RGB Color used in document profile you created in step 3. The document is then analyzed against the rules in this profile. The Preflight: Results window appears.

7 In the Preflight: Results window, under the Problems section, click the plus sign (+) (Windows) or the triangle (▶) (Mac OS) next to page 1. Then click the Uses RGB Color item under page one. If necessary, select Activate Snap. The item that uses RGB Color is displayed.

Use custom profiles to identify areas of problem or concern. You can then return to the original source document—in this case an Adobe Photoshop image that was placed into an Adobe InDesign layout—and correct the concern before printing.

8 Click the Done button to close the Preflight:Results window and click the Close button in the upper corner of the Profiles window to close it.

9 Choose File > Close to close this document.

Layers

Adobe PDF files created from some graphics software, including Adobe InDesign CS and Adobe Illustrator CS, may include layers that were built in the original document. You will use the Layers pane to enable and disable certain layers within a brochure.

1 Choose File > Open. Navigate to the Lesson20 folder and choose the file newsletter_export.pdf. Click the Open button.

2 Click the Layers tab on the side of the document window or choose View > Navigation Tabs > Layers.

3 Click the Eye icon (👁) to the left of the Column 1–English. Clicking on the eye hides it and turns off the layer for viewing and printing.

4 Click the empty box to the left of the Column 1–Portuguese. The Eye icon becomes visible. The elements on this layer are displayed on screen, and will print if the document is printed.

You can use layers in your design software to create separate versions of documents, or to control which elements are visible or will print.

5 Click the Eye icon to toggle the Illustrations layer off and click the Eye icon again to make the layer visible. Layers can include both text and graphics.

💡 *All the layers in this document were created in the original file before it was converted to PDF. Programs that can export directly to the PDF file format, such as Illustrator and InDesign, often can include more robust information in the PDF document, such as document layers and transparency. Layers and transparency are not preserved when files are converted to PDF by printing using the AdobePDF printer, nor are they maintained when creating PDF files using Acrobat Distiller.*

Separation preview

To determine which portions of this document will print on each of the color separations, you will use Acrobat's separation preview.

1 Click the Fit Page icon (□) or choose View > Fit Page.

2 Click the Next Page button (▶) or choose View > Go To > Next Page.

3 Choose Advanced > Separation Preview. The Separation Preview window opens.

The Separation Preview window shows all the colors that are included in this document for printing. The four subtractive primary colors used in color printing are displayed: Cyan, Magenta, Yellow, and Black (CMYK). Also, any special colors that will print are listed. These special colors, called Spot colors, are printed in addition to the four subtractive primary colors. Printing jobs that use spot colors need to be printed on equipment capable of handling more than four colors. This typically increases the cost of a print job. Because of the extra cost associated with spot colors, you may want to check PDF files to confirm that none are used in your documents if you did not intend to use them. The Separation Preview window can be used to confirm the colors used in Adobe PDF files. You can also use the Preflight process, described earlier in this chapter, to check for spot colors in PDF documents.

4 In the Separation Preview window, click once on the check box located to the left of the Pantone 300 C color swatch. The check box switches to a CMYK colored icon. Acrobat attempts to portray how the color will look if it is converted to a combination of Cyan, Magenta, Yellow, and Black–rather than if it were printed as a separate ink.

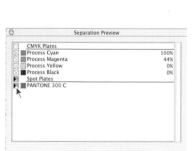

5 Click the same check box located to the left of the Pantone 300 C color swatch. The check box switches from the four colored icon and becomes deselected. All items on the page that would be printed using a color are hidden from view when its color separation is disabled.

💡 *The Pantone 300 C color swatch is only visible when viewing page 2. If you are not viewing page 2, or if you have not opened the newsletter_export.pdf file, this color swatch will not be visible.*

6 Click to deselect the Process Cyan and also the Process Magenta check boxes in the Separation Preview window. Objects using these colors are then hidden from view.

7 Click the CMYK Plates check box to display all the CMYK plates.

8 Click the Spot Plates check box for the Pantone 300 C spot color to be displayed on your monitor.

Note: Unless you use a color management system (CMS) with accurately calibrated ICC profiles, and have calibrated your monitor, the on-screen separation preview colors may not provide an exact match of the final color separation output.

9 Click the Close Window button in the upper right corner of the Separation Preview window (Windows) or the upper left corner of the window (Mac OS). Keep the file open.

Working with transparency

Adobe applications offer the ability to modify objects in ways that can affect the underlying artwork, creating the appearance of transparency. This can be accomplished by using the Transparency palette's opacity slider in applications such as InDesign, Illustrator, or Photoshop, or by changing the blending mode in a layer or with an object selected. Transparency works across Adobe applications, but you do need to be aware of a variety of settings and preparation steps before printing documents containing transparency.

Previewing transparency

When printing, objects with transparency are broken down, so any overlapping objects are converted into either separate vector shapes or rastered pixels. This retains the look of the transparency. This process of converting transparent objects into vectors and pixels is referred to as flattening. Flattening essentially eliminates the transparency while maintaining its appearance.

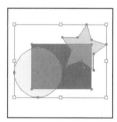 

Objects before flattening.   Objects after flattening.

Before flattening occurs, you can determine how much of the transparent area remains vector, and how much becomes rasterized. Some effects, such as drop shadows, must be rasterized in order to print correctly.

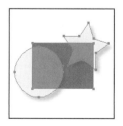 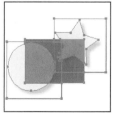

What is rasterization?

Rasterization is the process of changing vector objects, including fonts, into bitmap images for the purpose of displaying and printing. The amount of ppi (pixels per inch) is referred to as the resolution. The higher the resolution in a raster image, the better the quality.

Vector Object   Rasterized at 72 ppi   Rasterized at 300 ppi

If you received a PDF file but did not create the file, you may not know if, or where, transparency has been applied. Acrobat's transparency preview shows you where transparency is used in a document. This feature can also help you to determine the best flattener settings to use when printing the document.

1 If necessary, click the Next Page button (▶) to navigate to page 2. If the entire page is not visible, press Ctrl+0 (Windows) or Command+0 (Mac OS) to fit the entire page in your window.

2 Choose Advanced > Transparency Flattener Preview. The Flattener Preview window opens.

3 In the Preview Settings section, click the Refresh button. The Refresh button scans the content of the current PDF to identify if transparency features have been used. In this document, it recognizes transparency and outlined strokes. The Flattener Preview now shows a preview of the newsletter in the lower portion of the window. Keep this window open.

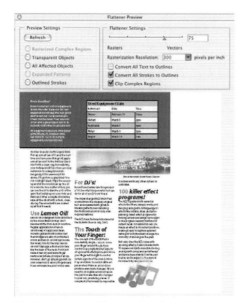

The Transparency Flattener Preview window.

Setting flattener preview settings

1 In the Flattener Preview window, choose the radio button to the left of Transparent Objects. The photo image and three of the musical notes are now highlighted in red, indicating that they have transparent properties.

2 In the Flattener Preview window, use the Flattener Settings to choose how much of the artwork you wish to retain as vector artwork and how much you want to rasterize. Click and drag the adjustable slider to the farthest position to the right. This maximizes the amount of artwork that remains as vectors.

Note: *The preview disappears as you select new settings. It will become visible again after you click the Refresh button.*

The settings vary from complete rasterization, which is obtained by dragging the slider all the way to the left, to maximum retention of vectors, obtained by dragging the slider all the way to the right.

3 From the Rasterization Resolution drop-down menu, choose 1200 pixels per inch. If it is necessary to rasterize portions of the document, this is the resolution that will be used.

4 Click the Refresh button and a new preview appears. Position your cursor over the image of the musical notes in the lower right corner of the window, and click to zoom in on the page.

Use the zoom capabilities to better identify smaller objects that are affected by transparency. If necessary, hold down the spacebar, then click and drag, to scroll within the preview area.

5 To zoom out, click the Refresh button to see the entire page.

6 In the Flattener Settings portion of the window, click and drag the slider all the way to the left. This causes Acrobat to preview which objects will be rasterized if this setting is used when printing.

7 Click the Refresh button, then click All Affected Objects radio button. Note that a significantly larger portion of the page is now covered in red. If a lower Raster setting is used, the majority of the document will be rasterized–or converted to a bitmap.

Note: Documents that contain many transparent objects may take longer to print when higher Flattener settings are used. This rasterizes fewer page elements.

8 When you are finished previewing how the various transparency flattening settings affect different portions of your document, you can note these settings for use when printing. Click Close to close the Flattener Preview window.

Advanced printing controls

Use Acrobat Professional's advanced printing features to produce color separations, add printing marks, and control how transparent and complex items are imaged.

1 Choose File > Print. The Print window opens.

2 Choose a PostScript printer to which you would like to print this document. If you do not have a PostScript printer available, choose Adobe PDF as the Printer, as this uses a PostScript print driver.

Acrobat is capable of printing to most output devices for general printing purposes. Because you are creating color separations, it is necessary to choose a PostScript printer for this portion of the lesson.

3 For Print Range select All (Windows) or Subset (Mac OS).

4 For Page Handling (Windows) or Page Scaling (Mac OS), choose Fit to paper and choose Auto-Rotate and Center. Keep all the other settings unchanged.

5 Click the Advanced button. The Advanced Print Setup window opens. Note that there are four tabs along the left side of this window: Output, Marks and Bleeds, Transparency Flattening, and PostScript Options.

6 Confirm the Output tab is selected along the left side of the Advanced Print Setup window, and choose Separations from the Color drop-down menu.

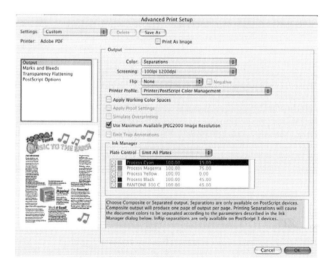

7 In the Ink Manager section, scroll through the inks and locate Pantone 300 C. Click the check box to the left of the Pantone 300 C name. The check box changes into a CMYK color swatch, indicating that this color will be printed as a combination of CMYK color values.

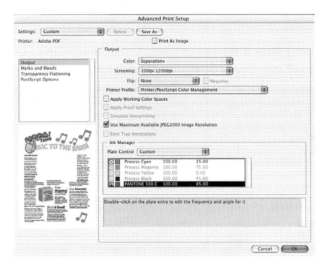

For Pantone 300 C, a close approximation of the color is made by mixing Cyan and Black. Because you converted this color to a CMYK mixture, Acrobat will mix these two colors to simulate the dedicated ink that is used to produce Spot colors. Because these two colors are already used throughout this newsletter, it is more cost-effective to use them to represent a spot color, rather than adding an entirely new ink in addition to the CMYK colors that are being used.

Acrobat also lets you globally convert all spot colors to their CMYK equivalents by choosing Convert All Spots to Process from the Plate Control drop-down menu.

8 Click the Marks and Bleeds tab, and click the All Marks check box to turn-on a variety of marks that image outside the edges of the document. Keep the Advanced Print Setup window open.

Flattening transparency

Determine the flattening settings for your PDF in the Advance section of the Print window.

1 In the Advanced Print Controls, click once on the Transparency Flattening option on the left side of the Advanced Print Controls window.

2 Acrobat displays the same options that you reviewed in the Transparency Preview window prior to printing. You have already determined which settings will impact certain portions of your document in the Transparency Preview Window. You can enter these settings in this window.

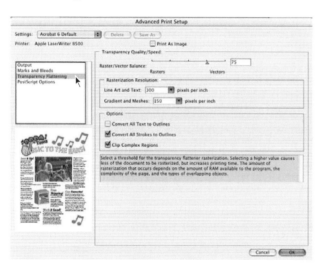

About flattening options

Convert all text to outlines

This option ensures that the width of all text in the artwork stays consistent. However, converting small fonts to outline can make them appear noticeably thicker and less readable (especially when printing on lower-end printing systems).

Convert all strokes to outlines

This option ensures that the width of all strokes in the artwork stays consistent. Selecting this option, however, causes thin strokes to appear slightly thicker (especially when printing on lower-end printing systems).

Clip complex regions

This setting ensures that the boundaries between vector artwork and rasterized artwork fall along object paths. This option reduces stitching artifacts that result when part of an object is rasterized while another part of the object remains in vector form (as determined by the Raster/Vector slider). Keep in mind that selecting this option may result in extremely complex clipping paths, which take significant time to compute, and can cause errors when printing.

About rasterization resolution

Gradient and meshes

Use the Gradient and Meshes drop-down menu to determine the ppi of gradients and meshes–which are sometimes called blends. These will be rasterized, and should have a resolution appropriate to your specific printer. For proofing to a general purpose laser printer or inkjet printer, the default setting of 150 ppi is appropriate. When printing to most high-quality output devices, such as a film or plate output device, a resolution of 300 ppi is sufficient for most work.

Line art and text

Because line art and text involves a more sharp contrast around its edges, it needs to be rasterized at a higher resolution to maintain a high quality appearance. A resolution of 300 ppi is sufficient when proofing, but this should be increased to a higher resolution for final high-quality output. A resolution of 1200 ppi is typically sufficient for high-quality output.

3 Choose the Save As button at the top of the Advanced Print Set-up window to save these flattening settings.

When settings are saved, you can re-use them on future jobs, avoiding the repetition of re-entering the settings you use for certain jobs or specific output devices.

4 In the Save Print Settings window, type **newsletter** and click OK.

The settings are now available from the Settings drop-down menu at the top of the Advanced Print Settings window.

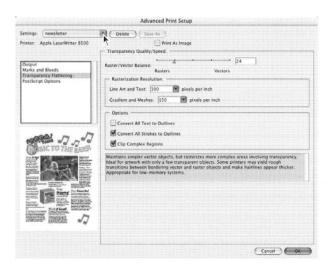

5 Click OK to exit the Advance Print Setup window. Then click either the OK button to print this document, or click Cancel if you prefer to not print at this time.

Setting up color management

Using color management can help you to control consistency throughout your workflow. Color management essentially assigns profiles, or characteristics for different devices, to your document so that you get more realistic results throughout the entire production process.

1 If the newsletter PDF is not open, choose File > Open. Navigate to the Lesson20 folder and choose the file newsletter_export.pdf. Click the Open button.

2 Choose Edit > Preferences (Windows) or Acrobat > Preferences (Mac OS) and click the Color Management tab along the left side of the Preferences Window.

In the Color Setup section you have several presets available to make color management less complicated.

3 From the Settings drop-down menu, choose U.S. Prepress Defaults. This selection allows Acrobat to display colors as they generally appear when printed using North American printing standards. By using a Settings selection, all the options in this window are changed.

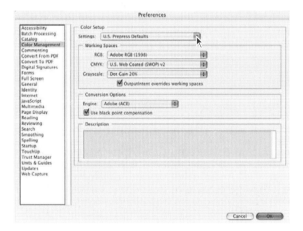

4 Under Conversion Options, confirm Adobe (ACE) is selected for the Engine.

The Adobe ACE is the same color management engine used by Adobe's other graphics software, so you can be confident that color management settings applied in Acrobat will mirror those applied in your other Adobe software.

5 Click OK to close the Preferences window.

6 Navigate to Page 1.

7 Use the Zoom-in tool (🔍) to focus on the picture of the band.

8 Choose Advanced > Proof Colors. Note a subtle color shift occurs when you choose to proof the colors on your screen using this option.

The proof on your monitor is called a Soft Proof, and it uses the settings you selected in your preferences.

9 Choose File > Close to close the document.

Congratulations! You have finished this lesson.

On your own

1 Print one copy of the English language version of the newsletter, and one copy of the foreign language version. Use the Layers pane to switch between these layers before printing. Use the layers to print text-only versions of the document, or to print only the graphics.

2 Open the Transparency Flattener Preview window and test various settings to determine how the increasing the amount of Raster or Vector content impacts more or less of the document. Try these same settings when printing, and note that the more vectors that are used, the longer the print time. But these settings generally provide a higher quality output.

3 Create a custom preflight profile to identify if fonts are not installed in a PDF document. Also create a preflight profile to identify images below 200 pixels per inch.

Review questions

1 What is the purpose of Acrobat Distiller, and how is it useful for high resolution printing?

2 What problems can Preflight detect within a PDF? Does it correct the problems it encounters?

3 How are layers useful for print and prepress? What concerns arise when printing a document with layers?

Review answers

1 Acrobat Distiller is used to convert PostScript files to PDF. PostScript files are generally created by using the Print to File option with a PostScript print driver. Any document that can be printed to file is then able to be converted to PDF with Acrobat Distiller.

Because you can easily convert a PostScript file to PDF with Acrobat Distiller, you can use the same PostScript file to generate multiple PDF files for various uses. You can convert the same PostScript file to PDF using the various Default Settings for experimentation, or to meet the needs of posting a PDF on-line and also delivering a different PDF to your printer.

2 Use the Preflight command to check for all areas of concern within a PDF. For example, if you posting PDF files on-line, you can look for items that might make a PDF file too large–such as embedded fonts or graphics that have too high a resolution. If you are using PDF files for print and prepress, you can check for fonts that are not embedded, low-resolution graphics, and incorrect colors.

3 Layers provide the ability to easily create various versions of a PDF document. But not all prepress workflows accept layered PDF files, and they introduce the possibility of printing the wrong layer if your printer or service provider is not expecting to receive a layered PDF file. It is a good idea to always communicate with your printer or service provider before using layers within a PDF document.

Index

Training and inspiration from Adobe Press

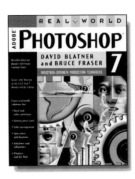

Classroom in a Book

The easiest, most comprehensive way to master Adobe software! *Classroom in a Book* is the bestselling series of practical software training workbooks. Developed with the support of product experts at Adobe Systems, these books offer complete, self-paced lessons designed to fit your busy schedule.

Each book includes a CD-ROM with customized files to guide you through the lessons and special projects.

Real World Series

Get industrial-strength production techniques from these comprehensive, "under-the-hood" reference books. Written by nationally recognized leaders in digital graphics, Web, and new media, these books offer timesaving tips, professional techniques, and detailed insight into how the software works. Covering basic through advanced skill levels, these books are ideal for print and Web graphics pros.

Idea Kits

The how-to books with a twist: Each features projects and templates that will jump-start your creativity, jog your imagination, and help you make the most of your Adobe software—fast! All the files you'll need are included on the accompanying disk, ready to be customized with your own artwork. You'll get fast, beautiful results without the learning curve.

Other Classics

Adobe Press books are the best way to go beyond the basics of your favorite Adobe application. Gain valuable insight and inspiration from well-known artists and respected instructors. Titles such as *The Complete Manual of Typography*, *Adobe Master Class: Design Invitational*, *Creating Acrobat Forms*, *Adobe Photoshop Web Design*, and *Photoshop One-Click Wow!* will put you on the fast track to mastery in no time.

The fastest, easiest, most comprehensive way to master Adobe Software

Visit www.adobepress.com for these titles and more!

Adobe Certification

Adobe® Certified Expert

Adobe® Certified Training Provider

What is an ACE?

An Adobe Certified Expert (ACE) is an individual who has passed an Adobe Product Proficiency Exam for a specified Adobe software product. Adobe Certified Experts are eligible to promote themselves to clients or employers as highly skilled, expert level users of Adobe Software. ACE certification is a recognized standard for excellence in Adobe software knowledge.

ACE Benefits

When you become an ACE, you enjoy these special benefits:

- Professional recognition.

- An ACE program certificate.

- Use of the Adobe Certified Expert program logo.

What is an ACTP?

An Adobe Certified Training Provider (ACTP) is a Training professional or organization that has met the ACTP program requirements. Adobe promotes ACTPs to customers who need training on Adobe software.

ACTP Benefits

- Professional recognition.

- An ACTP program certificate.

- Use of the Adobe Certified Training Provider program logo.

- Listing in the Partner Finder on Adobe.com.

- Access to beta software releases when available.

- Classroom in a Book in Adobe Acrobat PDF.

- Marketing materials.

- Co-marketing opportunities.

For more information on the ACE and ACTP programs, go to partners.adobe.com, and look for these programs under the Join section.

Production Notes

This Adobe Acrobat Professional 6.0 Classroom in a Book was created electronically using Adobe FrameMaker and Adobe InDesign. Art was produced using Adobe Illustrator and Adobe Photoshop. The Minion, Minion Pro, Myriad and Myriad Pro families of typefaces were used throughout this book.

References to company names and telephone numbers in the lessons are for demonstration purposes only and are not intended to refer to any actual organization or person.

Images

Photographic images and illustrations are provided in low-resolution formats and are intended for instructional use only. Illustrations of the Acrobat user interface vary from chapter to chapter, representing Windows XP and Mac OS X.

Update team credits

The following individuals contributed to the development of new and updated lessons for this edition of the Adobe InDesign Classroom in a Book:

Project coordinator, technical writer: Christopher G. Smith

Production: AGI Training: Luis Mendes

Proofreading: Jay Donahue

Testing: AGI Training: Carl S. Leinbach, Larry Happy, Brian Reese and Cathy Auclair

Content Development: Jeremy Osborn (Lesson 17), Christopher G. Smith (Lesson 18), Greg Heald (Lessons 19), and Jennifer M. Smith (Lessons 20)